LIFE ON EARTH AND BEYOND

THE ESSENCE OF KARMA

Prof (Dr.) Kanhu Charan Patra

Powered by

24by7Publishing.com

This book **'Life on Earth And Beyond – The Essence of Karma'** by Prof (Dr.) Kanhu Charan Patra is self-published by the author.

All the printing & distribution process of the book is powered by

24by7 Publishing
13 New Road, Kolkata - 51, India
https://www.24by7publishing.com
mail@24by7publishing.com
+91 9831 470 133
+91 9433 444 334

MRP: INR 595.00
First Published in November, 2023
Version 1.00
ISBN: 978-81-964745-9-1

Powered by

24by7Publishing.com

ॐ ॐ ॐ

This book is dedicated to the Great Spiritual Masters who have made significant contributions to the welfare of humanity and protected us.

About The Book

A friend asked me a very pertinent question – *why should I read your book when there are plenty of such books in the market?* I was happy and thankful for his genuine question.

Why one should read this book? In the present day, the materialistic life has made us so busy that we have almost forgotten the very purpose of our birth on this earth. Most of our precious time is directed towards enhancing our image through acquiring power-positions-property that we know for sure is purely temporary. Of late, people have become aware that our life on this earth is temporary and our permanent home is the Astral or Causal world.

Then, the next question is what to do. A survey has shown that towards the end of life, most of us (over 95% are not satisfied with what we have done in this life and regret it ("The Top Five Regrets of the Dying" by Bronni Ware). At this old age, time and energy have almost run out. Failure in achieving the objective (I should have done this) is one of the carryover karmas that one has to finish at some stage of one's life cycle. We must learn how to decide our priorities in life through our free will (intelligence given to us). And this comes through the knowledge that we need to acquire at the right time in our life.

During the last 3 years of the Pandemic, I enjoyed reading many good books {(i) *Living with Himalayan Masters – by Swami Rama;* (ii) *An Autobiography of a Yogi – by Paramahansa Yogananda;* (iii) *The Laws of the Spirit world – Khorshed Bhavnagiri;* (iv) *Apprenticed to a Himalayan Master – A Yogis Autobiography by Sri M,* (v) *Karma by Sadhguru,* (vi) *Good Karma by Jaya Row - to name a few*}, which has enhanced my knowledge. I also used the opportunity to browse the internet for months and listened to the discourses of the great masters through YouTube for 100s of hours. Let all this knowledge be available as a single source of information as a book so that it can be useful to someone at some point of time in life. *This book has topics beginning with the essence of Karma in life, the journey of the soul (Atama), the creation of the Universe (how this beautiful universe came into being, who created it, and the evaluation of life forms on earth), the search for life on other planets, the journey of our life after death, the karmic laws that are the guiding principles, personnel experiences, and introduction to a few great spiritual masters.*

Information on spirituality is impossible to prove - one has to believe it. For example, God cannot be shown. His presence is to be felt and believed (Swami Vivekananda). Happenings with the great masters are impossible to be demonstrated again. One has to either believe it or discard it. Some information in this book is unique. They are collected and compiled from various sources that I am sure should be valuable. The book should serve the requirements of some spiritual seekers.

I shall be still happy if information from this book can change the life of even a single spiritual seeker toward His path.'

I wish that the income generated from this book would be exclusively used for social causes only.

Preface

The last three years of restricted life have benefited me at least in one aspect: I could read many books on the meaning of our life on earth. To put this knowledge into a hard copy, I started writing this book with the positive notion that someone shall use this resource on a fine day that may change his path in life towards Him. Though I have authored a good many books on the subjects of my research related to water resources and hydraulic engineering, I find writing this book is bit difficult.

With my background as a teacher at NIT Rourkela, I thought the book should start with an introductory chapter on the essence of karma in life, the journey of the soul (Atama), the formation of the Universe, the scientific and spiritual exploration of the possibilities of life on the Exoplanets, and our connection with them. Some of the pertinent questions about the continuity of our life after death, the Karma we should do as human beings, and the powers of the great spiritual masters are tried to be addressed. Finally, the personnel experiences are discussed. Some information in this book is unique; they are collected and compiled from several sources.

When I started writing this book, many questions came to my mind: (i) Who created this beautiful Universe and how so perfectly? (ii) Is it going to have an end? (iii) What happens to us after our death? (iv) Why at the same place and time two infants taking birth have two extreme facilities, and so on...

Our present-day scientific knowledge is quite incapable of answering the questions on the continuity of our life after death. However, many great spiritual masters, with their extremely focused minds, have transgressed to outer space while in meditation and have acquired this great knowledge. Many such great masters have the perfect knowledge of converting any material to any other material that we are incapable of understanding. They have demonstrated this quite often and with ease. Of course, it is not possible to prove scientifically; we are to believe it as it happened. Like a small child is surprised to know that water can change to ice and a vapour state, we, with our present level of scientific knowledge, are also surprised to know this change of material from one type to another.

I salute these great masters who have revisited Earth after death to meet their disciples with their physical bodies in flesh and blood with the knowledge of decomposing and recomposing their astral entities. As revealed (by Swami Yukteswar) - An autobiography of a Yogi by Yogananda, enlightened souls can travel in space from one living planet to another in no time.

The main purpose of this book is to spread spiritual awareness so that the people at large become good and helpful to each other. I shall still be satisfied if this book can impact even a single individual and change his/her course in life for the good of others. Many times, I hear people saying, "*I have no time*". I feel sorry for them. We give our full time to achieving objects that we cannot carry and, at the same time, do not have time for things for our permanent home and life there. What a contrast!

Acknowledgement

The very purpose of writing this book is to create spiritual awareness, leading to peace and harmony in society. I reiterate to say that I shall be very happy if this book can change the life of even a single reader and advance him a step towards Him.

I am grateful for all the books, reading materials, information available on the net, speeches - discourses by great teachers, and all other information that is available on YouTube and other sources that I have referred to in preparing this book. I record my special thanks to all the authors, publications, and channels to which I had referred while writing this book.

I am especially thankful for all the internet sources (en.wikipedia.org, vedicfeed.com, www.indiatvnews.com, pujanpujari.com, refwww.boldsky.com, godbless-u.ning. com, www.reikihealingfoundation.net, en.m.wikipedia. org, article.sapub.org, and others, to name a few), which I have referred to and used in preparing this book for spreading spiritual awareness. By referring to these articles here, I am only working towards their very purpose of spiritual awakening among the readers.

I am thankful to my wife Gita, daughters Sonam and Suman, Son-in-laws Rajesh and Karan and my grandkids Diya and Aditya for their tolerance and understanding during the preparation of this book.

I am also thankful to Prof. K Umamaheswar Rao, Director NIT Rourkela, Colleges S P Singh, and all others who have helped me in preparing this book.

My thanks are due to my esteemed REC-81 friends, who are so dear to me, my first PhD student, Dr K K Khatua,

Sachin, and all others, including the current students Avinash, Rosysmita, K Uma Maheswar Rao, Partha, Abinash Patra, and Nibedita Patro for their contribution.

Any suggestion for improving the book will be highly received and appreciated.

The very purpose of this edition is spiritual awareness.

Prof. K C Patra, Professor HAG

Civil Engineering Department, NIT Rourkela – 769008
Prof_kcpatra@yahoo.com kcpatra@nitrkl.ac.in

Contents

Chapter - 1

The Journey of the Soul (the Aatma)

(Every individual born here has a specific quality, potential, and purpose to perform as per his agreed blueprint. Never underestimate yourself – always be happy)

As per yogic science, there are Dasa Dwar, (10 Gates), that is, Seven Primary Chakras, and three major Nadis in our body. A major part of our consciousness lies in the Primary Chakras. However, the consciousness sticks inside the 9 major doors, they are holes in both of your excretory organs, a hole in the belly, two holes in the nose, two eyes, one mouth, and Brahmarandhra. Your Prana is all around the doors, chakras, and Nadis due to Vyana Vayu. The Prana is collected from the body and the soul leaves through any of these openings.

Now, if we believe the Garuda Purana, a Hindu scripture, maybe the Aatma starts receding from the body almost 4 hours before the due death time. The leg sole located below the feet gets detached indicating its severity from the earth. Then the feet become cold. When death arrives, the silver chord connecting the soul to the body gets detached. The soul becomes free of the body, it becomes very light and moves up from the body.

Some of the souls are too attached to the body and they refuse to leave the body. In this case, we see some slight movements in the body, even after the person is dead. The soul has to go up as the astral chord is cut.

The Aatma (soul) leaves the body after death broadly through three routes (you can sense the location by touching the point of the just deadbody soon after the death – it is slightly reddish and warmer). Relation between the locations of exit points of Aatma from the body with its incarnation in the next life is as follows:

(1) For those who have done good karma or good deeds in life, the Aatma or the soul leaves the body through the holes present in their facemouth, ears, eyes, or nose and they go to the higher realms. These soulsare reborn into good families in their next life.

(2) For the very high spiritual persons or the people who have attained knowledge or those who leave the body during meditation (e.g. Swami Vivekananda), the Prana leaves the body through the imaginary hole called Brahmarandhra present in the centre of the head (you can feel the impulse by touching your centre of the head) and these people attain **Moksha** or salvation. They are relieved from the cycles of rebirth.

(3) For people who have done only sins or bad Karma, the Prana leaves the body through the holes present below the abdomen, that is, either through Anus or urine hole or through the stomach centre and they go to the lower realms. These souls are reborn as lower human beings or beasts or animals in their next life.

The soul never admits that it is dead and shouts, "I AM NOT DEAD" but the sound is not audible as the air is no longer the medium of the soul's sound transfer. At the same time, the soul can hear all the voices of the people in and around the room. With time, the soul understands that it is dead and in no way it can come back. It goes up and stays close to the roof at about 12 feet up from the earth. It can hear and understand everything. Along with the body, the soul goes to the cremation ground at this level of 12 feet above and observes all that is happening. After cremation, the body is lost and the soul feels free. Now it can travel anywhere as the bondage with the body is lost. The soul may be attached to earth materials or family and stays close to its attached items. After the 7th day, it moves up to the periphery of the Earth plane and crosses the Earth plane. The body must be cremated as soon as one dies.

Others say that it has to cross a big tunnel within 12 hours of death and therefore these 12 hour is very important. We have always to be in love with the departed so that it goes with satisfaction without being angry or hurt. The astral realm is waiting for the soul after the tunnel journey. The family needs to give food to the soul for his journey till it reaches the astral world. The astral world is highly illuminated and very pleasant. The mass prayers on the 11th and 12th days of death with homa are the ritual signifying our part of the assignment after death.

Between the 12th to 15th days, the journey of the soul is said to be complete and marks the festive of the joy of meeting with theancestors, close friends, and relatives from this or all the previouslife. There is a great reception to the soul there and they hug each other like we do when we meet someone close after a long time.

The guide who is mostly our ancestor takes the soul to the Karmic board for review of the Karma of the life that just ended.Since there is no physical body, the soul becomes his judge,feels sorry for the wrongdoings, happy for the good works it had done, and angry for the punishment he had received from others. The final judgment becomes the basis of his next life. Thus, it becomes a judgment for himself depending on his karma on earth. Based on this, his complete detailed structure for the next life is created as his blueprint. Every minute detail of the next life of the soul is printed *(For example, a person should have severe headaches throughout his life and no medicine can cure if he had smashed the head of someone else in his previous life. If the sufferer forgives, then he may be free from his headache).*

There is a cooling period between this and the next birth, which depends on how soon the soul decides to cast off the karma. The soul enters the mother's womb during 4-5 months of conception. The time of the entry of the soul into the womb and birth time is a perfect match with the horoscope and the creation is incredibly perfect. For the initial 1-2 months of the birth of the infant, the soul is in direct contact with the astral world, after which it gradually severs the contact and after one year it is complete. We meet friends, relatives everyone here after birth depending on our blueprint. They are the side actors for us as the soul has prepared the blueprint and exchanged karma with them from their previous lives.

From the death time and up to the 12th day, we have to respect the departed more and offer lots of food of their choice so that it can leave the world happily with satisfaction. That is why we have so many things to do up to 12 days and go for mass prayer.

If a soul does not reach the astral world in 12-15 days after death, the life of the dead soul becomes miserable as it has already left the earth and not reached its destination. Prayer is very important. If the rituals after death are improper, or the soulhas a strong attachment to the earth's world, then it may refuse the journey. Then it has to live on earth as a **Ghost** for many more years. When the soul dies, it rises as smoke.

Bhoot (Ghost): Due to unsatisfied desire some souls do not go to the astral realm and roam as ghosts. As soon as their desiresare met they transcend. **Pretas** *are ghosts but due to the wicked karma they have done while alive they are not able to get outof Preta's bodies even when their desires are met.* Later they suffer a lot and want to get out of the suffering but it is difficult to transcend them because of their evil karmic deeds done while alive. These beings are desperate to get out of the Preta body due to the intense suffering they have to bear. **Pichas** are wicked spirits, who have done a lot of bad deeds while alive and also want to do the same after they are dead. They enjoy the suffering they are subjected to. They are not willing to get out of their Pichas body and they believe that they enjoy suffering and suffer even more. Pichas is the most deadly of the three and can bring a lot of suffering to whomever they are close to as they enjoy suffering and excruciating pain. They are worthy of the sufferings.

It is important to know that death is just a break between this life and the next life, we never die. Death does not end everything. We are meeting again, so never grieve or feel sad as it may harmthe journey of the dead to the astral world.

Another theory suggests that for 40 days the soul continues to wander on the Earth after death. During these days, the soul visits all the places it likes and at the end of 40 days, the soul finally departs from this world. In some other beliefs the time lapse between this death and birth in the next life is zero. The soul, as soon as it leaves this life gets implanted in the womb of the mother for the next life. Those with divine vision can seethe immortal Aatma in every manifestation.

In Bhagavad Gita, it is mentioned that after the death of a person, he/she has to undergo new bodily formations. It is to maintain the cosmic law of Karma. The dead get different lokas,or planes as per the Karma done in a lifetime. In the realm of the God of death known as Yama Loka, the record keepers guide and transfer the souls from one realm to the other.

A death is classified as ***Akal Mrityu,*** *if a person does suicide or dies by accidents including fire, water, etc.* As per the Bhagavad Gita person suffers more after death by suicide. It is like disrespect for the creator if someone does this. The journey ofthe soul never takes place if the body dies by suicide. It certainly has to live the lifetime associated with the earth.

*There are various Yogis who leave the body in meditation.*The cosmic body is already formed in an individual who practices meditation. Cosmic beings come to pick up the soul in their vehicle to take them to their worlds. It is one of the best forms ofdeath as the journey of the soul for 13 days does not apply.

Just a few moments before the last breath, the soul, is covered with a causal body, and then over it, the electrical body leaves the old physical body that leaves together, which is called death. When the Soul leaves the body, the causal body carries the Karma with it. By the strength of Karma carried in the causal body, the soul discovers the mother's womb, where it is to live. The birth of the child and the course of life as a whole follow the preceding Karma. While the old karmas are being discharged, new karmas are also being accrued at the same time. The soul covered with the new causal body and then the electrical body leaves this second life's physical body at the time of death following the inclusion of these new karmas in the soul. This keeps the cycle of rebirth going.

If one believes the Hindu cosmology, the universe is divided into multiple worlds called Lokas. It is said that after a person's physical death, their spirit travels through several sub-worlds, the first of which is PretaLoka, an inferior realm. The departed spirits stay here between the period of bodily death and its judgment.

PretaLoka means the 'world of the departed or spirits'. In Vedic writings, PretaLoka is a stage between death and rebirth. The BhuLoka, which is the gross physical world, is divided into four sub-worlds: MartyaLoka is where the soul lives in a physical body, PretaLoka is the first resting place for the soul after physical death, NarakaLoka, is where the soul faces judgment, and PitraLoka is the place where the soul experiences their karma.

Different opinions prevail on the sanctity and truth of the Puranas. Critics feel that there is an exaggeration of the concepts of heaven and hell. Heaven with a rosy picture of grandiose while hell is a place of punishment and suffering. **The Samskaras Govern a Man's world and life.** *To get the best behavior from a man, sages knew the right way would be through reward and punishment. Therefore, they came up with the concepts of Swarga and Naraka.* The righteous souls or jivas are bound toward heaven after death and the immoral or evildoers towards hell. By portraying graphic descriptions and dire consequences of punishment, the sages extol the theory of cause and effect. It is made very clear that no one can escape the clutches of nature either in this birth or the next one. Balance of deeds will be met at some time or another. Our returns are based on our investments. No one can be scot-free. *Hell and heaven may be fictional mythological abodes,* but a rationalist and a wise person understand the law of action and reaction.

The diseases and illnesses we suffer are based on the actions of our previous lives and our relationship with our bodies. Hell, and heaven, a life of misery or bliss in the present life in itself, is based on our minds and thoughts. A man needs to think twice before sinning.

Liberation is the ultimate goal in Hinduism. A permanent solution to the process of rebirth for human beings is for the reunion with Brahman, the Supreme Self. This is possible through the control of mind and body, renunciation, devotion to God, and complete surrender to Him. The final liberation is possible when humans withdraw themselves from their desires and attachments and engage to attain the highest world of Supreme Brahman. Followers of different sects of Hinduism have different Abodes about the Supreme God. For the Shaivites it is *Kailash*, for Vaishanavites, it is *Vaikunth*, and for the Jnanamargis it is *Brahmalok*. The literature of these specific followers gives the impression that they are not the same but of different worlds, each inhabited by different classes of beings.

The universe is made up of many worlds, levels, and planes, some of which are known and some of which are unknown, some of which are close to our area of awareness and sensory knowledge, and some of which are far beyond. These worlds are inhabited and governed by a variety of forces, entities, energies, and deities, with mysterious happenings.

With Japa, Kirtan. fasting, tapas, charity, and being good to others, the Rajasic and Tamasic life is renounced. Life becomes Sattvic, where virtues like tolerance, love, compassion, and kindness prevail.

Chapter - 2

The Essence of Karma in Life

Most of us have seen the veracity of our life in society. It generates many questions. We feel that the world in which we are living is very hostile, bad, and cruel and then question its creation. In some other situations, we do have questions about our present incarnation and its mysteries. Why terrible things do happen to some good people, while some bad people enjoy fortune? These bring more questions within us about the very creation of God. Why there is pain and suffering in this world? Instead, we should have a beautiful world, where there is peace and happiness all around. Let us answer these with the viewpoint of Karma and how it is connected to the vital areas of our living and address human inquiry.

Ancient sages in India pondered over life and its various mysteries. They discovered that "*every cause has an effect, and every effect must have a cause.*" If one thinks deeply about his past, he can certainly be sure that he is the root cause of his present and will be the creator of his future. This chapter may skin out some of the misunderstandings and allow you to see the world from a different prismatic angle.

As you know karma means actions. Most of us consider karma as a bad word that creates fear and psychosis in us. When one is born, he brings within a blueprint of his life to which he has agreed to live. It is the Prarabdha karma which is a part of his Sanchita (total) karma taken out and given to him for this life. When one says "*This is my Karma – it means that he is responsible for his fate and no one else.*" Karma forms the natural force of our existence. It is the software that you have developed for yourself and continuously updating without any knowledge of its physical, mental, and energy forces. Your subconscious mind stores all these Sanchita karma from the very beginning of your first incarnation on this earth.

We are unaware that each one of us is gifted with enormous potential. If one seriously looks within, it can be seen that solutions to most of our problems are in our minds. Swami Vivekananda once said at best he may have used up to 5% of his brain capacity in his entire life. If you take the case of Einstein, then, as per the information from his brain mapping, he used only around 2.5% of his brain power, despite, being the greatest scientist of our times. One must always try to use this God-gifted inherited potential, but alas most of us are not aware of this great wealth.

A magnetized piece of iron can lift more than 10 times its weight of iron, but when not magnetized, it is at its zero potential. Some people have magnetized their brains and others do not. This miracle lies in one's subconscious mind. You do not have to acquire it, only try to learn its use. Within this subconscious mind, there is infinite power, wisdom, potential, intelligence, and continuity.

Here are some examples of the uses of this great potential. Take the case of Arunima Sinha, the Indian mountaineer who despite being a female, amputee could become the 1st female in the world to climb Mount Everest. Hari Budha Magar, a double amputee reached Mount Everest on 21st May, 2023. With examples of blinds and other disabled persons climbing Mount Everest, which is like a miracle to most of us, just think about the source of getting the willpower and energy. It is the strong willpower drawn from the subconscious mind.

Everyone has only one mind, but it has two distinct functions and characters. One is the subconscious mind and the other is the conscious mind, which is in constant conflict for most of us. The conscious mind is our physical mind that is interested in our current materialistic world while the subconscious mind is the spiritual mind that is always guiding us for the right path in life. The power of the subconscious mind is infinite, while the conscious mind has limited power. The subconscious mind is capable of communicating with the infinite energy of space and drawing power from it, but you need to train it on the right track.

Your mind is like a fertile garden. If you want to harvest good fruits, then you need to show the required seeds and make them fit. You cannot expect to harvest good fruits if you are sowing thorny plants. It is essential to sow good thoughts in your mind so that good things can be harvested. It has been said over again that "*as you sow - so you reap.*" When the mind is positive and thinks correctly, then there are always outputs with magic powers. The essential requirement is to control the thoughts so that you sow good seeds in your brain field. What you are now is created by you only either consciously or subconsciously through your mind.

When you feel upset or disturbed or fearful then realign yourself from this negative alignment and align with the universe. This force of the Universe may be called God's angels or spirit or inner guidance. "*Close your eyes and try to transmit yourself to the space of the universe which has all positive powers. Peace shall prevail in you when you are connected to the superpower.*" You must be very calm and peaceful when you get up in the morning. Chant your mantras in appreciation of the supreme power for all that you have. If you honestly count, He has given you more than you deserve. Begin the day with happiness and love for Him, you shall get all positive things on the day.

The greatest obstruction to our progress is fear which is just the opposite of feeling good. We have been misguided by society that '*getting good things*' is limited and difficult. Therefore, we are addicted to fear. On the contrary, "*getting good things in life is easier.*" If you try to change the environment that affects you, it may take your whole life and you are not likely to succeed. *Change yourself*, the cause and the effect will be outstanding leading to progress, and peace of mind which you need for a happy life.

Our actions depend more on us and are less predefined by fate. However, there are three thought processes to the approach to life with one group feeling that each individual's life is written before birth, which is fixed and cannot be altered. Others believe in free will and to them "everyone is entirely responsible for his own life and has the power to create his own life and destiny." Then, of course, there are those, who believe that life is a combination of fate and free will.

Before 1947, India, Pakistan, and Bangladesh were one nation and long before even Sri Lanka, Nepal, Bhutan, and Burma were a part of the great Bharat. The thought of separation of these countries from the main motherland must have first germinated in the minds of some individuals leading the divisions of the great country. The greediness for independent living separates couples, families, organizations, and nations leading to painful parting ways. These lead to enormous financial as well as emotional loss. A positive thought can bring peace and prosperity into our lives. A classic example of positive thinking on unity is the way the people of East and West Germany had shown us. A verse from Rig Veda says, "*Ayam nijah param veti ganana laghuchestasam, Udaracharitanam tu vasudhaiva kutumbakam,*" meaning thereby that the narrow-minded differentiates between mine and yours, while the open-minded consider the entire universe as one family.

The following example that I witnessed can be good for understanding the issue. In a small town in Odisha, the two brothers were in serious differences over the distribution of their father's assets. Finally, they decided to appoint a third person to resolve the conflict. The elder brother asked the younger one to name his arbitrator. The younger brother said, "When the elder brother is there, how can any other person be a better arbitrator for him than the elder brother himself?" He cannot think of a better person than his elder brother to look after his interests. The separation never happened.

The root of everything in our life is our thoughts, each of which is added together in shaping our future. The state of the mind (either calm or agitated), the state of intellect (whether there is clarity or confusion), etc. are the outcome of our thoughts. The thought only builds our character and the creator of our destiny. When a person thinks of construction and technology he becomes a civil engineer. One who thinks of stocks and shares becomes a stockbroker. Another person thinks of medicine and becomes a doctor and so on.

The first and foremost thing in life is to be happy. If you are not happy with your world, you cannot be successful. Happiness and success go together. It is not possible on your part to change your entire environment or the world around you to become happy. Therefore, by changing your thoughts, making a shift in attitude, or altering your feelings, the world automatically changes for you.

Everyone knows that life is temporary with no guarantee for the next minute. Therefore, one must enjoy what the world offers. Depending on your interest in happiness, do plenty of shopping, travel as you can, and eat the best dishes, but at the same time, you must not forget to build good things within as that is the only reserve you have stored to carry forward with you to the next life. *These reserves are the good thoughts, positive feelings, honest actions, and soothing words that will assure you a happy and prosperous life.* You should always try to improve spiritually so that your next birth in a better world is guaranteed. You should not downgrade yourself spiritually so that you are to be born in a slum in the next life, which can be close to your present house. Your subconscious mind records all these.

People go to so-called spiritually elevated personalities to listen to them to know more about life. It is called *Satsang.* It should never be the purpose of hanging around a good person but making a conscious effort to inculcate positive thoughts to clear the negativities. It is recommended to read uplifting books and expose yourself to spiritual thoughts. Don't waste your time watching TV as the breaking news only breaks you more. Watching good and inspiring movies is positive. Make a strong foundation for your next life.

Everything in life starts with *Vasana.* It is the vasana that gives rise to *thoughts,* the thoughts give rise to *desire* and finally, the desire generates *actions.* At some point, a thought came to my mind but from where I got that thought? I got it because I had Vasana for it. Thus more desire means more actions and more actions means more vasana. These form a complete cyclic order forming a *loop* All of us act following our Vasanas or nature. An elephant is mostly cool, a monkey is never stable, and a tiger is ferocious: all creatures are bound by their nature. All these characters are found in human beings. Some people are aggressive, others are gentle, many are brilliant, while there are dull ones too. But humans are intelligent and therefore have the adaptability to change. You can take thousands of examples starting with Steve Jobs to your very neighbour who has changed themselves and become great in life.

Never think that everything in life is your fate and is predefined. God has given you free will and is the sensitive mind in you to think rationale and act. When you know that everything is originating from you, then you should be enthusiastic and confident. It is the potential of your free will to create your destiny. *Whenever there is a problem then look within, trace back to the cause, and solve it.* Always try to make a conscious effort to make a happy future.

Take the example of Nelson Mandela, who was subjected to intense torture and misery in jail for almost three decades. When released, he said, "*if he didn't leave behind the hatred and negativity, he would still be in that prison.*" The persons who tortured Nelson Mandela continued to remain prison guards throughout their lives. But Mandela became a world leader inspiring millions.

As an intelligent human being, it is necessary to decide the purpose of life and work towards it. Your precious life is to be dedicated to positive works only, and when it happens, you have no time left for negativities. Under any circumstances, never be pulled down from your good mission. Like an animal lover who understands the nature of each animal and loves all of them, you being an intelligent person must adjust to the nature and behavior of others and act accordingly, without demanding changes in them.

In present-day life, adjusting to people is very important for a peaceful living. As an intelligent being, you have to assess the people around you, the environment, and the administration to which you need to adjust yourself. Your thoughts, emotions, and actions either take you to a new height or lead to misery. Correct yourself, if you are entertaining hateful thoughts. Never be negative in your thoughts and blame others for your failure in life. *You are gifted with enough strength, that nothing can disturb you except yourself.* The right thing to do is change your attitude. You can then be a happy person.

I have seen people constantly complaining about others. Everyone including yourself has shortcomings. Separate the person from his bad qualities. The person may be heartily good. Do not emphasize his bad things and create problems for yourself, rather appreciate his positive things and live happily, the choice is yours.

Swami Vivekananda once said, "*Conquer the mind and you will conquer the world.*" Towards this, I have an example. One day a distant friend abused me in front of others. I had a choice either to have a conflict with him or neglect it. I decided not to react and therefore the situation never aggravated. He later realized his mistake and was sorry for his bad utterances. It brought in a close friendship between us. If I would have reacted, things would have taken an ugly turn. Always think that others are free to say what they want and to react or not is solely a personal choice. You chose not to take it, so you are free. If you accept it then a problem comes in. Do not react to the things that are thrown at you by others as you have no control over them. You certainly have absolute control over yourself.

Through constant and positive actions, one can overcome a shaded past and build a bright future. When bad things happen, instead of being depressed or disheartened, try to correct the situation with positive thoughts. The change may not be visible immediately, but that will happen for sure. Strange things do happen in life. *The effect of your past karma pushes you in a particular direction and is known as destiny.* One should never look for instant results and become discouraged. Just keep on making positive efforts and be happy, success is bound to come. Have enough faith, confidence, and patience.

Someone defined the law of life as "*When you are giving, you are gaining much more, and – when you are grabbing, you are losing a lot*". You must have seen that the wealthiest person in the world at times feels deprived of certain things, while a person in the slum feels happy and abundant. Always be grateful for all that you have received in life as a gift from God.

It is a state of hypocrisy if one shows his intense love for an unknown and unseen God when he does not love the people around him with whom he lives. Human beings bring untold suffering and misery to fellow human beings and also to the animals including slaughtering them for their pleasure. There is no protest.

There should not be any confusion that our present life is not a birth, but a rebirth. Many have remembered their past life. I have heard from Sri M through the YouTube channel that he has remembered many of his past lives in great detail. Lord Budha has remembered his 100 past lives. Why we have taken this rebirth or reincarnation? The reason is very simple. With the passage of each life, our load of desire increases. This accumulation of desire is called Sanchita Karma. We cannot get the Moksha or the complete release from the life cycles until this accumulated karma reduces to zero. According to a global study in October 2021, more than 50% of people believe in reincarnation. Rebirth means one leaves this body and goes into another. Moksha does not happen when you have the desire unfulfilled. *In my present reincarnation, I remain essentially the same, while I take a new body with this new environment.*

It is a well-established fact that "*Every cause has an effect and for every effect, there is a cause.*" If you have read the book "The Top Five Regrets of the Dying" by Bronni Ware, you can understand that at the time of death, each one of us has the regrets of the unfulfilled desire. These desires do not vanish, it has to be enjoyed by the person. And it is these thoughts that bring him to the next life of incarnation. These are the causes leading to its effects. Remembering the problems of one's lifetime is the carryover factor. Thank God that you have not given us the memory of our past lives as the animals do. The world then would have become more destructive and revengeful.

In each minute of our lives, the desire forces us to remain active. It is my desire arising out of thirst that I have to go to the dining hall to drink a glass of water. We desire and therefore we move out of our house or do anything for that matter at any instant of time be it going to the office, shopping, or the cinema. The whole day's activity performed by you is your sheer desire.

In a similar sense, it is the desire that takes us from life to life. We have taken this birth with a small bundle of desires called Prarabdha Karma which is a small quantity taken out of the total accumulated Karma (called Sanchita Karma) that must be experienced in this lifetime, come what may. *Essentially by death, we are transferring the Karma or the desires or the Vasanas of the mind, and the intellect from one body to another as we cannot fulfill them in this life.* Suppose you have got a strong Vasana to be a top bureaucrat that generated in you towards the end of your life, then you are to be reborn as a bureaucrat to fulfil this desire.

A person, while completing the agreed assignment of the Prarabdha Karma of the present life, starts accumulating more karma by his strong desires for other things that he could not fulfil in this life. God again gives him another opportunity to move on to another body with a conducive environment that is best suited to fulfill the next bundle of his Prarabdha Karma that is taken out from the large stock of Sanchita Karma. He is not permitted to die unless and until his Prarabdha Karma which was agreed to be accomplished in this life is completed. Once done, he must leave this life and move to the next incarnation to complete the other set of his Prarabdha Karma. Nothing can prevent it. One must have seen in situations of accidents that some are dead, while others escape without any scratches on their body. Sometimes the person who is not to die has just got down from the vehicle which met with a serious accident just seconds later.

The desires are the outcomes of one's thoughts, feelings, words, and actions at every moment that create a greater influence or impact on his body, mind, and energy levels. Next, depending on the type and nature of these impacts, the character of a person is built. A good character emits a good smell or Vasana and a bad one the vice-versa. And this decides the spiritual rise or the fall of a person in society. A spiritually advanced person is always happy and successful and they emit fragrance for centuries. People remember them for long. I have seen at some pilgrim locations that people remember every detail of simple monks who were living in those places/caves some thousands of years back, but the very rich ones living during that time are forgotten entirely by the masses. The memory of the people for those rich or powerful persons living at that time is short-lived.

You must have also seen people having extreme mental stress and nightmares. These are the people who have led a negative life of selfishness, performing desire-driven vicious actions. This is referred to as hell. If you have performed noble, unselfish actions, you will have happy, pleasant dreams, which are heavenly.

We have to take rebirth again as we have to exhaust all of our accumulated Karma in this or the next incarnations. During the passage of the soul from one life to the other, in each lifetime, we have the option of reducing or eliminating part or all of our karma. But our desire in each life becomes so strong that we subtract a few, but add a few more and end up with a greater load of Karma, than we were born with. Thus, one forces himself to many more lives in this mortal, grief-stricken world. Knowledgeable people understand the difficult life here and have the extra vision of looking beyond. They get rid of the desire and choose moksha, or freedom. They follow the spiritual path aimed at eliminating desire and performing selfless actions that take them toward enlightenment.

These great souls after death, are transported to Brahmaloka, a superior quality of heaven where life is millions of times better than the world can offer. If one is free from desires, he is the wisest person. When such great souls leave their bodies, they are spiritually so high that they go straight to the world of enlighted habitants. They are said to have got the Mukti or direct liberation. However, in the process, some nonsensitive aspirants are attracted to the desire or the Vasans of the materialistic world that delays their progress to Enlightenment.

There is no doubt that everyone in the world is looking for happiness. We do not exactly know what is the true happiness. We are born to be happy, cheerful, and satisfied in life. But instead of being happy with what we have, we run after desires. When one desire is fulfilled, we feel happy for some time and the agitation of the mind ceases for a while. With time, another desire comes in. It keeps on moving in cyclic order. *The desire is a never-ending process.* One should understand that the desire never lies on an object; it is a mental state. Happiness is within us, yet everyone is looking for it outside. Look within, introspect, and turn inward, you will find happiness and peace within yourself. At the end of life, one understands the damaging effects of the desire. In old age, when time has elapsed, most of us understand that everything we are cultivating, nourishing, and nurturing is a waste.

Desire is described as the devil. Unhappiness is the result of an unfulfilled desire that leads to restlessness and mental stress. One can have millions of desires, but nature is not obliged to fulfill them. The law is that "*you get what you deserve, not what you desire.*" Normally we do not accept the advice of great masters warning us against the ill effects of desire. We think that they are telling us against our enjoyment and this is one of the greatest misunderstandings causing suffering in the world. One must acquire, and enjoy as much of the world without desiring it. Spiritual developments are for peace, prosperity, and progress. When one is spiritual, the wealth of the world will be with him. Despite that, he is unaffected by the environment around him.

Desire and unhappiness are strongly correlated. As long as a desire remains unfulfilled, one is unhappy. The moment one gets it, he becomes happy, at least for that moment. *Is the material or the state of mind that brings happiness to you*? Unfulfilled desire generates stress in the mind that works against happiness. The desire for food comes when the stomach is empty. Therefore, emptiness is the root of the desire. From the very moment, we wake up till the time to sleep, from birth to death, all of us are consumed by a feeling of emptiness.

One must have fulfilled many desires in life, but has the feeling of emptiness gone or even reduced? No. Just think, why does the emptiness not go away despite fulfilling so many desires? *The Bhagavad Gita explains this phenomenon by saying that one must always feel full and satisfied.* When you are in the path of knowledge, then you understand the need to have zero desire within you. This leads to the ultimate purpose of life – the attainment of total and complete happiness within. While continuing to fulfil your desires, you must also give time to know your fullness.

The universal law is "*as you think so you become.*" Do not think only for yourself. By this, you are limiting your mind and intellect. You are becoming a limited, restricted, small being. Always try to fix a higher goal in life.

Selflessness is the highest quality of action. By this, you are working towards enlightenment. You are not driven to benefit yourself. The other approach to reduce desire is to love people. "*Love and affection bring in the best in others. By this, you connect with them at their best, and at the same time they, in turn, also give their best. Everyone puts their best leading to wonderful results.*" If your neighbour buys a luxury car, you be happy in the true sense. Feel one with the neighbour. He has worked hard to achieve this success.

Just think of the growth of the human population that has increased in an exponential progression from a near number of 100 crores (1000 million) in 1900 to about 800 crores (8000 million) in the year 2023. Have you wondered from where these souls have come? There can only be two sources of their trans-migration. The first source is the migration of water and animal kingdoms to a lower form of human beings. Lower form means that they are born either in very remote places that are cut off from the mainstream and they are less knowledgeable or they may be mentally challenged. The other source is the collapse of the other exoplanets from where the souls in large numbers are transported to this earth. As you know from the Bhagavad Gita souls cannot be created or destroyed by any force such as fire. In the journey of the soul from its origin to its end, which is considered as a merger of the soul with the Brahma, there cannot be any dead end or break in between. It has to continuously change its abode from one body to the other so that it evolves spiritually.

From the past, through the present, and to the future a continuity of the soul is maintained. Then comes the explanation of rebirth. What is a rebirth and why it is required? "*Birth and rebirth are only a change of the physical body so that it fulfils the quality and the quantity of the desires and attachments. It maintains its process of continuity so that all desires are fulfilled before its final journey to Baikuntha.*" For example, if you have a strong desire to be a great leader that you could not become in this life then God certainly gives you an opportunity in the next life so that your Aatma is satisfied. "*An unsatisfied Aatma cannot go to the Baikuntha. The type of thought you have in your lifetime shall continue to manifest as well in your next life unbroken.*" One should know that (i) life is a continuous process and does not terminate with the death of the body, (ii) death uncovers the hard cell of the soul, still the soul is covered by causal and over it the astral cover, (iii) the fate of the person in the next life is part (Parabdha) of the total Karma (Sanchita) which one has agreed to face in this life, and (iv) except the enlightened souls (those who got Moksha due to the highest state of devotion or deeds) the process of continuous rebirth and death is the must.

The mind of a person is always in the state of hearing, thinking, and doing either good or bad things. Following this, it gets channelized to the same Gunas in this and then to the next life. His life is shaped accordingly. "*The present state of the person is the outcome of his past actions, and the future is the projection of the present thoughts and actions.*" The quality of a person is divided into 3 Gunas viz. the Sattvik, Rajsic, and Tamasic which are always present in each of us in different proportions. Our personality is decided based on the quantum of this quality in us. Let us consider that your soul has started the journey to a higher state and you are climbing the ladder up. If you are Tamsic, you are on the ground floor. Then acquiring good habits, you are climbing to the next floor gradually and becoming Rajsic. You still climb up with acquiring more positive Gunas, you are going to the Sattvik floor. And finally, you go to the terrace which is the Mokshya. You are to climb the steps one by one. Now jumping from a lower to a higher floor is very rare but not impossible like Valmik Rishi. It is said that the higher floor or Realm is very sparingly occupied now and the lower floors are heavily crowded.

Spiritual things cannot be proved scientifically. Science can be good only where capturing data is possible to prove the outcome. Whereas, philosophy satisfies all the questioning of the intellectuals for which there is no need for scientific data. Science can only prove materialistic things, but what about its origin and how it came to be, science has no answer, but philosophy.

Your feelings matter in karma. If you are saying something with good intentions to your friend, but he is hurt, it still earns good karma for you and bad karma for him. Along similar lines, if you are saying something with bad intentions but he has no problem, then you are earning bad karma and he is earning good karma. Then what is the worst karma? It is the sum of (i) bad thoughts (from the mind), (ii) bad feelings (from the heart), (iii) bad language (from the mouth), and finally (iv) bad actions (physical) which are summed up to a great burden. If you are forcing someone for your benefit, then the karma earned is in the worst form.

Out of the five bodies we have (1. physical, 2. mental, 3. energy, 4. etheric, and 5. bliss) our karma is accumulated to the first three bodies only. Therefore, on breaking your physical body at death, karma is still with you in the mental body in the astral world and then on breaking the mental body, it is again carried to the causal realm in energy body.

Karma in itself does not give any punishment or reward to anyone, but it makes its way to your life. *If you see the animals, they are leading their life without intelligence and therefore they accumulate the least karma.* Whereas human beings are born with infinite freedom, options, and possibilities because of their intelligence (free will). However, they are pulled by the materialistic world and earn karma in the process. They live with their interest and never think that they are part of this great universe. When you think deeply, you can feel that you are a part of everything else in this universe.

In the process of growth of life, one develops a great sense of likes and dislikes that are solely responsible for the addition of karma. The present civilization has forced us to live a lifeless life. We are not free to cry or laugh loudly leading to a joyless life. *Those who cry and laugh freely, have a stress-less life and this kind of free-minded people earn less karma. If one lives happily in every moment, the karmic effect reduces to zero.*

There is extreme diversity in the society. Some are born rich and others are born poor, some are healthy, others are handicapped, and so on. "*You are suffering only because you and only you have created it for you.*" Think deeply about this, you have the answer. Your karma is the cause of your response to what is happening to you. If one has no job, he is suffering and then when he gets a job, he again complains after some time that he is suffering. Similarly, if one is married, he is suffering, and when he was unmarried he had the complain that he was suffering, and so on. "*If one controls himself both psychologically and emotionally, he can be guaranteed 100% free from karmic influence with good fate. Karma is nothing to do with the morality of your life, it is to do with one's cause and effect. That way, ignorance, action, and no action all add to karma.*"

You may have had a disastrous day yesterday, but when you have got up fresh in the morning today, please do not manufacture more karma for yourself by revengeful actions. Your misery of yesterday is waiting to give more bad karma to you. Are you interested in getting more of it? Whatever had happened has happened, already.

Then comes what you should do. Now karma is the action. You know that what you are now is your processed product. It is by your actions and responsibility only. Even in society, when you see an unfed child begging in the street, some pain comes to you, even though his parents have manufactured it. This is the karma of the society of the area which has to think for it. It is seen that you have done something very bad some years back that has appeared to trouble you. You call it fate but it is your karma as well.

Some turn to *astrologists* to know their future. These Astro-readers say your future is based on your present state and the inheritance. You can turn it around 100% by the simple action of spiritual practices. That is in your hand. There are plentiful examples of this. Then comes your *horoscope*. It is a reading of your possible obstacles and how to crossover them. It cannot give any possibility of your sure roadmap of life. If you are on the spiritual path, even the best astrologist can't predict your future as you are the creator of it.

Someone asked you a silly question "*Who are you*?" The answer may look very simple but is a difficult one. Like your body is a collection of food from the earth over the years, your mind is also a collection of information that you have stored over the years. You are represented through your memory. If the memory is lost you are lost. A mad person has almost no memory. And what is that memory and where it is stored? The human body has some 40 to 50 trillion cells of different sizes and shapes. Over one year these cells get completely replaced. Then how does this memory gets stored in the physical (brain/body), mental, and energy systems get transmitted from one cell to another? It is very intriguing and the design of such millions of features in the human body is mindblowing.

There is a clear division between memory stored in the brain and memory carried by the body. The memory in the mind can compute, and process, while the body's memory can perceive and give signals to the mind's memory. The exchange of karma is the maximum in physical intimacy. When a female bears a child, this intimacy or karmic memory shifts from the husband to the child. As mentioned earlier, sexuality is the highest catcher of memory and therefore carries a big amount of karma. Since every one of us has a huge load of karma with us, let it be not over-burned with more karma through sexual practices. This is why many good spiritual persons are not involved in these activities.

The allotment of Prarabdha karma, which is part of the vast accumulated karma (Sanchita) is different for different individuals. When a child is born, you can see his response and behaviour concerning his brothers and sisters are different. This allotment varies from person to person depending on his capability to dispose of the quantum in the present incarnation. When someone is in good spiritual practices, he is not only trying to stop earning bad karma, he is adding positive karma in his store.

To become a karma yogi, one needs to be trained under an accomplished teacher, the environment should be conducive, and there should be dedication by the student. Be always conscious of yourself and never think that there is God around you, who is responsible for all your activities. When one understands that he is responsible for his karma, and no one else, everything becomes easy for him. *Karma veer is the person who has done his best, capable of being at the best and doing the best.* This inner journey has to be undertaken oneself. When an enlightened person accepts someone as a student, then he can guide him in such a way that his karma, which otherwise would have taken a hundred lives to work out can be accomplished within a few minutes. But these could be rare cases.

Our karma is limited to the first three stages of our bodies, i.e., the physical, mental, and energy levels which are our places of abode in *Bhur, Bhubah*, and *Swaha* (the earth, the astral or Pitrulok, and the heaven or causal world respectably), and beyond this level, our body may be etheric and/or bliss body, where there have no karmic effects. You have to dissolve all the karmic load before your soul leaves the energy level to the etheric level.

The very meaning of *karma yoga* is not to keep yourself busy, but it is a process of doing things so that you are free or liberated from the cycles of birth and death. Karma yoga also does not mean that you always do good or social service. It is about doing good always with good feelings and happily without any intention. *Doing work is karma and doing work so that it liberates you is karma yoga.* You may be content with the work you are doing, but if the work is in the context of creating a better living in the society around you then it is karma yoga. It also tells us that one should not look up to others for help, or look down on others to whom we are helping. Do not give up everything that you have. Karma yoga is the selfless attitude of doing good to the society where you are living.

Our lifestyle has changed significantly over the years. Has anyone seen your parents laughing freely each day? What we see in our family has almost 100% impact on the development of our personality. The anxiety, tension, fear, and all other discussions in the home are carried by the kids in their lives, and with this, how can we expect a better society from the next generation?

Have a deep embrace with the creation even for a minute each day. Surrender to him, you shall see outstanding results. Can you try to sit in a still position and maintain a blank in your mind for a single minute? It is very difficult unless you are an accomplished yogi. If you can, your karma has no impact on you. You are liberated.

We keep on working throughout our lives with the desire to acquire more PPP (position, power, and property). In the present-day context, the losers are those, who have no desire. One should have the desire but desire for enlightenment only and not for PPP. The world exists today because a minor fraction of the great spiritual entities are meditating for world peace.

How can you know that someone is under constant emotional stress? For such a personality, observe that the left eye is slightly smaller unless he is born defective. Through yoga, your body is made fit for taking up more karma now so that your future karma is reduced. Physical yoga is where you burn the excess karma you have collected over the years. People do a lot of breathing exercises. The positive effect of it is that it destroys or burns a lot of one's karma.

When your activities benefit society, it is good karma. For example, when you discover a medicine to cure people of fatal diseases, or you create a machine that can be used for the large benefit of society, it is good karma. Personally helping individuals to relieve their pain (physical) or suffering (psychological) is good karma as well, but when you see an injustice made to an individual on the road and you can help but neglect, this inaction is bad karma.

If you are living for others, not affected by your interests, and always thinking good for others you are in the path of liberation. It is very difficult but possible. In some yogic practices, one can go back to the previous lives and recount the layers of the past, working them out with intense awareness. Reaching this state is difficult.

The child selects the parents where it is best suited to discharge his Pradrabha karma. For the same parents and with the same environment the kids grow up to different personalities. This event can be seen in the womb of the mother. The movement of the infant in the mother's womb is different for her different kids. Depending on the karmic load the response to the same input is different for different persons. One can easily notice that born to the same parents and in the same environment the response and behavior of even the twin brothers are different. You may have seen that a father is a criminal, but the child is spiritual. This is because you have chosen it to be like that.

When death comes to someone when he has vibrant energy within (a youth), the body then has to be pacified through the process of rituals. Maybe the person takes birth immediately to accomplish the desires. But when a person dies at a very old age with minimum energy, there is no hurry for immediate rebirth. He stays in the higher realms for long before the rebirth.

Then comes the epitope, the highest state, when your love for human beings shifts to love for God. Connect with him and you get the enlightenment, the ultimate freedom from this painful world.

Finally, we all know the story of the great monarch Bharata who gave up his luxury to his son and retired to the forest. When he was about to be enlightened, he saw a deer being killed by a hunter soon after it delivered an offspring. Bharata saw that the infant would die without help so he took care of it. Instead of thinking of God, his thoughts were attracted to the deer. Even on his deathbed, his attention was on the deer. As a result, the desire for the deer made him go through an entire incarnation as a deer before he got enlightened.

(I am thankful to the great masters and authors, whose works are referred in this chapter; specifically, "Karma by Sadhguru, Good Karma by Jaya Row, and others.")

CHAPTER - 3

ॐ *The Universe is created with incredible perfection and dimension. The sun is another star amongst the 400 billion stars present in our Milky Way Galaxy. Again, there are nearly 200 billion such galaxies in our Universe. Besides, being on Earth we are continuously in motion at a mind-blowing speed of millions of km/h in a resultant path in space that is rather impossible to calculate. We all agree that the Big Bang had happened; which is the responsible creation of the universe.*

For most of us, both God and the universe are mysteries. The human body, the universe, and nature all are created with intense complexity and are mind-boggling. The main question is: who created whom? Did God create man or man created God? The DNA of the body is unbelievably complex and therefore designed very carefully, and so is the complexity of our nature. We cannot sustain ourselves on earth without the smallest insects like bees as pollination cannot happen without them. Everything is neatly designed, from the macro - the vastness of the universe, to the micro - the role of the micro insets. And if there is a design, there must be a designer. Let us thank Him first as without Him, we are non-existent."

Chapter - 3

The Universe and Evolution of Life on Earth

Universe – The Mega Creation

The universe is created with incredible perfection and dimension. Even with our present-day scientific knowledge and advancements, we are just incapable enough of reaching out to a tiny fraction of its vastness both in its special extension and scientific magnanimity. Within the scope of our present-day knowledge, we have put forth various theories on its creation and continuous evolution, but with huge limitations. Scientists are almost entirely in agreement that the Big Bang happened but differ in the ways of their explanations of how it happened. The prominent theory of how the Big Bang could have happened may perhaps have the following steps (The Hot Big Bang Model).

- At its beginning, the Universe had no dimensions and was extremely hot and dense.
- The Big Bang caused expansion, which resulted in a decrease in the universe's temperature. The dispersion of the temperature is a result of this cooling.
- The majority of the elements found in the universe today were generated within the first few hours of the expansion of the universe.
- As a result of gravity, the largest objects in the universe began to rotate, giving rise to galaxies.

- Atomic collisions caused clouds of hydrogen and helium to begin condensing within these galaxies, which sparked nuclear fusion events. Stars were created as a result of these reactions.
- These stars died and collapsed, causing enormous stellar explosions that released additional elements into the vast universe. There are now more stars and planets due to these elements.

Two distinct rulebooks describe how the universe operates. The dynamics of the expanding universe, galaxies colliding, and planets in orbit are all beautifully explained by the general theory of relativity. The other forces— electromagnetism and nuclear forces—are handled by quantum mechanics. When it comes to explaining what happens when a nuclear atom decays or when a light particle strikes a solar cell, the quantum theory is a good option. The formulations of the theories of relativity and quantum mechanics are fundamentally dissimilar. For more than a century, there has been a simmering conflict between the two branches of physics. Events are continuous and deterministic in general relativity. Events in quantum mechanics are created by the interaction of subatomic particles in jumps (quantum leaps), with probabilistic.

When one attempts to scale the theory of relativity down to quantum size, it produces absurd results and eventually describes gravity with infinite values. Similar problems arise when quantum mechanics is scaled up to cosmic dimensions. Even in what appears to be space, quantum fields carry a certain amount of energy, and the amount of energy increases as the fields get larger. $E=mc^2$ is Einstein's formula for the relationship between energy and mass. In other words, building up energy works exactly like building up mass: when you build it up to a certain size, it turns into a black hole that causes the universe to collapse in on itself.

Space-time, according to Einstein's theory, isn't flat and doesn't move linearly. Consider placing a heavy object on a length of stretched-out fabric; the fabric will sink under the weight of the object. Similar to how time bends due to gravity, space-time also travels with a slight curve rather than in a straight line. The majority of things in the universe are explained by Einstein's general theory of relativity. However because it is unable to explain how the universe began, it is insufficient. Quantum theory plays a role in this.

Quest for a Unified Theory of Creation

Over the brief history of humanity, our understanding of the cosmos has evolved. Before we have a single theory that can account for the entirety of the cosmos, though, we still have some distance to go. When it comes to singularity occurrences and subatomic particles, the laws of general relativity are inapplicable. On the other hand, quantum mechanics is applicable in every situation, but there is no coherent theory that unifies it with gravity. Hence, a unified theory must incorporate both the principles of quantum mechanics and general relativity.

One can never completely disprove a theory; instead, one can only be sure that the predictions the theory consistently makes are by the data. It should be possible for mankind to fully understand the principles that govern our universe once a unifying theory has been found. Then and only then will our quest for comprehension be completed. As of now, the key concepts in understanding our universe are given in the figure below.

The latest is the String Theory (Unified theory), which is the combination of all the above theories (Fig. 3.1) that could bring breakthroughs in our understanding of the universe. It is said that it involves 26 dimensions instead of just four dimensions in our universe.

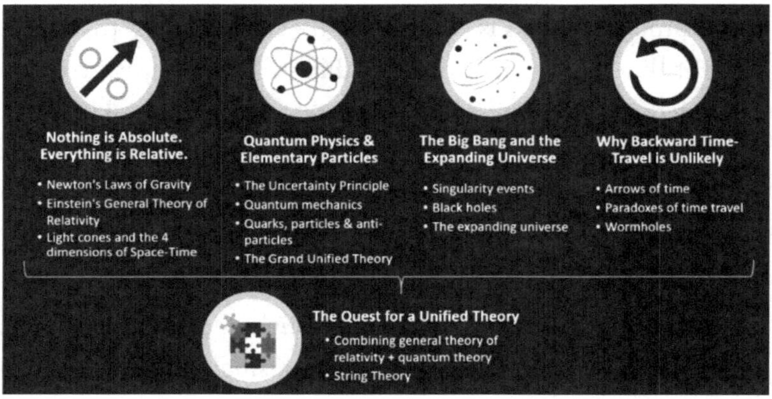

Fig.3.1: The String Theory of Explanation on the Universe.

Possibilities of Earth-Like Planets

To determine whether there is likely to be life on other planets in the Milky Way, scientists have been searching for exoplanets (planets that orbit stars outside of our solar system) for years. A planet must be rocky, roughly the same size as Earth, circle Sun-like (G-type) stars, and be in the habitable zone to qualify as Earth-like. Also, it must travel in the range between its star's habitable zones, where the planet is neither too hot nor too cold for life to thrive. It has been determined that around 4,000 exoplanets have the proper size, those orbits around their stars. These exoplanets may have liquid water and perhaps even life. Research using data from NASA's Kepler Mission, which was published in *"The Astronomical Journal,"* suggests that there are more Earth-like planets than previously thought in our galaxy. In the Milky Way, millions of planets like Earth orbiting are the G-type stars. The analysis only took into account planets that have a regular orbit around the stars.

Up to 400 billion stars make up our Milky Way, with 7% of them being G-type stars. (Astronomer Jaimie Matthews from UBC). This implies that, at the very least, six billion stars in our Galaxy may have planets similar to Earth. How many Sun-like stars can support an Earth-like planet, is the next query. The estimate of 4000 exoplanets appears to be rather low.

Facts about the Universe

The following lists some of the amazing facts about the Universe.

1. Earth makes a full rotation about its axis once a day. Its circumference is roughly 40,075 km. Thus if you are located at the equator you are moving at a speed of 1670 km/h, which reduces gradually to zero at the poles.
2. Earth orbits the sun once in 365 days in a nearly circular path. It covers this route at a speed of 1.07 lakh km/hr
3. Proxima Centauri is the closest star to our earth and is 40,208,000 million km or 4.246 light years away from the Earth.
4. The Sun, the Solar System, and the Milky Way rotate once every 230 million years at a speed of 200 km/s, or 720,000 km/h. When compared to other galaxies, the Milky Way also moves through space.

   The Sun and solar system have orbited the Milky Way galaxy's nucleus roughly 20 times over their 4.6-billion-year lifespan. This is referred to as the *cosmic or galactic* year. It is the amount of time needed for the Sun to complete one orbit around the Milky Way galaxy's centre.

5. In the area around our Sun, the Milky Way galaxy rotates at a speed of 7.56 lakh km/sec, or 2.1 million km/hr. The area of the sky that is bounded by the constellations of Leo and Virgo is roughly where we are travelling.
6. The Milky Way and Andromeda are separated by roughly 2.5 million light-years. The two galaxies are moving 402,000 km/ hr toward one another, propelled by gravity. Even yet, it will be four billion years before they finally meet.
7. In our Milky Way galaxy, the sun is just one of 400 billion stars.
8. There are 100 to 200 billion galaxies in our Universe.
9. The diameter of the Milky Way ranges from 100,000 to 120,000 light-years.
10. The solar system has a radius of 143.73 billion kilometres measured from the Sun.
11. The observable universe has a sphere-like shape with a 93 billion light-year diameter. There are multiple universes in space. There could be one to a billion parallel universes. We have no technical know-how to arrive at the count.
12. Scientists estimate that the Milky Way alone contains between ten million and a billion black holes, which is based on the number of stars large enough to form these black holes.
13. There is no centre to the cosmos. The cosmos has been expanding outward from a central point of detonation ever since the Big Bang, which occurred roughly 13.7 billion years ago.

14. Galaxies perish when star creation stops within them or when the gas necessary for star formation is gone. Red dwarfs, which are the smallest and coolest stars, exist for a few trillion years while stars like the sun only last for 10 billion years.
15. Only 0.00000005% of the sun's total energy is received by the earth which maintains life sustainable.

The above facts have assured us at least one thing our solar system is too small in comparison to the vastness of the universe. Furthermore, being part of the galaxy, we are in constant motion at a very high speed in a resultant path and direction that we are incapable of calculating. Even most of us are unaware that we are moving at this incredible speed. It is the gift of God that we never feel this speed. There has never been an accident amongst the trillions of stars moving at very great speed continuously in the generated paths. Our solar system in the Milky Way Galaxy can be seen in Fig.3.2 and the location of the Milky Way Galaxy in the Universe is shown in Fig.3.3.

Fig. 3.2. We in Our Milky Way Galaxy

Fig.3.3. Location of Milky Way Galaxy in the Universe

The Universe

According to the Big Bang theory, the cosmos has been expanding since space and time co-emerged some 13.7 billion years ago. The size of the observable universe, which has a current diameter of around 93 billion light-years, can be determined, even though the size of the entire universe's space is unknown. *The question of what caused the Big Bang remains unanswered if you think the universe was created in that manner. Yet the mystery surrounding the origin of the stuff that the Big Bang put in motion continues to this day.*

The development of observational techniques revealed that the Sun is one of the Milky Way galaxy's few hundred billion stars, which is one of the few hundred billion galaxies in the cosmos. There are several stars with planets in a galaxy. Since galaxies are evenly dispersed throughout the universe at the largest size, there is neither an edge nor a core. Galaxies of smaller sizes are grouped in clusters and superclusters that create enormous filaments and holes in space, creating a structure that resembles a foamy mass. The idea that the universe had a beginning and has been expanding rapidly ever since was suggested by findings made in the early 20th century.

According to the Big Bang theory, the initial matter and energy have become less dense as the universe has expanded. The inflationary epoch, the first period of accelerated expansion, lasted for 10-32 seconds. The first subatomic particles and basic atoms were able to form as the universe continued to expand and progressively cooled. Under the influence of gravity, the dark matter eventually accumulated and created the foam-like structure of filaments and voids. Huge clouds of hydrogen and helium were progressively drawn to the areas of the universe where dark matter was the densest, resulting in the formation of the earliest galaxies, stars, and everything else we see today.

The movement of galaxies has revealed that there is far more matter in the universe than can be explained by the observable objects—stars, galaxies, nebulas, and interstellar gas. Dark matter is a name for this invisible substance ("dark means that there is a wide range of strong indirect evidence that it exists, but we have not yet detected it directly"). As per wikimail.com, "The most popular theory of the universe is the Lambda Clod Dark Model; or ΛCDM. It is known as the standard model of Big Bang Cosmology. It suggests that about 69.2% ± 1.2% of the mass and energy in the universe is a cosmological constant, which is responsible for the current expansion of space, and about 25.8% ± 1.1% is dark matter. The ordinary ('baryonic') matter is therefore only 4.84%±0.1% of the physical universe. Stars, planets, and visible gas clouds only form about 6% of the ordinary matter, which indicates that almost 99.7% of the mass in space is not a part of the stars, planets, and visible clouds."

Regarding the outcome of the universe, there are numerous opposing theories. According to some physicists, there may be many more universes outside our own that also exist. Even in principle, the Universe is immense, enormous, and gigantic as far as the most powerful telescopes can observe it. There are hundreds of billions or trillions of galaxies in the universe. Each of those galaxies has approximately a trillion stars (on average), and from our perspective, they are dispersed throughout the cosmos in a sphere with a diameter of 93 billion light years.

The four main building blocks of the cosmos are the physicochemical laws, energy, time, and non-Euclidean space. Although time and space are combined to form space-time entities in relativity, we will utilise them independently in this context. The universe is controlled and managed by physical laws, which use energy to generate, modify, move, contract, expand, and carry out all physicochemical reactions in the time dimension through space. The universe is spontaneous and operates according to unbending, error-free predetermined laws.

Time and space are relative to the observer; they are not absolute. It is impossible to tell if two events that occurred at different periods occurred in the same location because everything is continually moving with everything else. Moreover, time is relative; that is, it travels at various speeds depending on who is seeing it. Since they are woven into the fabric of space-time, space and time cannot be considered independently. All events have to be represented in space-time about four coordinates: (a) a point in time, (b) a point in space, (c) the position of the observer, and (d) the velocity of the observer.

For the first time, scientists have recently discovered that astronauts age more slowly during extended simulative space flight than they would have if their feet were firmly on Earth. Hawking seemed to acknowledge God's involvement in the universe's genesis. Writing in his bestseller *"A Brief History of Time"* in 1988, he said: "If we discover a complete theory, it would be the ultimate triumph of human reason – for then we should know the mind of God."

Now it nearly confirms that there are uncertain numbers of earth-like planets in our own Milky Way Galaxy, but the presence of life on these planets is yet to be explored. Our present knowledge is quite incapable of exploring the facts. But at the same time, how could our spiritual Masters be capable of communicating with the living beings of the outer terrestrial planets? Are they scientifically so great? Is spiritualism a different science altogether or it is just magic? Now here are the experiences of some of the experiences of great living and past masters who have witnessed the facts of life existing on the outer planets (Exoplanets).

Evolution of Major Life Forms on Earth

The first multicellular organisms appeared roughly 610 million years from now, even though the world was formed about 4.6 billion years ago. The Cambrian Explosion, an event lasting 10 million years, saw the evolution of numerous diverse species of organisms. Certain environmental changes that made the Earth's environment more conducive to a larger range of life forms may have contributed to this abrupt burst of development.

About 500 million years ago, fungi and plants first emerged. Arthropods quickly followed them (insects and spiders). Around 300 million years ago, amphibians followed, then 200 million years ago, mammals, and then 150 million years ago, birds. Several ancient creatures have gone extinct, according to fossil evidence. It is typical for species to go extinct; in fact, 99% of all species that have ever existed on Earth are thought to have vanished.

Geologic time scales are used by geologists and other Earth scientists to pinpoint certain points in Earth's history. Figure 3.4 depicts the basic timeline of the 4.6 billion-year-old Earth, whereas Figure 3.5 depicts the geologic time scale of the emergence of plant and animal life on Earth.

Figures 3.4-3.5 indicate the formation of the earth and the evolution of life on it. Human beings evolved on earth some 2,00,000 years back and the life of so-called intelligent humans started only some 10 - 15 thousand years ago, as evidenced by the great epic of Ramayana. The timeline of the evolution of human beings is an indication of our Modern civilization.

The Astonishing Nature - Did Life Start by Accident?

Many scientists believe that life on Earth started by accident. They think that it was caused by a series of small steps and chemical processes. But more and more scientists realise that DNA is so complex that it cannot have originated from a series of accidental chemical reactions.

The argument is that no computer software can come into being by accident, without a design, and without programmers working on it. Our DNA is as complex as computer software. Life did not come into being by accident. DNA contains so much information that you need volumes of books to write it down. Could all this information stored in our DNA have come into being by accidental chemical processes?

Random processes only lead to chaos. If one writes down a series of random musical notes or combines some random musical notes, he can never get a nice melody. It will be a terrible collection of separate sounds. Then, if life cannot have come into being by accident, it must have been designed. The body is unbelievably complex and therefore designed very carefully. And if there is a design, there must be a *designer*.

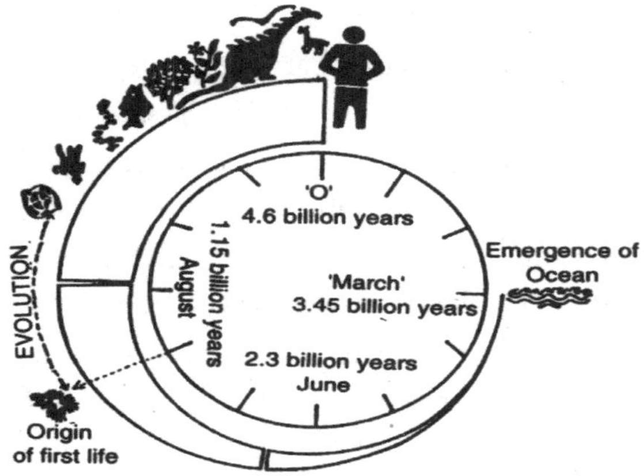

Emergence of oceans and life forms on geologic time-scale.

Fig. 3.4: Timeline of a 4.6 billion-year-old Earth

Fig. 3.5: Geologic time scale illustrating the timing of events

The beauty and complexity of the world and the universe are mind-boggling. There is endless space with billions and trillions of stars and planets on one side and a tiny earth with an enormous number of different plants, animals, and people on the other side. You can see that everything in nature is made with enormous attention to detail. Every plant, animal, and human being is so complex that even after centuries of research scientists still have a lot to discover. There are countless stars and planets, too many to discover them all. The design is very creative and brilliant.

A flower cannot reproduce without insects and insects cannot live without flowers. Many flowers have beautiful colours and others the fragrance by which they attract insects. Bees and other insects pollinate many of the plants we eat. Without these bees, we do not have food. This is just one of the countless examples that show how everything works together to make life possible. The Creator of this must be incredibly creative and brilliant to be able to come up with all these things.

Put the human body under a microscope to examine it. There is a vast world there as well. Replicating cells combine to form organs and limbs. The result of this entire interaction assures that humans can exist. The human body has about 37.2 trillion cells having 200 different sizes, shapes, and structures of which 50 to 250 billion cells die each day for each adult. Every year our body gets full replacement of the entire cell structure. Be it the human body, nature, or the universe, it is intricately put together with fantastic accuracy. After all, change does not create order, only chaos. Life cannot arise from dead chemicals; no scientist has yet demonstrated that.

Every night when we go to bed, we expect the sun to come up again in a few hours. We are not afraid; it will stay dark. We trust in these regular patterns of day and night and summer and winter. We can also rely on the laws of nature, such as gravity. These laws are unchanging. Science could not exist if there were no fixed laws of nature. In nature, everything works according to fixed patterns of cause and effect. Nothing happens at random. Gravity always pulls you down when you jump, never up. If the laws of nature were arbitrary, we would end up with chaos. Life on earth would be impossible and the universe would not exist. The Creator is very reliable.

The endless universe shows how great and powerful the Creator is. He could have stopped after having made the world with living plants, animals, and humans. He gave man the ability to make his own choices. We cannot live without the people around us. We need each other to be able to get things done. The bond with our family and loved ones goes deeper than just needing one another for food and drink. Relationships and love between human beings form a special part of our existence. They give life extra flavor. The Creator is still involved in His creation and never left us. A question comes to us *"Why there is so much misery in this beautiful creation"?* I shall respond to it later.

He gave people the ability to respect and love Him, or do what they want and ignore Him. Every human being is born and therefore has a mother. How would your mother feel if you chose to ignore her and deny that you owe your life to her? You can ignore your mother, but that does not change the fact that you were born. How would the Creator feel if you chose to ignore Him? There are several reasons why we cannot see Him.

The Purpose of Life

The world has more than 4,000 religions and most of them have a different picture of the Creator. One could study all religions of the world to find the truth, but studying more than 4,000 religions is so Hercules a task that a whole lifetime is not enough. God has given us freedom. You cannot give love to dead objects, or robots, but you can give it to creatures who can respond to that love. God expects your sincere attention, but He does not force you. He wants you to react from the heart to His love for you. Therefore, look at the Lord before it is too late. Just call him now, while he is near. If you look for God, He will give you His attention.

Deep in our hearts, we know whether something is right or wrong. All over the world, it is wrong to kill another human being. And nowhere in the world is stealing someone else's possessions acceptable. Animals do not have these moral values. When one animal kills another, it does so because it is hungry or because it is being attacked. Animals also do not lie to each other. Human beings know that certain things are right or wrong. An honest judge (God) will pass judgment based on the law. He will punish the guilty to compensate for the harm the victim suffered.

God is reliable because He made the unchanging laws of nature that remain unchanged in every situation and circumstance. If moral laws are broken, a reaction must follow. In case of a major offense, a judge is asked to determine the penalty. If someone is murdered, for example, family and friends demand that justice be done. The killer must be punished. If a judge lets the murderer go free without punishment, friends and family would never accept it. God made the moral laws, if one breaks the laws, action must be taken. Because He is the highest authority, He must act when we break His laws. Offenders must be punished, whether the crime is murder or something else. But God does not act as soon as an offense is committed. Later we will try to discover the reason for this. It seems obvious that God cannot just ignore when one of His creatures is murdered. But God also loves. Couldn't He just ignores or forgives our smaller mistakes?

By breaking His moral rules, you try to offend the Creator. Every offense you commit, minor or major, demands a reaction. On the other hand, one's actions must make Him proud. Show your appreciation for your Creator. He wants your attention, straight from the heart. Things you do must make you proud. Gossip about others is normal but hurts people a lot. Never be jealous of what others have and you do not. No one does everything right always. One may think to make up for the bad things by doing enough good things. Many mistakes cause damage that cannot be repaired. We have ourselves or maybe our family as our priority and that is the reason we keep ignoring what the Creator wants us to do. Working for ourselves and our family keep us occupied every day. With time, we accumulate more punishment. You will be punished on the day when God will show his anger and he is always right.

Our freedom of choice allows us to choose between good and evil. Every day we choose to lie, deceive, gossip, argue, envy, misuse power, and more; and do illegitimate sexual desires. We are proud and short-sighted and think mainly about what makes us feel good right now. We are even addicted to certain habits.

God is the source of truth and justice; therefore, He cannot overlook your wrongs, even though you are truly sorry and promise to do better. If He just forgave you, He would no longer be just and reliable. God made us because He loves us. He loves His creatures and wants to share His love with us, more than we can ever realise.

Religion and God

Both God and the cosmos are mysteries. Who created who is the central query? Man created God, or did God create man? Virtually everyone questions, whether there is a God at some point or another in their lives. If your family was religious when you were growing up, you most likely heard some explanation for why you were created. God was created by man with humanistic traits so that he might share in his suffering, disappointments, worries, stress, and anxiety. Man-made God is self-aware, possesses spontaneous absolute power (almighty), can suspend all natural rules, creates everything at once, and upholds justice. Although having absolute power, God always abides by the laws of nature. The physiochemical rules of the universe are never disregarded or broken by God. God lives simultaneously in the present (∞), future (∞ +1), and past (∞ - 1). You might be able to travel through time at the speed of light, but it's impossible to travel into the future. The speed υ is equal to infinity in both the past and the future, and the differential of time for motion, *dt*/*dx*, is equal to zero.

There are many different religions and gods, and throughout history, many groups have created their gods. We must first familiarise ourselves with various religions to understand diverse Gods. Many super-religions have been created through cultural tradition. Hinduism, Jainism,

Buddhism, and Sikhism are the four primary faiths of India. Taoism and Confucianism are the two main religions of China. Indigenous ethnic religions are present throughout the world and include Asian shamanism and traditional African faiths. Some new religion that is revitalizing an older faith has been around since the 19th century.

In his book "A History of God," Karen Armstrong examines the origins of the three main monotheistic religions—Judaism, Christianity, and Islam—as well as Hinduism and Buddhism. From its early Middle Eastern origins up until the present, the concept of God has undergone an evolution.

There could be 330 million Gods in Hinduism. They hold that there is a primary God called Brahman and that all other gods are various manifestations of the primary God, Brahman. Some other Hindus hold the view that there are independent gods in addition to the primary God. The bulk of Hindu deities have numerous heads and hands, which stand for their extraordinary strength and talent. The primary Hindu deity, Brahman, controls and maintains the cosmos. Eventually, everyone who is good will ally with Brahman.

Various Gods, each with a distinctive power; in Hinduism, Brahman (the Creator) is revered as the God of creation. The God of life preservation is Vishnu, while the God of destruction is Shiva. Ganesh (wisdom) has a human body and an elephant head. He is the deity that Hindus revere the most. The Goddess of time and annihilation is Kali (force of time). The Goddess of wealth and prosperity is Lakshmi (prosperity). The main character in the Hindu epic Ramayana, Hanuman (devotion), is renowned for helping Rama. The wife of

Brahman, Sarasvati (art, music, and knowledge), is seated on a white lotus blossom and is heard playing music.

Men create an all-powerful God to fill all their needs as a result of their materialistic aspirations. In this regard, man was never able to comprehend the true nature of God and the cosmos. The only kind of God that a man can deal with is the one who can grant all of his desires. Man has made a strong, forgiving, and artificial God out of his greed, selfishness, infantile imagination, joys, and anxieties

The intention of this chapter is:

1. *To introduce the readers to the knowledge on the beginning of the Universe and how and when it evolved from a small super condensed object to its incredible perfection and dimension, and from where this matter had come in the vast space.*
2. *To make the readers aware that we are continuously in motion with a resultant velocity of millions of km/h that we are not experiencing.*
3. *To make one understand the complexity of the human body, the universe, and nature that are mind-boggling; everything is neatly designed, from the macro - the vastness of the universe, to the micro - the role of the micro insets.*
4. *To know that similar to the evaluation of life on Earth, there are at least 4000 such earth-like planets (Exoplanet) in our Milky Way Galaxy alone, where life is possible as opined by the astrophysicist.* ***Then, is there any link between life on those planets and life on Earth? Present-day science has no answer to this.***

This defined the intention of this book: – to establish a link between our life on earth and the life on the Exoplanets – Do we go there after our death – what are the types of these planets

– what should we do (karma) here so that we can be taken to a comfortable exoplanet and possible answers to many such questions.

CHAPTER - 4

ॐ *"The Universe is so vast and complex that we are not at all capable of exploring even a tiny portion of it. Our present-day knowledge is just good, only to partially explore our natural satellite 'the moon'. We are yet to reach successfully to our nearest planet Mars. Exploring the possibilities of the presence of life on other exoplanets, beyond our sun family is just a daydream.*

Though many stories of Aliens and their UFOs visiting Earth are making regular news, no one has seen an Alien for sure, to date. However, I heard many stories about living beings from outer space visiting some of the great spiritual masters in their own specified vehicles with due permission to take advice.

Here is a live demonstration of a meeting with an Alien who has visited the earth as witnessed by no other than the great Guru Sri M. The Alien had come to take advice from the teacher of Sri M, Maheswarnath in the Himalayan Arundhati cave near Hrishiksh."

Chapter - 4

Life on Exoplanet – A Live Witness

Life on Other Planets

There exist a large number of earth-like planets (Exoplanet) in this universe, where the environment is quite favorable for the evolution and sustenance of life. Our scientific knowledge is very limited to exploring these facts. Over the last 3 decades, there has been a quantum jump in the advancement of our knowledge of science, still, we have not yet fully explored our natural satellite the moon, and the other planets in our solar system, leaving aside the exploration of the great universe. If God is the creator of this universe, then he must also be the Lord of all planetary systems existing in this universe. The science of today is incapable of exploring the existence of life on exoplanets, but the spiritual masters in India had the capability of exploring the universe time and again.

There has been a quantum jump in ICT technology over the last 2 to 3 decades that has made global information available instantaneously at just fingertips. The YouTube channel is flooded with information by the narrators who are the patients in their near-death state, describing their journey into outer space. These describers have revived back from the near-death experiences from the coma state. Of course, these facts are either to be believed or rejected which is left to the viewers. These may be the stories of facts or friction. Some of these may sound like stories of friction. However, I am picking up information available from the description of the great Himalayan Masters, the spiritual Gurus, and the established Yogis, whom I consider the enlightened yogis. This information is made available to us in their biographies and discourses. While going through the great volumes of the biographies and recordings of the great sages, I emphatically say that life exists on other planets, as we live here on this earth.

The Fireball from the Sky

Sri M has documented his great experiences with the extra-terrestrial beings when he was with his Guruji Sri Maheswarnath Babaji. In his book *"Apprenticed to a Himalayan Master – A Yogis Autobiography"* the experiences are vividly described. Also one can hear the recorded version of Sri M himself speaking on the YouTube channels, available free. Part of the information in this chapter is taken from the above reference. Before we go through this, let me introduce in brief about Sri M.

There is a small ashram in the village known as Madanapalli in the state of Andhra Pradesh, India which can be reached from Bangalore in a three-hour drive covering a distance of about 120 km. There is an engineering college named MIT (Madanapalli Institute of Technology) that I had visited on invitation which provided me the opportunity to visit the great ashram in the village. Of course, I could not meet the busy teacher Sri M (fondly called Madhu by his great Guru Maheswaranath Babaji) on the day of my visit, as he was out of station for spiritual discourse.

With regards to a very brief introduction about Sri M, he was born on November 6, 1948, to a Pathan family in Kerala.

His original name was Mumtaz Ali Khan. At the age of 9, while standing in the extreme corner of the courtyard of his house in Ambujavilasam road, Thiruvananthapuram, in the evening hours, he suddenly saw a tall, extremely fair and well-built, barefoot man, with a white cloth wrapped around his waist. The saint simply put his hand on the shoulder of Sri M and asked *"Do you remember anything"?* (Which can be considered as a reminder of his past life) after which he suddenly vanished. From this day onwards Sri M developed a great affinity with the Snowclad Mountain of the Himalayas. At the age of 19, he could not but start a journey to the Himalayas in search of a true guru and eventually met the same person he once met at the courtyard of his Kerala home almost 10 years before. Of course, the search took a long time. Both of them had roamed the great Himalayas cress-crossing from Badrinath to Kailash-Manasarovar over three and half years and witnessed many strange happenings.

Sri Maheswarnath Babaji had lived far exceeding 200 years by the time Sri M joined him as his disciple. On the advice of the Babaji, Sri M has dedicated himself to spreading the knowledge of spiritualism and therefore is a frequent traveler across various countries as well as places in India for SATSANG – the spiritual discourses. He is the most invited person on the date to deliver talks on spirituality. Most of the time he is busy with spiritual discussions, discourses, and initiating Yoga practices. He has authored many books that are international bestsellers. This simple-living man has a family who lives in Madanapalli Ashram.

He is jean clad spiritual preacher who takes no financial help from any donor. He remembers many of his past lives. His life is full of incredible experiences, out of which I shall try to discuss a happening with him in the presence of his Guru,

Sri Maheswarnath. Once, Sri M and his Guru were descending from the Kedarnath temple towards Rishikesh passing through Sonaprayaga, Guptakashi, and Rudraprayaga. They reached the Vasishtha cave in the evening. However, they preferred to stay in another cave nearby known as Arundhati cave, located just behind a big banyan tree. It has a large flat rock at the entrance that acts as a veranda to the cave. On the third night in the cave, a strange thing happened. Though Sri M was about to sleep in the cave, he could hear a thunder-like noise. When he looked beyond, he saw a huge fireball approaching the cave emerging between the two clouds in the foothill of the Himalayas at a far distance. In no time this fireball reached the cave and landed near the Dhuni with a good sound. Sri M gathered courage and sat behind Babaji, his Guruji, who was in a sitting posture in the cave looking out.

Something unbelievable happened. The fireball of about two feet in diameter split vertically into two parts from which a very large snake-like creature emerged. The great cobra looked transparent and was glowing like blue electric filaments. The monster hissed softly as it knelt down and gently stroked Babaji's feet with its hood. Then Babaji blessed the creature by holding its head in his right hand. The blue cobra sat facing Babaji after straightening up, and the hissing conversation went on for a while. After that Babaji called Sri M and introduced the cobra as the deputy chief of the SARPA LOKA. The snake hissed and then on the instruction of Babaji Sri M bowed to the snake, (the Nagaraj). The snake hissed again and touched the forehead of Sri M with its forked tongue. This created a mild electric shock flowing in the body of Sri M. Then the snake moved into the ball, and the ball closed and left the place with a rumbling sound as it had come. In no time it vanished into the clouds.

This looks like a story of friction or imagination. Sri M questioned its reliability and Babaji replied like this: There is a star system with seven planets and eighteen moons in the Milky Way. Naga Devatas, the highly advanced hooded snakes, live in one of the worlds called Sarpa Loka, which is home to them. The Nagaraja, the planet's vice leader, is the one who arrived here. The five-hooded golden snake known as Anantah in ancient Indian writings is the planet's ultimate head. Long ago, when humanity in this world was in an infant stage of mental evaluation, these Nagas from the Sarpaloka were frequent visitors to the earth and spent a long time teaching and educating human beings. They had deep wisdom. They taught the kundalini energy initially. The great saint Patanjali, who gave us the Ashtanga Yoga Sutra was a Naga. With time, humans have started to misuse the teachings of Nagas and acted against them. The supreme Naga Chief recalled the Nagas from the earth. Overnight the Nagas were transported from Earth to Sarpaloka. The Nagas that you see today on earth are some of the families of the old Naga heirs who could not go back due to old age and ill health.

This small happening, before the eyes of the teacher Sri M establishes at least one thing; there are living beings on the other exoplanets as well. Initially, I too had taken this as a friction story but after knowing the reputation and spiritual exposure of the simple living genus, Sri M, who remembers many of his past rebirths and is the most invited Kriya Yoga teacher across the globe (please read about Sri M, his works, listen to his You Tubes discourses before rejecting this friction like a story), I consider this as the live record.

Sri Saibaba Visited Sarpaloka

Another connecting experience of Sri M and his Guruji is with Sri Saibaba of Siridhi. We know Sri Saibaba as the great saint of recent times. Books on Sri Sai Baba describe short stories about his great spiritual powers. Everyone present at Siridhi was shocked when Sri Saibaba abandoned his physical body for three days before returning on the fourth. Since his body showed no signs of life throughout those three days, everyone assumed him dead. Sainath informed the close public that he had gone to another planet to settle a dispute which was known as the SarpaLoka. Sri Saibaba left his body in the year 1918 but much later Sri M and his Guruji visited and met him at Siridhi and spent a night with him (YouTube talk by Sri M).

These stories may indeed create an impression by some readers that the stories are near friction and gossip. Towards this Babaji replied to Sri M *"Truth is stranger than the friction"*, and clearly said that by the time the story was made public, there must have been an expanded knowledge of outer space and the other planets. The Discovery of water and other living conditions on other planets may substantiate this later.

The contents as discussed are not storytelling. I have read some books of Sri M, listened to his spiritual discourses for 100s of hours, and his honesty with popularity. To know him, first one has to know his work. He has a small ashram and is extremely busy with discourses. He remembers many of his past lives, like Lord Buddha, remembered his 100 past lives. I do not have an iota of disbelief in him.

As we know similar to the evolution of life on Earth, there are at least 4000 such earth-like planets (Exoplanet) in our Milky Way Galaxy alone, where life is possible as opined by the astrophysicist. How could Sri Maheswarnath (as his age by then was more than 200 years) the Guru of Sri M, could know about the Milky Way, in which there is the existence of a stellar system with seven planets with eighteen moons in which one of the planets is called Sarpaloka. This planet is inhabited by highly evolved hooded snakes called Naga Devatas. The person who came here is the Nagaraja, who is the deputy chief of the planet". **This is a witness by no other than Sri M who in a small way links life on those planets and life on Earth. Present-day science has no answer to this.** *I never disbelieve the words of such saints who had never come to the public and had spent their lives in caves.*

CHAPTER - 5

ॐ *"The great Guru of Paramahansa Yogananda, Sri Yukteswar resurrected after his death and appeared in flesh and blood in front of his disciple and informed him that he is directed by God to serve on an astral planet called 'Hiranyaloka – an illuminated Astral Planet. There are many astral planets, the guru continued. The inhabitants use astral planes or the mass of light to travel between them. The astral world is made from the subtle vibrations of light and colour and is very large. There are countless astral solar and Steller systems. Their planet has an astral sun and moon, more beautiful than the physical ones.*

The yogi continued: inhabitants of Hiranyaloka have already passed through the ordinary astral sphere, where nearly all beings from Earth must go at death. There they destroy many seeds of karma connected with their past actions in the astral world. Only more advanced devotees in the astral world are pulled by cosmic law to be reborn in Hiranyaloka, where Sri Yuketaswar is helping them. Some souls are also returned to Hiranyaloka from the superior causal world. Hiranyaloka is somewhere between Astral and the causal words."

Chapter - 5

Life on Exoplanet - The Hiranyaloka

Earth and Other Living Planets

Most of us must have read the great edition "Autobiography of a Yogi" by Paramahansa Sri Yogananda. It is a beautiful autobiography and very informative. An interesting live discussion between Paramahansa Sri Yogananda and his Guru Sri Yukteswar is beautifully depicted in a chapter in this autobiography. Based on the information given there, this chapter discusses the life of human beings after death and how they live in their allotted exoplanets.

The Resurrection of Sri Yukteswar

In the autobiography, chapter (No. 43) *"The Resurrection of Sri Yukteswar"*, gives a detailed account of life in exoplanets, and is very relevant in the present context. Paramahansa Sri Yogananda is the disciple of Sri Yukteswar. He was born on 10th May 1855 and entered Mahasamadhi at 7:00 PM on March 9th, 1936 in his ashram in Puri, Odisha. Sri Yukteswar founded two hermitages, one in Serampore near Kolkata, and the other in Puri. He was the disciple of Sri Lahairi Mahassaya (1828-1895) of Banaras. Sri Shyama Charan Lahiri was one of the greatest spiritually accomplished teachers and a married enlightened person who lived in Banaras City. It was seen that angles were seen flocking around his bed when he was in deep sleep. His wife was the first disciple of this great soul.

Once, someone tried to take a photo of Sri Lahairi Mahassaya and failed. Sri Lahari said, "I am spirit; can your camera reflect the omnipresent invisible"? This Yogavatar, after a continued request finally permitted his body to be photographed. The master had never permitted a photograph again. Sri Mahavatar Babaji is the guru of Sri Lahairi Mahassaya. One can understand the great spiritual height of Sri Lahairi Mahassaya by reading the book "Autobiography of a Yogi" by Sri Yogananda.

Mahavatar Babaji the Great Guru of Yukteswar

The birth and life of Mahavatar Babaji are not documented in history. "The deathless avatar has resided for untold years in the remote Himalayan regions of India, revealing himself only rarely to a blessed few," Paramahansa Yogananda mentioned these facts in his autobiography. Mahavatar Babaji is the one who brought back the outdated scientific meditation practices known as "Kriya Yoga." Sri Lahiri Mahasaya received Kriya initiation from Babaji, who stated, *"The Kriya Yoga that I am giving to the world through you in this nineteenth century is a revival of the same science that Krishna gave millenniums ago to Arjuna; and that was later known to Patanjali and Christ, to St. John, St. Paul, and other disciples."*

In the year 1936, Paramahansa Yogananda was in Bombay to take a western voyage, which was canceled at the last moment. Devotees on knowing the cancellation of the trip arranged several public addresses in the city of Bombay. On June 19, 1936, in the same Hotel in Bombay, where he was staying, Paramahansa Yogananda was roused from meditation at 3 PM with sunlight transmitting into supernatural splendor. Sri Yukteswar had arrived in flesh and blood and had taken Mahasamadhi on March 9th, 1936. Discussion between the two great souls continued for almost 2 hours.

Yukteswar: I constructed a brand-new body, identical to the physical body you have seen thus far, totally from cosmic atoms. I was raised from the dead in an astral world. Astral planet residents are more adept at upholding high standards than people on Earth. You can join me there with your family members. I am instructed by God to serve on an ethereal planet named *"Hiranyaloka – an illuminated Astral Planet"*. There I am aiding advanced beings in overcoming their astral karma and achieving freedom from astral rebirths. The Hiranyaloka inhabitants have attained a great level of spiritual development during their earthly incarnations. No one may reach Hiranyaloka until he has passed on earth the state of Sabikalpa Samadhi to the higher stage of Nirbikalpa Samadhi (*In Sabikalpa Samadhi the devotee has acquired realization of his oneness with spirit but cannot keep his cosmic consciousness expect in the immobility trance condition. By practicing meditation regularly, a yogi can attain a higher level of Nirbikalpa Samadhi*), when the final remnants of his material or earthly karma are destroyed (though he may still retain some astral and then higher karma).

Life on Astral and Causal Realms

The sacred Gayatri Mantra indicates the existence of three worlds of living abodes. The great sacred Mantra is cited by most Hindus and is uttered as:

Om bhūr bhuvaḥ suvaḥ tat savitur - vareṇyaṃ
Bhargo devasya dhīmahi dhiyo yonaḥ prachodayāt

The first three words of the mantra after OM (or AUM) are the BHU or BHUR (earth or the physical realm OR PritibiLoka), BHUBAH or BHURVA (PitruLoka or the Astral World), and SWAH (Causal World or the Swarga Loka) through which the soul needs to evolve with good Karma before it finally merges with the supreme infinity.

"{Gayatri Mantra English Translation: We meditate on the glory of the Creator; who has created the Universe; who is worthy of Worship; Who is the embodiment of Knowledge and Light; Who is the remover of all Sin and Ignorance; May He enlighten our Intellect.] **{Meaning:** O, Divine mother, our hearts are loaded up with darkness. Kindly make this darkness distant from us and advance brightening inside us.}"

The usual astral realm, where almost all creatures from Earth must travel after death, has already been traversed by the residents of Hiranyaloka. There, they eliminate a large number of karma seeds related to their previous astral world deeds. Most of the persons enjoy the beauty of the astral world; they do not feel to advance further for the more spiritual path. Only more advanced devotees in the astral world are pulled by cosmic law to be reborn in Hiranyaloka, where Sri Yuketaswar is helping them. Some souls are also returned to Hiranyaloka from the superior causal world. Hiranyaloka is somewhere between Astral and the causal words.

The Discussion Continued

Every human soul is encased successively in 3 bodies: The 1st is the idea or the highest causal body, the next is the subtle or the astral body, which is the seat of men's mental and emotional nature, and then the gross physical body. Man has been blessed with his physical body (senses) on Earth. His astral body interacts with his thoughts and emotions, and the body itself is made up of lifetronics (Prana). The world of thoughts is a lovely place for a causal body. Sri Yukteswar's task is to assist astral entities who are getting ready to join the causal realm.

The guru continued. "There are many astral planets. The inhabitants use astral planes or the mass of light to travel from one planet to another, much faster than electricity or radioactive energies. The astral world is made from the subtle vibrations of light and colour and is very large. *There are countless astral solar and Steller systems.* These planets have an astral sun and moon that are more beautiful than the physical ones. They are very luminous. Astral day and night are longer than Earth day and night. The astral world is extremely beautiful, clean, pure, and orderly. There are no dead plants or barren land, and there are no weeds, bacteria, snakes, or others. The temperature in the astral world is even throughout. Sometimes eternal spring and very occasional white snow and rain of many coloured lights. There are bright seas, a Rainbow, a River, and other natural beauties."

Numerous astral worlds are home to millions of astral creatures, ranging in species from fish to animals to demigods, according to their karmic backgrounds. Evil spirits are restricted to bad zones, whilst good ones are free to move. Various vibratory quarters are assigned to different grades of spirits like in earth fish stay in the water, worms inside the soil, and birds in the sky. The astral world is divided from very dark to very light zones or realms. In very dark zones bad souls are parked while in the lighter to brightest zones good to very good souls are parked, depending on their karmic evaluations.

Above the dark astral prison, all others are shining beautifully. Beings in the astral world can modify or enhance anything that God has created. The will of the astral inhabitants is so strong that instantly, they can change the form of any material at will, without any natural or chemical process. There is no murder in this world and everyone lives happily with harmony and equality. They can dematerialise or materialise their forms at will. No fixed, definite natural laws can bind them around. They can produce an astral tree, mango, or any desired fruit or anything at will. Everything is vibrant with God's creative light. There are no male or female beings in the astral world. The astral body is not subjected to cold or heat. The astral body is capable of changing its forms by life-tronic force and mantric vibrations.

There is a brain with six awakened Sushma or astral axis that is connected to it. The heart draws cosmic energy from the astral brain and pumps it to the astral nervous system or life-tronic forces. The face and figure of the astral beings are similar to the previous earthly sojourn. By shear intuitional feelings, all the astral beings see, smell, taste, and touch.

They pose three eyes; the two horizontal ones are partially closed and the third vertical eye placed on the forehead is open. Any organ of the astral body can do any function such as the eye can smell, taste, hear, or sense. If there is a cut in the body, it can be immediately repaired by mere will. They celebrate when a being is liberated from the astral world to enter the causal or the higher level of heaven. At this time, the lord appears in the form of the devotee who had worshiped and pleased him. Friends and relatives invariably recognize one another. The beings of the astral world can see the people in this physical world, but only the higher spiritual persons on the earth can see the astral ones. Communication among astral inhabitants is through astral telepathy and television without any communication error or misunderstanding.

Earth-liberated astral beings meet their relatives like fathers, mother, wife, husband friends, etc. that they had during various previous births on earth from time to time and as they come to astral realms in due course. There is no mistake in recognizing all of them who were once dear to him in any previous births. In the astral world, the life span of the beings is much higher than Earth with normal advanced beings and it may be between 500 to 1000 years measured in Earth's standard of time. Dwellers stay in the astral world by their physical karma which determines them to return to Earth after a specified time. They can also move up to the causal world depending on their Karma in the astral world. The astral world is free from unwanted death, disease, and old age.

Astral death means the disintegration of lifetimes which is a life of astral beings. The cycles of astral and physical births and rebirths are the destiny of unenlightened beings.

The gross physical body has 16 elements, the astral has 19 and the causal has 35 ideas as required by God. The power of unfulfilled desire is the root cause of all men's slavery. Physical desire is the ego and the sensory pleasure. It is much more powerful than astral attachments and causal perceptions. Causal desires are fulfilled by perceptions only – they can materialise anything and everything by mere thought and instantly. A soul is invisible and therefore has to be covered by a body every time. When the physical body is dead, the soul is still covered by the astral and then the causal covers to prevent it from joining the omnipresent.

Even in the causal world, many beings remain for 1000s of years. When the soul is freed from the three bodies' coverings, it no longer is subject to the laws of relativity and unites with limitless without losing its unique identity. To eventually leave these bodies, other entities must go through innumerable earthly, astral, and causal incarnations. After the ultimate liberation, a person might choose to become a prophet to lead other people to God or they can opt to live in the astral universe like Yuketeswar. The savoir Sri Yuketeswar sometimes absorbers some of the karma of others in his higher astral world of Hiranyakloka terminates their cycle of reincarnations, and takes them to the higher causal world.

Karma essentially means the unfulfilled desire that a soul must completely work out before he is continuously allowed to stay in the astral world. In this astral world, there are 2 types of living souls: temporary visitors for the unaccomplished desire of earth-leaving souls and lower-bound souls from the casual world. Those who are freed forever from all material longings need no return to the physical or earth world but they shuttle between the astral and causal world to work out. Even the beings in the casual world must complete their astral karma or they have to return.

An awakened conscious being is in all three vehicles. In the physical body, there is a strong sense of testing, smelling, touching, and listening. Visualizing is essentially the astral body. When a body is in deep meditation or introspection, it is in a casual body. Yuketaswar said, he can dematerialise his body and can travel instantly by light express from planet to planet or astral to causal or physical cosmos.

A man works about 16 hours a day in his physical vehicle. When he sleeps, he dreams and is in the astral body, effortlessly creating any object he can in the astral cosmos. A dreamer is in astral and is not fully refreshing. If he is in deep sleep for several hours without any dreams, he is transferring to the causal world and is reviving. After enlightening the knowledge of the astral and casual world, the great Yuketaswar dematerialised his body into lifetronics and disappeared to his place of abode, the Hiranyaloka.

This chapter has a reference to the ***"Autobiography of a Yogi"*** *by Paramahansa Sri Yogananda which was published in 1946. It has since been translated into 45 languages. In 1999, it was designated one of the* ***"100 Most Important Spiritual Books of the 20th Century"*** *by a panel of spiritual authors. The Autobiography has been an inspiration for many including George Harrison, Ravi Shankar, and Steve Jobs.*

The great Guru of Yogananda, Sri Yukteswar resurrected after his death in flesh and blood and informed Sri Yukteswar that he was directed by God to serve on an astral planet called "Hiranyaloka – an illuminated Astral Planet". An interesting live discussion between Paramahansa Sri Yogananda and his Guru Sri Yukteswar is beautifully depicted in chapter ***43 (The Resurrection of Sri Yukteswar)*** *in the autobiography. This chapter discusses the life of human beings after death with a detailed account of life in exoplanets and is very relevant in the present context. Since this autobiography is very authentic, there is no room to disbelieve the fact that there are many Exoplanets where life has existed and continued since the beginning.*

CHAPTER - 6

ॐ *"Information for this Chapter is taken from the book "The Laws of the Spirit World" published by Khorshed Bhavnagiri in 2009, which was compiled from the daily communications by the departed souls Ratoo and Vispi between 14/04/1981 and 28/01/1984 in the form of automated writings.*

A detailed account of life in the seven types of realms where we have to go after our death from the earth is mind-blowing. The book has become a national bestseller. The karmic actions of the individuals on earth decide the allotment realm to the soul. Each realm has 10 stages numbering from 0 to 9 with realm 1 being the darkest - a horrible place to live where very bad souls are parked. Realm 2 is still dark, while Realm 3 is better but still no light. Realm 4 has day and night like Earth and the souls in Realm 5 look good. There is always light in this realm and is the beginning of a good world. Realm 6 is very beautiful and always lighted while Realm 7 is the brightest and the beauty is beyond imagination. The souls have very light bodies like clouds and are the most perfect. The book has answers to most of our questions and is in more detail than the Garuda Puran or the Autobiography of a Yogi.

Chapter - 6

Life on Exoplanets - Realms our Permanent Home

Journey of Life after Death – The Karmic Actions

During the years 1980 – 1981, there was regular news in the media that two accidentally departed brothers Ratoo and Vispi were in spiritual communications in the form of automated writing with their parents in presence of the relatives, friends, and guests including media personnel at their Bombay residence. Photographs and video recordings of their communications created sensational news in the ensuing years. The daily recordings of the automated writings are published in the form of a book titled *"The Laws of the Spirit World"* by their mother Khorshed Bhavnagiri in the year 2009 after due permission from the departed brothers. The discourses started on 14/04/1981 and probably ended on 28/01/1984. The book is the original script of the two departed brothers in automated writing. Some of the information was verified during the period of recording of discourses and was found to be correct. The book gives a beautiful account of various grades and types of Realms that exist, and where people are housed after they depart from the earth. Life of the departed souls from Earth on these realms or exoplanets is vividly discussed in the published book.

Two young brothers namely Ratoo and Vispi Bhavnagri, while returning to Bombay on 22nd February 1980 had met with a fatal accident and both of them died on the spot. The spirit soul of the younger brother Ratoo emerged first from the physical earth body and he saw his maternal grandfather standing to receive him. After a few minutes, his elder brother's soul emerged and joined them. The two brothers were taken to the hall of rest by their grandfather and then they were asked to lie down on a cloud or feather-like couch on which they were fast asleep. There, they were calmed down as they had met with an accident and therefore a sudden departure from the earth. When they came out of the hall of rest, they met many of their departed friends and relatives from their previous lives.

While going through the narration of the life on these exoplanets from this book I find that most of the information from all these three following sources is almost matching.

1. Live discussion by the great saint Sri Yuketaswar to his dear disciple Sri Yogananda at a Bombay hotel on 19th June 1936 (In chapter 43 of the autobiography, "The Resurrection of Sri Yukteswar"), from the edition "Autobiography of a Yogi" by Paramahansa Sri Yogananda giving a detailed account on the life in exoplanets.
2. Daily communication by Ratoo and Vispi, in the form of automated writing compiled in the book titled "The Laws of the Spirit World" published subsequently by their mother Khorshed Bhavnagiri in the year 2009, and
3. Description of life after death in the "Garuda Puran" in Hindu Mythology.

The Seven Realms

The narration of life in the spiritual worlds by the two brothers is in good detail and vivid. There exist SEVEN Realms or the places of living in the spirit world and in each realm 10 stages numbering from 0 to 9. Realm 1 is close to the earth and is the darkest - a horrible place to live. Here very bad souls are parked. There is not even a ray of light in this realm. Generally, the dwellers of this realm have heavy and deformed bodies and always crawl to move. Realm 2 is still dark, but not as dark as Realm 1, while Realm 3 is better, but still no light. Souls in these 3 realms always look older and imperfect. These bad souls try to capture the new entrants to this realm and try to make them slaves.

Realm 4 has day and night like Earth and from Realm 4 stage 5 the souls are permitted to move up or down to other stages of the realms. Souls in Realm 5 look good and there is always light or brightness in this realm and is the beginning of a good world. Realm 6 is very beautiful and always lighted. Souls here have very light bodies, and all of them live in love and harmony. Realm 7 is the brightest and the beauty is beyond imagination. The souls have very light bodies like clouds and are the most perfect. The authors of this book did not know after a soul makes a journey beyond stage 9 of realm 7. Souls after these realms have only onward journeys and do not return to earth, their spiritual journey is still continuous.

The souls take birth on earth for 70-80 years which is considered a short period in comparison to the length of their life in the realms. The souls are free to decide on birth on earth of their free will to complete their karmic debts to make faster progress in the spirit world. These earth-bound souls try to do good karma in their earth incarnation so that their journey in the realms is faster than otherwise would have taken much longer, even centuries to accomplish. The earth-born soul is purposefully not given the memory of their real home in the realms while they are in this earth's incarnation. Human beings have the conscious brain to act and do well. The subconscious mind present in human beings known as the spiritual mind remembers life in the realms, but it never reveals anything to the conscious mind unless he is a highly focused yogi. People on Earth need to understand that ***Earth is the temporary home and the real home is the realms.*** Over time the earth has become a bad place to live as the attraction of human beings for material gains, powers, and positions, lust for sex and other benefits has forced them to do bad karma. In recent years it has been communicated that the number of souls in the lower realms 1 – 4 is increasing drastically and is becoming densely populated, while the realms 5 to 7 are sparingly occupied. No one is perfect here on earth or in the spirit worlds, but continuously they try to evolve for good. Human beings have the brains to think and therefore they have the free will to decide what is right. Doing harm and bringing pain to others is never a good thing to do and by this bad karma is accumulated in the individual's account. God is always right and gives justice. One cannot hide anything from him. It was communicated that most of the highly acclaimed spiritual preachers on earth do not know what real justice is, and what God wants from human beings. God's real justice is not possible to be explained even in racks of books and years of discussions.

The Motive is Important for Spiritual Progress

If someone is really bad but later has made an honest and sincere confession to get changed from a bad to a good, then to such changed and self-realised souls God always graces. On the other hand, a person may create an impression that he is giving a lot on charity, a regular visitor to places of worship reads holy books, but he may not at all reach the lowest ladder of heavenly abode if he is doing all these with an intension to go to heaven but without a good feeling for doing good to others. If the motive of doing good is to become rich, become powerful, famous, or more successful then you are doing things for yourself, but not for God. Have a motive only to help others and that should be automatic and spontaneous from the heart. A tiny help may take one to a great height in the realms, but all the charity of yours without a good motive is not good at all. You can fool all, but not God. On earth, the realization is quick, and therefore the spiritual progress of self is faster in the spirit world.

Then there is always a question, Why do good souls suffer and bad souls go scot-free on earth? The reason is: that those good souls are under training and testing and therefore must gain experience. The more success the evil souls have on earth, the lower in the hell they go in the spirit world. Therefore, do not envy them, but you as a good soul, take the good things they are doing and appreciate them. One day, everyone is to die and face the laws of God, one cannot hide anything in the spirit world.

A treacherous person usually gets his permanent home in realms 1 to 3 depending on his karma. But if he has sincere repentance and asks for forgiveness, he may be born as a beast of burden, where he is better than realm 1, but as a beast, it remembers the bad karma of his previous life. A good-spirited person always tries to tell a bad person of his bad activities and tries to improve him, but in no case, he should be encouraged for his bad activities. Never help a bad person you know as by doing this, he shall be more encouraged to do bad things such as murder, stealing, etc. and you become a partner in his bad activities. Helping anyone in the streets is okay as you do not know him as good or bad. If a bad person repents, he deserves your help and you should help for his great change.

It is the wish of God to see that you are really happy.

He has given you the brain to understand and come forward with sincerity. There is a saying "God helps those who help themselves". Suppose a bad person who has done crimes, has self-realised and sincerely wanted to be good. In that case, God takes over and helps him out, but he has to suffer as he has to pay for his sins no matter what. There is nothing called excused for one's sins. But before helping him, it must be assured that he shall no more return to evil deeds. The karma he has acquired must be paid off. His self-guidance shall take him faster to higher realms than in a normal way. The inner motive of goodness is only important to God.

A simply neglected person on earth may have a much more advanced spiritual journey than a powerful person. There is no visibility of the vibrations of persons and the aura of souls in this earth's world. People are more interested in this temporary home than the real and permanent home which is the spirit world where one stays for centuries and continuously evolves there to higher realms.

On Earth as well as in the lower realms there are devils.

More importantly on earth, you have to live in a surrounding full of extremely negative people and fewer good ones altogether. In lower realms, all the devils stay together and in the higher ones only the good souls are put together. There is no mixing of them. In the lower realms, bad souls live together and harm each other in a group or individually and do not leave souls from these realms to go to higher levels. Genuine prayers from these realms are heard and Good souls from higher realms with due permission are deputed to go there and help out.

There is nothing to disbelieve that life does not exist after death. *Rather life is more vibrant in the spirit world than on Earth.* In the spirit world, there is no physical body, and therefore problems related to health are nonexistent. Spirit beings live in the astral world as we stay in this physical world with friendship, visits to places, and do a lot of readings, and save lots of time from health and safety issues. Everything is not perfect in the spirit world. Perfection comes as the spirits travel gradually to higher realms up to stage 9 of realm 7. With full perfection, the spirit beings merge with God.

The subconscious mind is the link between the earth's body and the spirit body. It stores records of all previous births. The conscience mind given to the human body is to drive the soul to do good. There is a saying "Whatever you sow, you reap". The journey of the soul from realm 5 to 7 is much slower than takes, even centuries. However, a soul taking rebirth on earth can pay off his karma much faster if on his earth he does good karma. However, there is a basic principle; spirits from realms 6-7 usually do not fall to lower realms. To be reborn on earth, the spirit needs to choose mostly the mother. A decision to be born with a rude mother for early disposal of karma involves risk and may lead to further problems for the soul. Spirit beings from higher realms are always helpful to the earth's living beings those who try sincerely to improve. Our sincere prayers are always heard and it is the spirit beings that come to help us when we are in trouble, but there is a limit to which they can be useful.

God Responds to all Genuine Prayers

Genuine prayers and desires are always heard and it gives outstanding results. God always wants to help all but being intelligent you should come forward with 100% sincerity so that help comes to you from the spirit world. The subconscious mind within you is the God within. It is not attached to you but it represents you. It punishes you if involved in evil deeds and takes you to higher realms if there is honesty within you to do good. Only you, the subconscious mind can place you in the realm you deserve by your karma. The higher realm beings can see the details of all realms including Earth, but the dwellers of the lower realm cannot see the higher ones until they reach realm 5 or above. The conditions for lower realm beings to visit higher realms are that there should be an invitation from someone from the higher realm, and it should be approved by the higher Good soul of that realm (Higher good souls mean in every stage there is a controller who is too good and remains in charge of the stage of the realm. Similarly, for each realm, there is a controller who is in charge of the entire realm. It is like a state and central administration of a country).

Then there should be a training following which a protective cover is given to the soul of the lower realm. This is because spirits from lower realms are heavier and the protective cover makes them lighter equal to the upper realm and the cover also protects the bright light of the higher realm. Souls from Realm 5 cannot go to Realm 7 but can go to Realm 6 for a limited visit. If souls from Realm 4 visit Realm 1 to 3, they should have the protective cover. Spirits from realms 1 to 3 are not permitted to visit other realms. If someone from this realm sincerely repents and prays genuinely, it is heard. In that case, it has to take birth to repay the karma. The journey from one realm to the next higher can be very fast if there is honest and genuine desire. It may take a few years to thousands of years to go to the next realm depending on the sincerity of the spirit being.

Souls from the spirit world always try to guide the earth dwellers and they are happy to help. They try to guide us through our subconscious mind but only a few of us can receive the messages as only a tiny portion of the subconscious mind works on earth. Of course, some good and gifted souls on earth can communicate with souls in higher realms directly like a two-way radio system.

Every realm has a high good soul who is the head of the realm. *Realms 1-3 are like hell and realms 5-7 are like heave*Life and the environment in realm 4 is like we stay on earth. The head of realm 7 is the head of all realms from 1 to 7. These heads are very simple and open-minded. The radiance from the realm heads is so scintillating that immediately one can know that he is a high-spirited being. If a spirit from realms 4 to 7 wants to go down to realms 1-3, he has to wear a clock cover so that he is invisible to the bad souls in the realm. If a soul from the higher realm visits the lower realm and he is not in protection cover, the evil souls from the lower realms capture him as a prisoner and mentally torture him. In this case, the head of the realm rescues the captured one. Souls from realms can go up rapidly if they do good service else continue for very long in the same realm.

An earth soul, if extremely spiritual can reach realms 5 – 7.

In this case, the body becomes lighter, deformations of the physical body are rectified, aches are gone, and no pains. Souls in realm 1 are the heaviest followed by reductions in weight gradually from realms 2 to 4. An evil body on earth may look good and handsome, but if he is placed in lower realms after death, the body becomes full of deformations. Similarly, a deformed earth body looks very handsome if he is in realms

5 to 7. By looking at the body in the spirited world, one can know his virtue.

A man on earth can be rich and powerful, but this is very temporary for a few years only. The permanent home is the spirit world and one should do more for this living there than for a temporary stay on earth.

Our Rebirth on Earth

Rebirth happens to complete the process of karma and also for those good souls who dare to take the bold step to rise faster in the spirit world. The earth is now in the hands of bad people and therefore everyone on earth is doing badly for money, power, sex, and other needs. Realms 5-7 are rarer now than 100 years ago and realms 1-4 are densely populated. In case a young one on earth dies, the reason being, their subconscious mind prays to the almighty to bring him back as he is a good soul. His prayer is heard but the mind does not know it. These good spirits take birth on earth with a mission to change the bad ones on earth but they fail as the earth is now full of evil persons. There is a saying *"God calls the ones who are loved by him"*. Some good souls try to reform the people on earth and suffer a lot. They stay up to 90 – 100 years but finally give up.

Lead a simple, honest, kind full, selfless, and clear life on earth. Never be evil-minded. If you are always good to others you are in a good realm after death. Once you reach realm 5 and above, you are protected by God not to fall. No one can reach these higher realms with fewer births. It may take 100s of births to pay off the karma. A famous person on earth has no value in the spirit world whereas a simple and unrecognized man on earth may be high in the spirit world. The soul who biases other souls towards evil is more affected in the spirit world than the victim himself. Never encourage the evils. The physical body is the hindrance between the earth and the spirit world. If one is determined to be in the higher world, he controls the physical mind and never sins. The basic principles are the same as it has been told again and over again viz. never harm or give pain to others, never take over others' rights or belongings, and never be jealous of others. Principles such as love for others, helping to your capacity, and being generous in the true sense pay you a lot.

Living on your own is good but it does not add any value to your life in the spirit world. Never waste your precious time on earth as you never know when your call will come. You are deputed to do certain works on this earth, if unfinished, you are to be reborn for the same purpose, which is again a very difficult task looking from the spirit world. The reason for lower souls to be born again and again is to pay off karma. Sometimes higher souls take a rebirth on earth of their free will either to protect their loved ones or to continue their spiritual mission.

Our subconscious mind is always engaged in guiding our conscious or the physical mind, but if the conscious mind does not listen to the subconscious mind and continuously does evil deeds, this subconscious mind stops or becomes dormant. For the soul of any level of the realm, if born on earth, there is every chance of being misguided in the present world which is full of evil people and the material attraction is very high. But once a soul is on the path of realization and prays to God for his sincere return from the evil activities, God can activate his subconscious mind which was dormant. A sincere prayer to God means that one is fully focused and his mind is in control. If one can keep his mind blank for a minute, meaning blank, he has achieved control. He can communicate with spirited souls and God faster. It is difficult to keep the mind fully blank for a minute, but through practice, it can be achieved. God only has the power to reduce the karmic punishment to milder.

For innocent kids, the subconscious mind is very active and in command. Babies up to the age of 1 or so are fully connected with their spirit world and are cared for by the spirit world. After birth, they observe their parents and decide to go back. After the age of 1 year, the babies lose contact with the spirit world.

Our subconscious mind is capable of remembering all of our previous lives since our first birth including our stay in the spirit world. *The conscious mind and the subconscious mind are always at loggerheads for all the residents up to realm 5. Dwellers beyond realm* 5 have extrasensory powers and they can remember their all previous births. Life on earth is very short and is meant for tests, training, and gaining experience leading to finally paying off the karmas. The subconscious mind does not allow you to remember past lives that may create a lot of problems on Earth. The great souls, whose subconscious mind controls the physical conscious mind, can remember past lives. The subconscious mind has no opening for earth beings, partially open for spirit souls in realms 6 or 7, but fully open for the souls beyond realm 7. Some good yogis are capable of controlling the conscious mind and therefore very capable of travelling across realms and remembering all previous lives. The death of the physical body is the death of the conscious mind. One needs to control his conscious mind through meditation and prayers.

The question of why a good soul from realms 5-7 sometimes seeks rebirth on earth is explained as follows: (i) Some souls take a faster route for their progress to higher realms as the progress between the realms is very slow. A journey from realm to earth (doing very good work on earth) and back to the higher realm is faster. (ii) Your close soul may be suffering on earth and you wish to help. While for souls from realms 1-3, it is an opportunity as earth life is far better for them than life in these lower realms. They are born as beasts of burden on earth and suffer a lot. In realm 4, there are souls fallen from higher realms and they take the chance with a rebirth on earth so that they can quicken their progress by doing good work on earth. **By committing suicide,** you are going against the will of God and you are falling very low.

Genuine calls for help are heard by the High good souls, even if the call is from realm 1. This help comes from spirits of higher realms as agents of God and they are known as His High Good Souls. Sometimes your loved ones from the spirit world come to your help. There are fixed laws for help from these good souls and if they need to break the laws for help, they seek sanction from the Highest Good souls and the result is like miracles happening to the soul on earth.

Anything done without any selfless motive not even a trace of it is termed a good deed and it gives the fastest growth in the spiritual world. While doing a good deed, never think of any return. The best is to forget it completely after the good deed is performed. If one expects returns from the good works done to others, then it works negatively and takes him to a lower plane in the spiritual path than growth. Assure yourself that your motive is not at all selfish when you take up good works like you do good for your relatives and close ones.

Sometimes we are jealous of others as we cannot tolerate the progress of others. This is bad. However, if someone is jealous of you as he cannot see your goodness or progress, then it is good if you expose him so that others know him and he cannot be jealous of others or harm others.

Try always to help good souls. For example, if a good soul requires help say financially, help him and refrain him from falling. However, never try to help a bad soul, he will consider it as your weakness and further exploit you and maybe others. By helping a bad person, you are earning bad Karma as the person is encouraged to do more negative activities. Everyone on earth is different and therefore the same rules do not apply to all.

Always trust God, pray to him, and request for his guidance and genuine prayers never go unanswered. Never try to help evil people, rather try always to avoid them, or else they try to influence you and take you on a bad path. Again, do not trust the horoscope or astrologer's predictions or predictors. The mind is greatly affected by these false predictions and the subconscious mind becomes dormant by such regular beliefs. To get blessings from the spiritual world, always try to be cool, calm, and relaxed. Sincere prayer and full faith in God shall certainly pull us up from the problems on earth. Souls from the spirited world always try to help earth people through the subconscious mind. Everyone on earth does some sin and has no option but to face it. Help always comes from the spirit beings for the people who are innocent and good and face suffering due to bad people on earth.

Prayers should always be short and should be done sitting in the same place because this place gets positive vibrations from your daily prayers. Long prayers are never fully concentrated and therefore should be avoided. Reaching God means you focus with full concentration. Suppose you pick up a stone from a roadside, wash it, keep it on your table, concentrate on the stone, and pray for it, then positive vibrations are received by the stone from you and it gets positively charged which is reflected when you are meditating with focus on it. It shall give wonderful results.

Nothing happens in this world before its due time. If you are under tension about the early arrival of the result, you are wrong. These tensions rather give you unrest and harm subsequently. Earth is full of evil souls. You are to stay with these souls. God is always in helping good souls, have faith in him. God's justice is always perfect.

Death never happens to the soul but to the physical body only and of course to your ego. Life on earth is just a stopover of the infinite journey of the soul, then how can there be death for you? After death, your body becomes more vibrant, more alive, and more loving. Spirited bodies have no body pain, aches, or gender. Having cast off the physical and astral body, the souls become a lighter causal body and life is much better in the spirit world. There are no negative souls in the higher causal world. Live is just like we stay on earth and the souls feel happy if the earth's people communicate with them. The spirit (causal) world is above the astral world and is the real home. Earth is a temporary stay like schooling. When one dies on earth, it retains the earth-like body appearance in the astral world but is much lighter, and then when the soul further advances, the body becomes lighter like a bird's feather and he looks younger.

There is nothing hell or heaven in the spirit world. Earth has 3 dimensions and therefore the 3rd universe to dwell in. These universes are created by the vibrations of the spiritual beings as the good souls did not want to stay with the bad ones and they want separate places to stay depending on their karmas. On earth, both the good and negative souls stay together which allows the good souls to help and improve the bad souls. If bad souls do not exist on earth, then what the good souls shall do? Earth is the testing ground of faster-growing good souls. There is nothing called permanent stay in any realm. Improvement and changes are a must.

Purposefully God has made people on earth not to remember anything of the spirit world. If it happens, the earth's body cannot balance the lightness of the spirit bodies in the spirit world. Further, souls will not be interested in staying on earth, even for a second after knowing their past. Spirit world is the truth and earth is the test place. *After death, the subconscious mind remembers all the activities on earth and carries them to the spirit world. The present characteristics of the souls are the sum of all the previous characteristics the soul had acquired over the previous births.* That is what you have trained to your soul over several births. The negative qualities acquired on earth by a person are still continuous in the spirit world, though on a very small scale in higher realms. There is free will for every soul. *If a negative soul does not want to go to realms 1-3 then it can continue to stay in astral form as ghosts for a very long time,* however, as ghosts, they acquire more bad karmas and further fall. They continue to go down till serious realization comes and souls from higher realms come to help them.

Hall of Rest and Hall of Learning

For the cases of accidents and sudden deaths, the souls are taken to the **HALL OF REST** and are given the healing rays to calm them down. Similarly, the traumatized souls are de-traumatized in the hall of rest, and by the time they come out of the hall of rest, they are cool and ready. *However, from realms 1 to stage 4 of Realm 4, there is no hall of rest.* Once the soul is allotted a place in the spirit world, the other spirits assist them and help. **HALL OF LEARNING** is the place for higher realms and spirit beings to study there on God's laws, the nature of the universe, and others. From realm 4, stage 4 onwards there exists both the hall of rest and the hall of learning. Higher spiritual souls come to these halls for spreading God's love and wisdom including exchanging information on other planets and dimensions. The hall of learning is blessed with cosmic powers and is a great place to learn in the realm.

Spirits from realms 7 stages 5 can come to earth in any form with permission from His masters to help the people on earth and they have very high spiritual powers. But spirits from realms 5 and 6 can help earth souls only from their realms. They cannot come to earth to help. When a soul takes birth on earth, a spirit guide is assigned from the realm. He continuously guides. But if the earth's soul falls too low, his subconscious mind becomes dormant, the spirit guide can no more help. God gives everyone protection from falling, but free will is supreme either to elevate you or make you evil. Now you have a subconscious mind to which you shall listen. People still fall and become evil because they listen to their conscious minds and not to their subconscious minds.

A soul mate is a group soul of family members and friends that take birth along with you for exchanging spirituality, and grow together and lead a better life. There can be many group souls for you. Every soul is given a name. But in the spirit world, once you reach there, the earth's name continues as your spirit name. In the hall of learning, your karmas are written in **AKASHIC** records. These records are written by your subconscious mind when you are in deep sleep without dreams. When you rise or falls from realms and stages, these record move with you. No one can read others' records. Documents and visuals from all previous lives are available in your Akashic records.

Spirit souls do not need food for survival but nectar is useful to provide positive energy. They need prayers and a water bath to further purify them. When they come out of the water from a lake, they feel fully energized. That is why you can see many spirits visiting the sacred Manasarover Lake for dips in the early morning time of Brahma-Muhurta which starts 96 minutes before sunrise at the location on Earth.

Every soul takes birth 100s to 1000s of times to evolve and progress spiritually. As has been said before, all the souls in realms 5 to 7 are very good and therefore do good karma. It takes centuries to climb from realm 5 to 6 or from 6 to 7. If a soul in these realms has still some bad karma to dispose of then it has to take birth on earth to do good karma to jump into higher realms. It has a great risk associated, as the earth is full of evil spirits and the chance of falling is more. Of course, opportunities for doing good services on earth are plenty. *With permission of the High good souls of the realm, one takes birth on earth to a prefixed mother with pre-decided surroundings, the date of birth, and the due date of return.* A soul in a mother's womb is in continuous touch with the spirit world. If the soul observes parents to be bad then he can decide to return and another soul of a lower level occupies the womb. If no soul is interested in the parents then a still baby is born. The child after birth is again in touch with the spirit world through the subconscious mind till the child develops spoken capacity. After this, the subconscious mind cuts off the link between the baby and the spirit world.

Sleep and Spiritual Connection

When you are in a dreamless deep sleep, your soul rises from your body and is connected through a silver cord. You meet your close departed souls of this or the previous births somewhere between Earth and the spirit world. They are in constant touch with you, guide you, and console you. This chord returns you to the body when you get up from deep sleep. If you suddenly get up from deep sleep, there is a feeling of sudden fall. Your spirit guide protects the silver chord from evil spirits as they may cut it and enter the body through its connecting point which is a point on the head of the body.

When a soul takes birth on earth, he is given the option of three return dates to the realms. The first two are probable and may pass off with mild illness or accidents, while the third one is a must. If there is some karma remaining to be fulfilled, then there is something called borrowed life. For this, the soul is in touch with another soul who has finished his karma and is permitted to spare his earth time for his friend. This happens with the arrangements made by the subconscious mind.

When a child dies, it goes to the spirit world as a child and is taken care of by the spirit mother. They grow up there very fast. The grown-up adults go there on their own, while full adults do not believe that they are dead as they travel there in the same appearance. The subconscious mind can be aroused by sincere prayers, keeping the mind blank for 1 or 2 minutes. This should be done during day hours only. To blank the mind, sit facing preferably north but never south, and try to listen to the distant sounds. Thoughts may come but do not force them out. Pray when you are alone. There should be some light where you are blanking; it should not be done in dark places.

Free will means you are more intelligent than animals and therefore have control over your mind, body, and spirit and therefore you are to face the consequent decisions. Here on earth, you are for a short period from your spirit world to repay the karma and undergo testing and training leading to the spiritual journey. *The very word evil is the reverse of the word live.* Evil invariably refers to a negative journey of the soul away from God.

Try always to keep fit by good and nutritious eating and not indulging in bad habits of drinking and smoking. One should not indulge in negative thinking or actions. Do not hurt others at all. Do not tolerate the bad works of others or encourage evil. Try to speak to evil-doers and it is up to them to accept your advice. Do not run away from the duties of parents and children. Honour your responsibilities to fulfil the mission of spiritual duties. Never commit suicide as by this you are going against God's wish and you may fall suddenly by 1 realm.

Never have belief in destiny, as it drags your future. Believing the destiny means you are fixing your results earlier and your karma has no impact. *The future depends on the present and if you are losing the present by thinking about destiny, the future will follow it.* Happenings with you are fully dependent on your karma, your present, and your past actions. It is you and not destiny, which shapes your future. If you have affected someone mentally, physically, emotionally, or spiritually you will be affected in that order of actions and so are the blessings. The results of good karma come in many forms like a happy family, good friends, comforts, finding a good guru, healing powers, good health, inventors, protections, skills, and ways to help others. Do not defer the debts; its carry forward is more painful. Do not be highly ambitious, nothing shall come to you beyond your capacity to handle in your lifetime. *There have been always tests, training, and karma accompanying living beings.*

Missions on Earth

Each human being has to accomplish three missions on earth and they are (i) To improve spiritually, (ii) To serve others without any self-interest, and (iii) To utilise his potential for the benefit of others. Earth is full of negative forces and therefore walking on the good path is more difficult here than in the spiritual world. Finally never tolerate evil as far as possible, but one should not endanger him or his family.

If you are on the right path and seeking the right master, you will certainly get it. To know that he is a good master for you, the first thing is that he shall not use his spiritual knowledge for his material gains or powers. Neither shall he be looking at your checkbook. You will receive the right master at the right time and unexpectedly.

When you are changing spiritually, you have more humility than before. Some good people lead a simple life and never harm others. But they do not live up to their potential. They are okay but not progressing spiritually. Never speak about your good deeds to others, ego comes in and you are losing the benefits of the good deeds. When you do good service to others, then you should thank God for the given opportunity. There are three missions in life: (i) selfless service, (ii) self-improvement and (iii) use the gift of talents given to you for the benefit of others.

Everyone on earth has a gifted power. This may be from some specialty you have earned in life, such as good cooking, singing, teaching, and others that should be used for others' benefit. Continue and complete your spiritual journey on earth as far as possible, or else life is a waste. Inspire others on their spiritual journey. All the testing and training in life is to crush the ego. There are two types of temptations: (a) the first one is physical things such as sex, drugs, food, money, power, etc. and (b) the second one is the temptation for pride, doubt, anger, revenge, jealousy, etc., which are worse than the first one.

A simple, honest, kind, selfless deed is more important than hours of prayers or thousands of charity. When negativity is high on earth prophets, saints, Rishis, and other such great souls are born to spread the messages of God. Unfortunately, with time these messages are twisted and take the shape of religion on earth and people use them for their benefit. People pray to God for cures for diseases, benefits, and protection from certain issues and personnel problems. But when these are not met, they lose faith in God. The basic point of their unanswered prayer is they are repaying for karma or they are not good for their spiritual growth. We are here not to test God's presence, but to believe him. If you are not seeing God, it does not mean that he does not exist. *Many times, you are on the spiritual path but suffering, while your neighbour is on the wrong path, but he is very successful.* You may then lose faith in God. It is just testing and training for you. Your successful neighbour is indeed falling spiritually.

Prayer should be intensive with selflessness, positive, and genuine. If prayers are for the spiritual growth of others, then it is the best one. As food is essential for the body, prayer is for spiritual growth. It protects you from all negative energies on earth and gives you the strength to move forward spiritually. *When you pray, your thoughts, words, feelings, and requests travel to the spirit world in the form of a ray of light. The brighter the intensity of the ray, the more intense the prayer. Millions of such light rays beam to space from Earth. Spirit souls intercept these lights and help them.* Just understand that prayer has a word RAY within. Every payer is listened to by God and it is the spiritual souls or angels who are deputed by God to respond to the prayers. Prayers are answered only when it is good for you, not from the earth's point of view, but from a spiritual point of view for your spiritual growth. *You may realise later that the unanswered prayer is indeed good for you.*

Always request God to give you what is good for you. Next, your prayer should be genuine and sincere with good motives. Third, the prayer must be selfless, non-materialistic, and should not interfere with your karma. Prayers do not wipe out your karma but give you the strength to stand for it. The powers of prayers are very intense and unbelievable. Prayer means you are speaking to God directly. Never feel lazy or think that time is consumed in prayers. It is the only good thing you are doing for your growth. The positive benefits of prayers are manyfold. Prayers must be short regular and intense and never pray in a fearful state. Praying at home is always better than at other places as by this you are cleansing your place of living. Prayers are never the same as rituals.

Pray in bed when you get up early in the morning before your feet touch the ground. It gives an extra ring of protection. Once your feet touch the ground, the protection is sucked by the highly negative ground. Before you sleep, pray once more in bed. Also, have short prayers during the days. Pray for yourself, then for the family members and others with a request to do what is good for them. *Always think positive, do positive, be positive,* and hope for positive. True success is not the name and fame you get on earth, but the spiritual successor. Always be humble and content and keep away from ego and pride.

No spiritual journey is possible without humility. Sometimes people have different levels of earthly success with the same amount of effort. This is something to do with your testing, training, and karma. Success is probably not good for you then. True success means spiritual success and not earthly success. Revenge is the lowest human quality and simply not acceptable in the spirit world. It is the greatest sin as it is planned. God has made everyone special and equal, so do not compare with others. When one compares, jealousy comes in. Then anger develops and finally, you start hating which drives you to revenge. People on earth always spend their time and energy on physical and material benefits which are temporary. Always surrender to God; his plans are always higher than what you plan for yourself in life.

The daily communications by the departed souls Ratoo and Vispi between 14/04/1981 and 28/01/1984 in the form of automated writings, which were subsequently published as a book titled "The Laws of the Spirit World" by their mother Khorshed Bhavnagiri in 2009, gives a comprehensive account of life in the realms where we have to live after our death from the earth planet. The book has become a national bestseller.

Information on the various grades and types of Realms that exist where people are housed after they depart from the earth depends on their Karma. A detailed life in each realm is scintillating. The karmic actions of the individuals decide the allotment of the realm to the soul. I believe this communication to be correct as I remember this automated writing was in the national dailies and newspapers in those years. Photocopies of some of these writings were published in the print media in 1981-1982. This once again confirms the very core question of the existence of life in the Exoplanets.

CHAPTER - 7

ॐ"Karma has a basic principle of cause and effect, "what you sow, you reap". Your actions are the cause and effect is its consequence. Any good work brings in positive karma and bad gives negative karma. Bad and good karma do not cancel each other, they are separate. One has to face both - one by one. Karma can germinate from thoughts, feelings, words, actions, and indirect instigations. It speaks about all that happens to us mentally, physically, and spiritually at every instant of our lives.

Everything we do, including our work, interests, deeds of kindness, and interactions with others, is part of our karma. But each of our activities has a consequence, and depending on what we do, the consequence might be either favorable or unfavorable. According to traditional beliefs, we might reap the consequences of our acts either in this life or the one following rebirth. The Buddhist Review magazine writes: "The seeds of karma shape our lives and our worlds." Therefore, for earning good karma "always feel positive, think positive, speak positive, and do positive."

Chapter - 7

Karma and Yoga

Meaning of Karma

The Sanskrit word "kri," which means to perform, act, or respond, is from where the word "karma" first originated. Karma, which is a Sanskrit word for "action," more widely refers to the Hindu concept of the global law of cause and effect, action, and reaction. The entirety of our deeds and responses from this life as well as prior incarnations, which all affect our destiny, is referred to as karma. Not all karmas have quick reactions. Some gather and unpredictably reappear in this lifetime or others. Everything we have ever done, said, thought, or caused has resulted in karma. It is also what we are thinking, saying, or doing right now. Therefore, Karma results from **five activities:**

(i) **From the heart** (the feeling: good feeling for others is good karma and bad feeling means bad karma),

(ii) **From the mind** (thoughts: good thoghts for others is good karma and bad thoughts means bad karma),

(iii) **From the attitude or words** (good words are good karma and bad words or scolding is bad karma),

(iv) **From the direct actions** (physically harming others is bad and excusing others is good)

(v) **From indirect actions** (others perform under our instructions).

According to a student's paper submitted to the Lincoln Community, **"Karma** is the universal causal law by which the present good or bad actions determine the future of an individual's existence. Karma represents the ethical dimension of the process of rebirth (samsara)."

The present births and life situations of an individual are the results of the accumulated effects of actions performed in previous lives. The dogma of karma essentially directs toward a goal for relief (moksha) from the cycles of birth and death. Karma has two main functions: (i) it provides the required motivation to lead a moral life, and (ii) it cautions us to live without doing any harm to others, rather than essentially directing us to help others.

If one's desire is incomplete, there must be a rebirth to complete the unfinished desire. Karma refers to a system in which positive results come from prior positive activities and negative results come from prior negative actions. This system of actions and reactions occurs throughout a soul's reincarnated existence, generating a cycle of reincarnation. Hindu texts categorise karma into three categories:

- **Sanchita or the accumulated karma:** It is the total Karma that a soul has collected over its entire life cycle of birth and rebirth. The total is indeed a very huge Karma.
- **Prarabdha or the Fruit-bearing karma:** It is the portion of accumulated (Sanchita) karma that is taken out and given to this present life. It is a particular problem in the present life.
- **Kriyamana is what we produce in the current life:** This is all the karmas that add to Sanchita's karma and consequently shape our future.

Some people think that only people who can discriminate between good and evil may do Kriyamana karma. Since they are unable to distinguish between good and bad, animals and young children are said to be bereft of creating new karma meaning that their actions cannot affect their future destinies.

As long as the stock of Sanchita karma lasts, a part of it continues to be taken out as Prarabdha karma for one's lifetime, and the balance is still waiting to be enjoyed in the coming reincarnations. This leads to the cycle of birth and death. A Jiva cannot be liberated (attain moksha) from the cycle of birth and death until the accumulated Sanchita karmas are completely exhausted. Acts of unkindness yield bad karma, called pāpa, and good deeds earn good fruits, called Punya. One becomes virtuous by good actions, and evil by evil actions.

I quote from Bhagavata Purana, where Vasudeva exhorts Kamsa to refrain from killing his wife, Devaki, by stating that "Death is certain for those who are born and when the body returns to the five elements, the soul leaves the body and helplessly obtains another form by the laws of karma, citing passages from Brihadaranyaka Upanishad. The soul materialises into an appropriate body whatever the state of the mind one remembers at the time of death; The soul and its subtle mind, intelligence, and ego are projected into the womb of a creature, human or non-human that can provide a gross body which is the most suitable for the state of the mind of the particular person at the time of death." This passage is similar in meaning to the Bhagavad Gita.

Karma has the principle in which "*cause and effect*" are inseparably linked in the moral sphere as in physical science. It follows that good actions have their reward and bad action gives punishment, either in this life or carried forward to the next life. The soul takes the next incarnation of life and in the new environment undergoes suffering for its past actions. One must know that karma does not go away, one must either reap the benefits or suffer the consequences of his past actions. If one refers to the Brihadaranyaka Upanishad, it states that "According as a man acts and according as he believes so will he be; a man of meritorious acts will be meritorious, a man of evil shall do sinful. One becomes pure by pure deeds and evil by evil deeds. And as is his desire so is his will; and as is his will, so is his deed; and whatever deeds he does that he will reap". Even the creator who made these laws of karma never violates them, but He gives courage and strength if requested to those who do sincere prayers.

Chandogya Upanishad distinguishes between a good birth as in a spiritual family and an evil birth, such as birth as a dog. Thus, the doctrine of karma explains why different life forms manifest, into wide levels of biological development.

KARMA has a basic principle of cause and effect, *"what you sow, so you reap"*. Your actions are the cause and the effect is its consequences. Any good work brings in positive karma and bad gives negative karma. It is a guide to the universal laws and no one can escape from this. Bad and good karma do not cancel each other, they are separate. One has to face both - one by one. As you know by now Karma can germinate from thoughts, words, actions, and indirect instigations. If one has done bad karma with someone and if he gets an opportunity to do good for him, then he must do it. This is an outstanding opportunity given by God else it shall be carried forward to the next life. The subconscious mind records all the karma of the present life in the hall of learning through Akashic records.

Charities never wipe out bad karma. When sufferings come, face it bravely as it is the result of bad karma. Sometimes others try to give you suffering as their free will, but you have to accept it. Always be thankful to God for all the good things that happened to you and remember him, both in good and bad times. Always be thankful to all who have helped you in your journey in this. If you have the strength, try to help others as far as possible. Karmic actions never compensate. For example, you are thinking badly of someone or trying to harm someone. This immediately initiates bad karma for which the person has suffered. Now you have realised the mistake and tried to do good. If you are lucky, try to get the same person and help him. If the person is not available, then do good, who needs your help. Then how it can be compensated? If the present receiver is a different person, then it cannot be compensated and if he is the same person then also it cannot be compensated as the person has already suffered. His suffering cannot be reversed.

You must have seen many situations in which a person born poor and suffered a lot during childhood has suddenly become famous or rich. And in another case, a person born rich has become very poor during a later stage in life and suffering. A healthy person meets an accident and becomes physically handicapped for life, and at the same time, a blind regains his vision by getting a donation of an eye from others. Why these things are happening? It is because the person is facing both of his previous karmas one by one. Therefore, karma has a separate accounting approach in bookkeeping, it has never had a sigma effect of compensating in nature.

Another situation of my experience is that in a locality of the jhuggi or slum area, there is a good maternity hospital. On that particular day and exactly at the same, two kids were born, one to a poor slum dweller and the other to a very rich family in the hospital. It is for sure that the newborn infants were from heavenly abode. Then the question is why such a great disparity right at the time of birth? If one believes the star positions, even then both have the same influences as they are in the same area, just outside the hospital compound wall. It has to do with karma carried forward from the previous life to the present life known as **Sanchita the accumulated karma. Be Focused, Fearless, Faithful, and Non-attached**. Attachment to the objects of the world is the cause of all misery. Non-attachment and refraining from the sense of ownership with sincerity are essential to get freedom from Karma. Non- attachment gives freedom and attachment brings bondage. Some great men are very capable of healing, which is done through Ichchha-shakti. Every human being has the potential of healing but the person who directs all the 3 channels, that is, the physical, mental, and spiritual in the right dynamics to the suffering parts of the body and the mind can heal any disease. Those who have spiritual powers can heal others on all levels.

The aspirant who is a genuine seeker of enlightenment should avoid crowds, publicity, and creating large followers. One should make his life creative and helpful, but at the same time, he should discipline himself to gain control over his mind, speech, and actions. A selfish person can never be great as he has built his limited boundary of ego. Selflessness is a great characteristic one can find in great accomplished persons of the world. Great persons are always fearless; it is the prerequisite for attaining enlightenment.

On the road to enlightenment, it is a positive development to be entirely free of all anxieties. The two necessary rungs on the staircase to illumination are faith and perseverance. The persons who are not aware of the potential within themselves are always dependent and fearful. It makes a person lonely. A perfect person feels that he is complete in himself. Under any circumstances, he never needs any external help or assistance. The highest of all companionships is the company of yourself. Enjoy the real self within and never feel lonely. The bondage makes a person dependent. Attachment to someone is mostly not love, but its misuse leads to selfishness, and seeking pleasure. Truth is the ultimate goal of life. One should not act against his conscience and not indulge in any actions that are against the conscience.

Some people are confused about God. They have their images of the type of God; mostly framing God as a human being. Even if God is shown to them, still they say that this is not God. What can be done to such a confused person who always thinks differently about God's existence?

Experience God

Swami Vivekananda once said, "If I have seen God, how can it be useful or good for you, for you, you have to try yourself." He further said, "I cannot catch your hand take you to God, and show you – it is impossible on my part to accomplish. "Therefore, direct experience is the only way out of spirituality.

Have you learned anything independently – No, whatever you learned is from others only, first from your mother, then your father, family members, teacher, friends, and so on. And they had learned from others in the same way. So, all you learn from others are the ideas of others. Indirect information from others is of course the knowledge, but for truth seekers, direct experience is the must. Real knowledge removes the suffering. Some people do not know even the alphabet but have great solutions to most intricate questions from the spiritual world, they had direct learning. Little knowledge or partial truth is always dangerous. In ancient texts (1000–700 BCE) of the

Vedic religion, karma referred simply to ritual and sacrificial action. The connection between the ritual and moral dimensions of karma is especially evident as a causal law, popularly known as the "law of karma." Many religious traditions – such as the Abrahamic religions that emerged in the Middle East (Judaism, Christianity, and Islam) - place reward and punishment for human actions in the hands of a divine lawgiver. In contrast, the classical traditions of India—Hinduism, Buddhism, and Jainism, much like the Vedic sacrificial theology that preceded them, view karma as operating according to an autonomous causal law. No divine will or external agent intervenes in the relationship of the moral act to its inevitable result. There is a beautiful message from Bhagavad Gita and it can be written as:

1. Whatever has happened, has happened for good
2. Whatever is happening is also for good
3. Whatever will happen, shall also be for good
4. What have you lost that you cry for?
5. What did you bring that you have lost?
6. What you have taken, has been from here.
7. What you gave has been given here.
8. What belongs to you today, belonged to someone yesterday and will be someone else's tomorrow

Karma is an ancient concept that was prevalent in various cultures, religions, and philosophies. According to Hinduism and Buddhism, the real meaning of karma is action. It refers to the actions of our mind, body, and spirit in every aspect and every moment of our life. Karma includes everything we do like our work, passions, charity, and others. However, each of our actions leads to certain results, which may be positive or negative depending on what we do. Following ancient beliefs, we can experience the results of our actions either in the present life or after rebirth.

The Buddhist Review magazine writes: *"The seeds of karma shape our lives and our worlds."* We can become aware of the delicate relationship between karma and our reality through mindfulness. Spiritual awareness can enable us to alter our karma which creates memories and desires, that then determine how we live. Actions, memories, and desires are the Karmic software that runs your life. The subtle energy created by your actions is stored within your memories and desires and is activated, sometimes immediately, but more often in the future.

Importance of Karma: Most people talk about karma and by this, they are referring to the great law of cause and effect. According to this law, whatever thoughts, or energy you put out, you get back, good, or bad. To get what you want, you have to be worthy of those things. It's the concept of what you reap, you sow. In Indian religion and philosophy, karma is the fundamental causal law by which good or bad acts decide the future modes of an individual's life. Karma denotes the ethical aspect of rebirth **(samsara),** which is widely accepted throughout India's religious traditions. In its most basic form, karma applies to all deeds and their consequences and is used to advance the soul and cause enlightenment.

How Does Karma Work?

The most common misconception is that "fate" acts in the same way as karma. However, this is not the case. If you do something bad, it does not mean that something negative will happen to you to "balance out." Karma is a force inside us that we can use for good or bad and not here to bring up unresolved issues.

Just like gravity governs the physical world, karma governs the divine realm. How karma works is by holding us accountable for our actions and, more specifically, for our intentions. The karmic process is nothing more than energy. It's the product of our deliberate thoughts and behaviour. We will be affected by the energy we produce now and in the future. It has nothing to do with rewarding or punishing people. Karma is impartial, and we have power over it.

It is worth mentioning that Karma is scientifically proven. We also know that our thoughts and feelings construct our reality. And, when we think positive thoughts or do good deeds, our brain reaps significant benefits. This can only have beneficial consequences and events in our lives.

Good and Bad Karma

The purpose of an action determines whether it has good or bad karma, and how it manifests.

Good karma is the result of actions and past impressions, whether it's a deed, a feeling, or an expression. Purpose directs the outcome of an action to be positive. Good deeds are rewarded either in this life or the next and they can also determine your karmic relationships.

Bad karma is the just opposite of good karma, and it is earned by negative actions, emotions, and/or words. Bad motives lead to bad behaviour, which leads to bad outcomes. Bad karma, like good karma, may be received in this lifetime or as a result of a past existence. If you find yourself on a bad spiritual path, then it is good that you have realised, try to correct yourself if you can, if not then try out online psychic readings.

In Instant Karma *there is an immediate retribution for a bad deed or a reward for a good deed. An example of good instant karma would be you are helping a person who is in urgent need and when you come home you get a long-standing problem solved. Instant bad karma is an instant retaliation for a negative thought or deed; for example, a person makes fun of a friend before other friends, and shortly after you are humiliated by your boss in the office.*

How Do Good and Bad Karma Work? All karma manifests in a positive or a negative form at some point in your life. Let us take an example of bad karma: A couple instead of living happily fights and gets divorced. The husband has made some false allegations against the wife. Later that person develops some type of chronic health issue. This is the good effect of karma for the wife and bad for the husband for which the wife would have suffered more. The divorce saved the wife from many other problems if they had stayed together. Although bad karma is what most people refer to as "what goes around comes back around", it's important to remember that this isn't the only form that the karmic body takes shape. In addition, karma's main purpose is not to make "bad people" suffer but to be a guide as to how people should lead their lives to reap good karma either in this life or the next one

However, there are occasions when you may decide to tell a lie with positive intentions. Although telling a lie goes against the law of karma but your motive is important. This poses a question: Will your positive intentions outweigh the negative karma of lying? In Buddhism, karma isn't defined as a good or bad thing. Karma is simply the product of decisions made in this and previous lifetimes. Meanwhile, Hinduism, Jainism, and Sikhism do believe in this distinction.

Difference between Karma and Dharma

Dharma refers to one's responsibilities in this life. Your dharma varies depending on your social status, family, and stage in life. Dharma's understanding can be both soothing and disturbing. On one hand, you may believe that by adhering to your family's and community's customs, you will be fulfilling your dharma. On the other hand, some doubt their dharma and seek true meaning outside of their community.

To help you further differentiate between dharma and karma, think of karma as the product of one's conduct to one's dharma. In certain ways, dharma can be viewed as the task of one of your lifetimes, and karma is the steps necessary to complete the task. Your dharma decides the type of karmic experiences you will receive as a result of your deeds. For example, going to war to protect one's country may fulfil one's dharma, but it may result in bad karma and misery for another who was supposed to stay at home and care for his children. Did you know that Dharma is something that takes multiple lifetimes to achieve, while karma is something that varies in each moment?

The Karmic Cycle

The karmic cycle describes how karma operates in people's lives through various circumstances and karmic experiences that we must go through to learn a solution. In a system of belief, one karmic cycle is said to last for 12 years. Different stages of life can be divided into 5 karmic cycles or stages as follows:

- **Childhood Cycle: 0 – 12 years:** Individual force constructs environments that assist him.
- **Youth Cycle: 13 – 24 years:** This is when the majority of the signs from your past life begin to appear, and you begin to pay off your debts in a meaningful way.
- **Adult Creation: 25 – 36 years:** As a person enters the adult stage of their karmic cycle, his karmic patterns are thought to be complete. What manifests are all of the mental, emotional, and physical health issues that have been aligned for that person in a previous lifetime.
- **Adult Expansion: 37 – 48 years:** At this point, the karma takes hold and the karmic life tests have been increased.
- **Adult Contraction: 49 – 60 years:** From this point forward, the cycle's power begins to wane. This is the worst of all the phases. Individuals have either fixed or postponed issues for the next lifetime.
- **Superannuation: 60+ years:** Some of the karma is experienced and the person either suffers or enjoys depending on the karma he has earned in this life.
- **Breaking the Karmic Cycle:** How can you break a karmic cycle? One approach is to do the right things over several lifetimes. You may like to get out of a cycle during your lifetime. Another option is to stay in your current situation, do your best, stay open and concentrate, and make yourself available to the process.

Sadhguru on Karma

The very process of life is the dissolution of karma. To make people understand it he explains, "Karma is the accumulated impression of past activity, either of thought, emotion or physical action". The quality of the karma that you gather is not necessarily in terms of action alone. From the moment you were born till this moment, the kind of family, home, friends, the things that you did and did not do – all these things influence you. Every thought, emotion, and action come only from past impressions that you have had within you. They decide who you are right now.

"KARMA means action or the imprint of action which remains within us. The actions that your father performed are working and kicking up within you not just in your situation, but within every cell in your body. It is not so easy to get rid of your parents! You may have noticed that when you were eighteen or twenty, you completely rebelled against your father or your mother, but by the time you are forty or forty-five, you begin to speak like them, act like them, and even look like them. That is a hopeless way to live because if this generation is going to behave, act, live, and experience life just the way the previous generation did, this is a wasted generation. This generation should experience life in a way the previous generation never even imagined. I don't mean you should do something crazy on the street, I mean the way you experience life can be completely altered. It can be taken to the next level of experience.

The problem has come not because of karma, the problem has come because you got entangled in it, and you got enmeshed in it. If a little distance comes between you and your body, between you and your mind, then whatever the karma, it has no impact on you. You can still make use of it to be embodied and live, you can still maintain a certain individual character but it does not become binding, it becomes a stepping stone."

Four Things to Know About Karma - How to Make it Work

When people hear the word "karma," most instantly know what it means. Though karma is commonly cited as a reason for having something good or bad happen in our lives, most people don't understand the true significance of this spiritual concept that has been around for thousands of years. Here's what you need to know about what it is, how it works, and what you can do for it.

1. Karma is not for Exchange

If something good or bad happens suddenly, people often say, "Oh, it must have been my karma." If something inconvenient happens or a situation does not pay out the way they thought it might happen then people say bad karma is in action. Similarly, when a good thing happens suddenly, people say "I think I have good karma now." Though this reaction is good, practically it is not so, it is more subtle and complex.

2. The components of Karma

Current karma (CK): A good example of current karma is when you are planting seeds on the farm which is your karma. This means you shall get the plants and the fruits by the seeds. If you have sown paddy seeds, you cannot expect to get wheat from the field.

Accumulated karma (AK): This type is already in the seed form, but has not come to fruition, meaning you haven't experienced it yet. Not all AKs will come to fruition in one lifetime. Think of it this way: In your karma farm, there are all different types of seeds, and some are harvested after 10 years, while others are harvested after 100 years. We have no control over this; the seeds just grow and manifest at their own pace which may be good/bad/neutral. Destiny is when AK comes to fruition.

3. Your karma is your choice

Before birth, each individual decides in the astral world to be born to fixed parents and the environment with free choice of selection. Your soul assumes a body, which it was able to pick and choose from different lifetimes and karmas. Essentially, your soul uses its past life learning to choose and create the life you are currently living. It knows what you can handle, and what you can't withstand. It knows your past, present, and future. It knows everything. You choose to have a certain kind of life, and that allows you to gradually move toward your soul's higher purpose.

4. Changing your karma is possible, but not simple

If you have bad karma carried forward with which you were born that was accumulated throughout your past lives, then you can't just replace it with good karma. No number of "good" actions will remove negative karma from your destiny. You can reduce the **intensity** of the negative karma you have by setting your intention very clearly and putting action in motion targeted toward the negative karma. This is where all the spiritual practices come into play, like meditation as well as charity and giving. If you do this effectively, when that negative karma comes to fruition, it will be less intense. The best can be to try to earn good karma. Take actions to make the world a better place, make someone else's life easier, or create positive influences. Through those actions, you have a chance to impact your destiny.

The 12 laws of karma

Everything is energy including your thoughts and emotions. In essence, everything you create has corresponding energy that comes back to you in some form. The 12 laws of karma can help you to understand how karma works and how to create good karma in your life. Let's look at each of these laws in more detail.

1. The great law of cause and effect

When most people talk about karma, they're likely referring to the great law of cause and effect. According to this law, whatever thoughts, or energy you put out, you get back. It's the concept of what you reap, you sow.

2. The law of creation

To make things happen in your life, you need to act, instead of waiting for something to magically come your way. You are in the making of what you want, based on your intentions. Consider how you can use your skills, talents, and strengths to create something that not only benefits you but others as well.

3. The law of humility

It is based on the principle that you must be humble enough to accept that your current reality is the result of your past actions. For example, if you're blaming your colleagues for your poor performance at work, you must accept that you created this reality by not performing properly as you could have performed.

4. The law of growth

Growth starts within you only and therefore try to focus on yourself. Do not try to control the people or things around you. To positively shape your world, you need to start with yourself.

5. The law of responsibility

You are to own what happens to you in your life. It has happened only because of you. You are the product of the choices you make.

6. The law of connection

This law is based on the principle that everything in your life, including your past, present, and future, are connected. "Who you are today is the result of your previous actions." And who you will be tomorrow will be the result of your actions today.

7. The law of focus

Focusing on too many things at once can slow you down and lead to frustration and negativity. That's why the law of focus encourages you to concentrate on one thing at a time

8. The law of giving

If you want to live in a peaceful world, you need to focus on cultivating peace for others. What you want to give to yourself is the primary.

9. The law of acceptance

To experience peace of mind, you have to embrace the present. This can only happen when you let go of negative thoughts or behaviours from your past. If you get too focused on past events, you'll keep reliving them.

10. The law of learning

Learn from past experiences and take steps not to repeat the mistakes. Do something different to stop the cycle.

11. The law of patience

Patience is the ultimate tool to win over. The person with more coolness and patience is more towards success. One must be consistent in our karmic deeds. Be consistent in your goals. Results shall follow.

12. The law of significance and inspiration

We all play a small part in this world and have something to contribute to society. What we share may sometimes seem small to us but can make an enormous difference in someone else's life. The law of significance and inspiration is a great law to focus on when you need a motivational boost or begin to feel like you don't have a purpose or matter. According to this law, every contribution you make will affect the world. You have been born with a specific gift, mission, and purpose that only you can bring into the world with your uniqueness. As you have a unique in your field, always share your skills and gifts to the benefit of others.

Karma and Yoga

Yoga teaches us to understand that everything is interconnected and, therefore, our thoughts and actions matter a lot. The Yoga-Sutras is a wonderful guide to help us mould our karma with more positive thoughts and actions. Through various yoga practices, we set ourselves up for making more thoughtful, compassionate choices, and actions through which we can steer our karma towards positive values in life. Yoga philosophy teaches us that doing our duty to the best of our capacities is essentially what we must do to balance karma.

Going through the literature of Yoga, one can find many ways of enlightenment from the cycles of rebirth, but broadly they can be grouped or lumped into only SIX main branches or paths. By following these yogic practices, they add positive karma to their account. It is not possible to discuss each of them separately in this volume, but a broad meaning of each of them is given here. These yoga practices are discussed in brief:

1. **Bhakti yoga:** It is a yoga of Devotion. It was first mentioned in the Bhagavad Gita around 300 BC, the word Bhakti comes from the root word 'Bhaj', of which the essence is 'to share'. This form of yoga is based upon the heart, love, and devotion toward a chosen deity. It involves Shravana - listening to sacred scriptures, Kirtana - singing devotional songs, Smarana - remembering the divine through meditation, Pada-seven - ritual worship or service at the feet of the Lord, Vandana - prostration before the image of God, Dasya - slavish devotion to the Lord, Sakhya - friendship through which the Divine raises the devotee to the status of a friend, and Atma-nirvana - self-offering.

    This Bhakti Yoga or the path of devotion is centred on self-surrender to God. People mostly adopt singing or musical ways of devotion to God. Self-sacrifice and deep reverence for God are the basis of the approach. People following this path have more humility, gentleness, purity, simplicity, sincerity, and honesty. The path seeks a day in and day out at the service to the Lord. People following the path are emotional and when they sing devotional songs or participate in spiritual discussions on God, tears are usually seen in their eyes. They are fully dedicated to God. They always collect positive karma and try to attain freedom from the cycle of rebirth. Here one starts with the Primary Practices of Mantra, devotional rituals, and meditation upon a chosen deity. This is good for Householders

2. **Hatha yoga:** It is the Yoga of Force. Many teachers equate Ha to mean the 'Sun' and Tha to mean the 'Moon' and the reason that the physical yoga practice is intended to 'balance' the Sun and Moon energies within us. Whilst the physical yoga practice is intended to bring about a state of equilibrium within the human organism, the real meaning and essence of Hatha yoga are to change the physical body and mind by way of experimentation, movement, and physical 'force'.

   Hatha yoga is anything that uses the physical body. It was first mentioned and practiced around 1100 AD and it is the most 'modern' branch of yoga. This branch of yoga in a way is derived from Tantra and the most widely celebrated 'inventor' of Hatha Yoga is Gorakshanath, who is considered a Maha-Yogi, or 'great Yogi'.

   The Hatha Yoga or the ***'Kriya or the Kundalini Yoga'*** is the energy of the body as the path of enlightenment in which people knowledgeable about the body, energy, and nerve channels follow the path. The body from the head to the hip joint in the spinal column is divided into seven chakras and by continuous yogic practice, they try to awaken the chakras starting from Muladhara/ Chakra through Sushumna to Sahashra chakra which is on the top of the head. Locations of these chakras in a human body are shown in Fig. 7.1. The Sushumna Nadi connects the first muladhara chakra to the seventh Sahasrara chakra, and is the path for the ascent of Kundalini energy up from the base of the spine to the crown of the head. It is considered the central channel for the flow of Prana throughout the body. The energy collected by this kriya yoga is essentially the vehicle for transferring life to higher realms and getting free from the cycle of rebirth.

There is however a finer difference between hatha yoga and kriya yoga. The biggest difference is that Kriya Yoga is focused on more than just the physical benefits of yogic practice. Hatha Yoga is the practice of performing yoga poses. The word "hatha" means "force" – thereby emphasizing the physicality of this type of yogic practice.

3. **Karma yoga:** It is the Yoga of Action. The word 'Karma' in this context is derived from the root verb 'Kri' meaning 'to do'. First mentioned around 300 BC, this form of yoga is the main focus of the Bhagavad Gita. *Karma yoga is based upon selfless service and acting without expectation of benefit.* It occupies a large part of Indian thought and through this practice union with 'the divine' is achieved through making any action an offering to God.

   Karma yoga suggests that we relinquish attachment to the consequences of our actions. Awareness of each thought, word, and deed is an important part of Karma yoga, which allows the practitioner to truly experience that moment in action. Through the practice of Karma yoga, yogis work and act to benefit the people to facilitate a unified and 'enlightened' world.

   Persons following this practice surrender all their results of actions to God as they believe that it is he who is present in everybody's heart. It liberates one from bondage and thus from the cycles of birth and death. For this, the right actions with knowledge are a must.

4. **Jnana Yoga:** It is for wisdom or knowledge. This is the yoga of 'knowing', of realizing the truth of oneself. First mentioned around 400 BC, this is thought of as one of

the most direct paths to insight and illumination, but also as one of the most difficult. Priests and scholars are most likely to be considered Jnana yogis through their practice of constant inquiry. The study of philosophical and yogic texts, along with discrimination and inquiry are the ways these practitioners understand the depths of the body, mind, and spirit.

In this path of intellect, the persons are mostly in the company of sages. They aptly listen to spiritual discourses and sharpen their knowledge of spiritual paths. One needs to be non-attached while seeking this path of enlightenment. It is a path in which acquiring wrong knowledge from non-enlightened teachers may lead to bad practices that lead to downfall.

5. **Raja yoga:** It is the king of all yoga practices. It aims to 'control' the intellect and thoughts through meditation. A connection with 'God' or 'consciousness' is worked towards by un-identifying with the ego-based self and identifying with the universal true Self. Raja yoga requires much self-discipline. The concept of Raja Yoga follows the principles of eight-limb yoga or Ashtanga Yoga that were compiled by Patanjali. By practicing eight-limb yoga, the practitioner can reach an enlightened state of consciousness or samadhi.

   In essence, "Raja Yoga' is the yoga of mind and body control with a focus on meditation and energy. It encompasses teachings from all the different paths, and it is from Raja yoga that hatha yoga and modern asana practice developed. Since Raja yoga involves all three dimensions of human existence (physical, mental, and spiritual), it enables practitioners to achieve balance and harmony on all of these levels. A Raja Yogi follows the following 8 steps and advances to the higher realms.

Yama – Niyama – Asana – Pranayama – Pratyahara – Dharana – Dhyana – Samadhi

Yamas has five social observances and these include ahimsa - the nonviolence, Satya - the truthfulness, Asteya - the non-stealing, brahmacharya the chaste, and aparigraha - the non-possessiveness.

Niyamas has five moral services: Saucha – the purity, Santosha - the contentment, tapas – the self-discipline, Svadhyaya - the self-study, and Ishvara – the Pranidhana (devotion or surrender).

Asana - Yoga postures.

Pranayama - Breathing techniques as a means of controlling Prana (vital life force energy).

Pratyahara - Withdrawal of the senses.

Dharana - Concentration.

Dhyana - Meditation.

Samadhi - Enlightenment or bliss.

These eight steps, commonly known as the 8 limbs of yoga, basically act as guidelines on how to live a meaningful and purposeful life. They serve as a prescription for moral and ethical conduct and self-discipline; they direct attention toward one's health; and they help us to acknowledge the spiritual aspects of our nature.

These eight limbs offer a systematic approach to calming the mind and finding liberation from suffering. Raja yoga is ultimately a means of transcending identification with the body-mind-intellect complex to understand the nature of the true self. Rajyoga is the most comprehensive path and, a highly evolved systemic science, followed by Swami Vivekananda in which the Karma, Bhakti, Kundalini, and Jnana yogas are combined. The chief practice of Raja Yoga is meditation.

6. **Tantra yoga:** The root word of Tantra is 'Tan' meaning 'to expand' or 'to weave'. It explores all aspects, sensations, and energies that weave through the body and mind and began as a religion around 500 BC. For over 1000 years it was the primary belief system of India in its less extreme forms and it was the first time the physicality of the human body started to become important within a yogic context. Before this, much of yoga practice was based upon worship, visualization, and meditation.

Many people confuse Tantric yoga with 'spiritualised sex' which is untrue. Tantra yoga includes many rituals. Much of Tantra is kept in obscurity, with the practices and rituals passed along secretively through oral tradition from guru to Sishya ('student' or 'disciple').

"One should never seek to practice classical Tantra without a guru because no Tantric texts exist that provide thoroughly accurate details of any ritual. Each text omits an essential step or includes false information, and only through a guru can the reality be handed down from teacher to disciple over generations."

Influence of Food and Breathing

When diet is wrong medicine is of no use, and when the diet is correct medicine is of no need.

~Ayurvedic Proverb

Eating well and practicing yoga can maximize our health benefits. **One should eat a vegetarian diet as far as possible,** as animal protein contains too much uric acid and toxins that get deposited in the tissues and joints. Practicing Yoga is the most beneficial when complemented with healthy food habits. Eating the right food is an essential part of living. What we eat, not only influences our physical well-being, but also our emotions and thoughts. Yoga does not dissect food into proteins, carbohydrates, or fats, instead, it classifies them according to the effect they have on the body and mind, into three types – **Satva, Rajas, and Tamas.**

Tamasic food is those which dull the mind and bring about inertia, confusion, and disorientation (Ex Non-vegetarian diet, Stale or reheated food, oily food, sugary food, and food containing artificial preservatives fall under this category). ***Rajasic food*** brings about activity or restlessness. They stimulate the body and mind into action. In excess, these foods can cause hyperactivity, restlessness, anger, irritability, and sleeplessness. Overly tasty foods (Ex. Spicy food, onion, garlic, tea, coffee, fried food) are Rajasic. ***Sattvic food*** makes you feel light, energetic, and enthusiastic. They purify the body and calm the mind. Cooked food that is consumed within 3-4 hours can be considered Sattvic (Ex. Fresh fruits, green leafy vegetables, nuts, grains, fresh milk, and certain spices)

Not just the right kind of food, it is vital to eat the proper quantity of food at the right time. Over eating leads to lethargy while under eating does not provide enough nourishment. Many times we know that our stomach is full but we are tempted by the taste of food. We might eat the right kind of food in the right quantity but if we are irregular with our timings then the whole system is on a toss. Therefore it is of prime importance to eat food at the same time every day and eat it at regular intervals.

The state of the mind of the person cooking/eating also affects the food. The energy in the food cooked by someone while he/she was angry will be lower than that of someone who cooked it with a feeling of love, contentment, and gratitude. Listening to some soothing music or chanting while cooking and eating can help retain the Prana (life force energy) in the food.

Breathing: During normal breathing, a healthy adult only takes in about 600 cc of air per breath in the lungs, the total capacity of the lungs being 6000 cc or 6 liters. In deep breathing, the practitioner can inhale up to the total capacity of 6 liters, which increases breathing efficiency per breath. Deep breathing involves efficient movement of the abdomen. The benefits of long breathing are many of which, the following are listed.

- Due to the slowing of respiration rate (from 15-18 to 4-8 breaths/ min), the heart rate/pulse rate is reduced. The blood pressure is also reduced. Deep breathing is very good for stress and related ailments.
- More oxygen is made available per breath, making the breathing most efficient.
- It relaxes the nervous system, which calms the mind by removing thoughts and emotions.

- Enhanced movement of the diaphragm brings in many good changes to the internal organs like the liver, pancreas, stomach, heart, and lungs which are attached to the diaphragm and move up and down during breathing.
- It is observed that animals who breathe slowly have more life span, so reducing the breath rate with deep breathing may help increase the life span of human beings.

Beginners can start with deep breathing practice in the sitting position. Initially, a ratio of 1:1 (inhalation and exhalation counts are the same such as - 4 seconds inhale and 4 seconds exhale or 5 sec inhale and 5 sec exhale) is good. One may practice it for 5 minutes initially, and gradually increase the time duration. After practicing it for 10 minutes every day, one can increase the ratio to 1:2 (exhale time twice of inhalation, say - 4 seconds inhalation and 8 seconds exhalation or 5 sec inhale and 10 sec exhale). A rate of **6 breaths per minute,** on average, creates a "resonant frequency" whereby heart rate and blood pressure oscillate 180 degrees out of phase with one another, while heart rate and respiration oscillate in phase with each other. **Slow breathing helps in expanding the lungs and increases efficiency in oxygen absorption and supply.** It massages all organs, strengthens the chest muscles, and improves digestion and the quality of sleep.

Monkey's respiratory rate is about 36 breaths per minute, while an elephant has 4-5 breaths per minute, and when resting, an alligator may only take one breath per minute. A normal breathing rate for an adult man at rest is **8 to 16 breaths per minute,** for an infant it is up to 44 breaths per minute. A whale lives for an average of 150 years and has - 6 breaths per minute. The normal respiratory rate for a cow is **10-30 breaths per minute,** and the average dog's breathing rate is between

18 to 30 breaths per minute at rest. Once a child reaches the age of 2, the respiration rate reduces from 44 breaths per minute to 26. A tortoise has - 4 breaths per minute, and they live for an average of 150 years.

As the breathing rate increases, the life span decreases.

The Bottom Line

The 12 laws of karma can serve as a guideline or road map to follow as you go through your daily life. These laws can help you understand how karma works, and the effect that your thoughts and actions can have on you and the world around you. Using karma as a set of guidelines in your life you try to be more mindful of your thoughts, actions, and deeds before you make a decision.

Yoga teaches us to understand that everything is interconnected and, therefore, our thoughts and actions matter a lot. The Yoga-Sutras is a wonderful guide to help us mold our karma with more positive thoughts and actions. Through various yoga practices, we set ourselves up for making more thoughtful, compassionate choices, and actions through which we can steer our karma towards positive values in life. Yoga philosophy teaches us that doing our duty to the best of our capacities is essentially what we must do to balance karma.

When we are born on this earth, we have to do karma to live. Karma has a basic principle of cause and effect meaning thereby that, what you sow, you reap. Doing good to others is good karma and harming others is bad karma. Your actions at any time should not make sad or tears to any other, be it a human being or animal. The ancient beliefs and the present examples amply indicate the results of karma we experience in our daily lives. Our karma as we are earning now is either to be faced in this life or can be carried over to the next life. Therefore, never earn bad karma at any time.

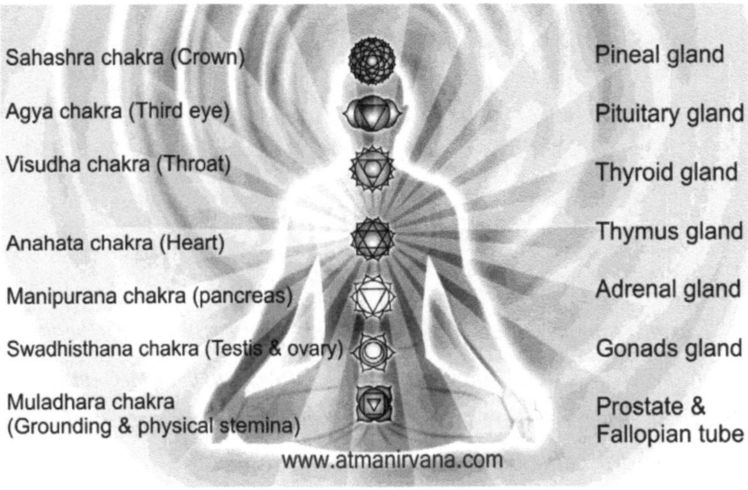

Fig. 7.1: Location of seven chakras in a human body

Karma germinates from thoughts, words, actions, and indirect instigations. The karma earned is never compensating, one has to face both - one by one. What we are now is based on our past karma and what we shall be is dependent on our present actions. Therefore, for earning good karma "always feel positive, think positive, speak positive, and do positive," and this is the Mantra.

CHAPTER - 8

ॐ *'Karma can germinate from the heart (feelings), mind (thoughts), mouth (words), actions (physical), and indirect instigations (order for actions). Whenever we are talking about others, we are earning karma, good or bad depending on what we think and speak.*

We put lots of effort into various works for its success. All of us have experienced that for some work, we get unprecedented results or benefits with less effort, while for other works, despite having put in enormous efforts, we get results much less in proportion to the efforts and sometimes we incur huge losses or failure in the mission. This is because we are not fit or our karma does not permit us for the assignment. God is supreme and he knows what is good for you. When we analyse the results later, we found that whatever had happened was good for us. Therefore, do good for others, whenever you get the opportunity, and thank God for the opportunity given to you.

Chapter – 8

Some Experiences with Karma

Some Facts and Examples

We know that *karma* follows the basic principle of cause and effect, *"what you sow, so you reap"*. The actions are the cause and the effect is its consequences. Any good thought or work brings in positive karma and bad ones bring in negative karma. It is guided by universal laws and no one can escape from this. Bad and good karma do not cancel each other, they are separate. One has to face both - one by one. The opportunity to do good should not be missed at all.

The stories of actions and resulting reactions (karma) are almost infinite as everyone has experiences of it. All of us have experiences of sudden loss or gain which are unexpected lines. When you get unprecedented results or benefits with fewer efforts you appreciate the good karma you must have done before, while despite having put in enormous efforts, you do not get good results or incur huge losses or sometimes great failures. You blame yourself for the bad karma that you think you have done before. However, some do not believe that there is something called karma. They do not admit it in public, but at some point of time in their life, they privately believe that there is karma and they are experiencing it.

You are gifted with an intelligent mind to think and make a decision which is known as the freewill. The intelligent mind is the conscious mind. When this conscious mind becomes dominant over the subconscious mind which is the spiritual mind or the mind of Aatama, then the person is more attracted to the the materialistic world and drags towards evil. God is supreme and everything is done in his direction. This is correct, but with one exception – the application of our free will or the conscious mind is given to us by God. Human beings are more intelligent than animals. Therefore, decisions are to be taken by you only. I have seen a situation where animals, which are given life by God and born on earth as the burden of the beast, are given the memory of the previous life so that they repent for the bad karma they have earned in their previous life. They take this tortured life to finish their karma earlier than staying in realms 1-2 for hundreds or thousands of years.

One day when I was driving, I had to slow down the car in the market. Suddenly a big buffalo came from nowhere and stood in front of my car. It put its head on the bonnet of the car and did not move for quite some time. I had no way out but noticed that the great buffalo was crying with tears continuously rolling down from both eyes. I was stunned. I came out of the car and showed my affection to the buffalo. After quite some time, the animal moved out. Here the question is why the beast at all came to my car. Why it was crying for my affection? What is the relationship? Is it out of my past life or a carryover factor of karma? I cannot know these answers as I have no power to transgress to the astral world and know my past. But I believe that this is related to our past life.

Someone asked a question if everything was under the the direction of God, then he is responsible for both the good as well as evil things done by me. I am only an instrument under him. God is my master and the owner of both of my activities.

Then why should I be punished? A good answer to this question is as follows:

I have engaged a driver to drive my car. One day I asked the driver to receive the guest from the airport. The driver complied and on the way made an accident. Now, who is to suffer? Is it the owner who is me or the driver? Here you agree that the driver should suffer, as he is given the power to drive with a fully conscious mind. I never asked him to make an accident. Similarly, God is our ultimate owner, and also, he has given us the free will or the intelligence in our conscious mind to apply break and control acceleration so that we do not have accidents at any time in our lives. Never blame God for the suffering which is earned by you. As you sow, so you reap.

What we earn should be fair and honest. Life on Earth is very short and temporary. But we give the maximum of our efforts and energy for earning wealth that we cannot spend at all and also cannot carry with us to the next life except the karma which is only the carry-over factor. More propriety means more tension leading to the generation of more negativity in mind. I shall try to record here another small experience of a successful businessman, the reality of which I had collected from some source.

A small businessman did very hard work and became rich. He was proud of his propriety and richness. One day, a friend of his who is good and spiritually minded visited him. He appreciated the great wealth earned by his friend businessman and advised him to do something so that his hard-earned money is carried by him to the next life as he has also become old. This has created a thought in him and he decided that he should look for ways to transport his hard-earned money to the next life. He engaged all his office personnel and fixed a timeline of 1 year. The entire office was after this solution to the problem. One year passed but no one could get any answer. After some time, an old intelligent man came to meet him. He requested the solution to this problem and replied like this. The visitor asked the businessman, have you visited America any time? The answer was yes. To this, the visitor asked, what do you do to meet your expenses in the USA- Do you use our currency? To this, the businessman replied I exchange my currency with the dollar and meet my expenses in the USA using the converted dollar.

A second question followed. Have you visited any time in the UK? The reply was also positive. To this, the visitor asked, what do you do to meet your expenses in the UK- Do you use our currency? To this, the businessman replied I exchange my currency with the British pound and meet my expenses in the UK using the converted pound.

Then came the final answer. The visitor said, if you visit the USA and UK in this world and cannot use our currency in these countries, then how you can use your money in the unknown world after your death if you cannot convert them into their currency? Karma is the only currency that is in use in that world and therefore you need to convert your propriety into the currency of karma so that you can carry it to your next world. Then the visitor gave a list of things to do. He requested to spend the money on the welfare of the people at large. This should help him to earn some karma that he can carry to the next life. But one thing he should never think at all is that this should be done without any intention or feeling for ego or desire to carry over. It is essential to do charities without any self-motive and ego, and then only the giving away can earn the karma. With this, the visitor left the place and the advice was well taken by the businessman. He became a changed person, loved by all.

Every one of us is earning karma at every moment of our lives except when we are sleeping. In deep sleep, our conscious and subconscious minds unite and work together. While we are awake, it is impossible to completely blank our minds for two minutes. If one can do it, he has attained a higher level of yogic practice. For most of us and for every action a decision is taken by either the conscious or the subconscious mind. For good persons, the subconscious mind controls the actions and for others the conscious mind. For evil persons the subconscious mind becomes dormant. We face issues of conflict in our minds on some decisions. Here is a minor example.

One day I was in a small market to purchase some items from a grocery shop. The bill was 270. I then handed over a currency note of 500 and was expecting a return of 230, but the shopkeeper handed me back 270 by mistake. I was in dilemma, whether to refund the extra 40 given to me by the shopkeeper or take it away. Initially, I thought not to refund which was the decision of the conscious mind. After walking out of the shop, I decided, I should return. This is where the subconscious mind prevailed over my conscious mind. The shopkeeper was happy and became good to me there afterward. He always honoured me whenever I visited his shop. This is not a question of the amount of money, but the primary attitude.

Understanding of What We Know – The Knowledge

The next question comes is our **knowledge** for which we are so proud. The first thing is what is knowledge? *Knowledge by definition is a familiarity, awareness, or understanding of someone or something, such as facts, information, descriptions, or skills, which is acquired through experience or education. In its simplest terms, to have* *known is knowledge.* Knowledge can be both theoretical and practical understanding of a subject. Our behaviour, response, attitude, talks, ... everything depends on our knowledge. The person who knows more and more becomes more humble. This is because he has entered into the vast ocean of knowledge and understands what he knows. But a person who has less knowledge feels proud mostly due to egoistic issues. Do we have absolute knowledge? No. None of us has absolute knowledge of any subject. We all have some relative knowledge.

The knowledge is so vast and we know so little. I appreciate the Nobel laureate Professor Eric Collins who once said and I quote *"My ignorance in my subject is many times higher than my knowledge in my subject and therefore I make mistakes."* Stephen Hopkins, the great space scientist said "Our knowledge of space science is almost zero – we almost know nothing of it." Then comes why we are so proud of our knowledge. What is the use of gaining knowledge that vanishes at death? The answer is simple. You have to gain knowledge that not only helps you to earn bread for life but should be fully used for the welfare of society. For example, you are a doctor, an engineer, a lawyer, or someone who knows a solution to issues related to the welfare of the people. By this, you earn your livelihood. But this should not be misused to earn money unfairly. You get your fees or salary for the use of the knowledge that solves the problems of individuals or society, but once you use the knowledge to earn evil money that becomes bad karma and you have to pay for it, either in this life or later.

Knowledge is always a thing of the past. If we say, someone is knowledgeable; what does it mean? It simply means that he knows the subject that has happened in the past. Only he has remembered the things that occurred in the past.

It is a memory. If memory is knowledge, then that is not going to help a person who is a spiritual seeker. For him, he has to experience himself.

Once Swami Vivekananda said, *"If I have seen God, then in what way it is going to be useful to you? I cannot catch your hand, take you to the Lord, and request for you. You need to see yourself. Individual experience is the only way out."* And this knowledge is not going to be useful in any way in your permanent life that is in the spiritual world which is your permanent home.

The use of knowledge for the benefit of the individual or society is good karma, while the purpose of earning extra money is evil. This is what you carry to the next life. Then the question may be, how do we know, that the next life exits and we carry forward our karma? The explanation is very simple.

You must have seen many situations in which a person born poor and suffered a lot during childhood has suddenly become famous or rich. And in another case, a person born rich has become very poor during the later stages of life and suffering. Why these things are happening? It is because the person is facing both of his previous karmas one by one. Therefore, karma has a separate accounting approach in its bookkeeping, it has never had a sigma effect of compensating in nature.

In the locality of the jhuggi or slum area, there is a good maternity hospital. On a particular day exactly at the same, two kids were born, one to a poor slum dweller and the other to a very rich family in the maternity hospital. It is for sure that the newborn infants were from heavenly abode. Then the question is why such a great disparity right at the time of birth? If one believes the star positions, even then both have the same effect. It has to do with karma carried forward from the previous life to the present life known as **Sanchita the accumulated karma.**

The consequences of one's actions to oneself are in proportion to one's good or bad intentions towards others. *To reap what one sow is a common idiomatic expression that means to experience an equal or the same kind of situation one caused others to experience. When someone reaps what he sows, everything happening to him results from things he has done in the past.* As you sow, so shall you reap. Yes, this is an old and true proverb. The meaning is that if you do good to others you will also be rewarded with good. And if you are bad and unkind, you will get the same from others.

As You Sow - So Shall You Reap

The meaning of "As you sow, so shall you reap" is that if you do good to others you will also be rewarded with good, and if you are bad and unkind, you will get the same from others. Here are some small but real events befitting the statement.

 # 1: There once lived a very poor girl with her parents in a small town. She worked as a servant girl in a rich Lady's house. One day as she was coming home from work, she saw a purse lying on the road. She recognized it at once. It was her master's purse. She ran towards it, opened it and found a little brooch which was made of gold and along with it was some money. She decided to return the purse and ran back to the rich lady's house. The lady was very thankful for getting back her money and the brooch. She presented the brooch to the little girl and also promised to increase her monthly pay. The girl was also very pleased.

As you see, if you do good, you will also be rewarded with good as the little girl was rewarded. It is not always that you are rewarded. Sometimes the person to whom you do good doesn't reward you. Then you should not feel bad. Because good deeds are not done for rewards but out of your goodness and they should be done wholeheartedly. Good deeds should be done anywhere you go. May it be school, home, or the in the market.

You should cultivate the habit of doing good things in your life. The students in schools should learn that if you find something, you must give it to the person to whom it belongs or in the office to hand over the same to the owner so that the student will feel very happy. Learn to do good things in your house by way of helping your parents, friends, and neighbours.

 # 2: A Collected Story: Once there lived a poor farmer named Fleming. One day, he heard a cry from a nearby wet muddy ground. He ran to that place to save the boy. There, he saw a terrified boy stuck to his waist in that black muck. He was screaming and struggling to free himself. Fleming saved the boy from what could have been a slow and terrifying death. The next day, a fancy carriage pulled up to the farmer's surroundings. An elegantly dressed nobleman stepped out and introduced himself as the father of the boy, Fleming has saved. 'I want to repay you,' said the nobleman. 'You saved my son's life.' 'No, I cannot accept payment for what I did,' the farmer replied, waving off the offer.

At that moment, the farmer's son came to the door of the home. *'Is that your son?' the nobleman asked. 'Yes,' the replied proudly. 'I'll make you a deal. Let me take him and give him a good education. If the boy is like his father, he'll grow into a man you can be proud of.* 'The farmer's son graduated in medicine from St Mary's Hospital

Medical School in London and went on to become the noted Sir Alexander Fleming, the discoverer of Penicillin. Years afterward, the nobleman's son was stricken with pneumonia. And what saved him -The Penicillin. The name of the nobleman was Lord Randolph Churchill, and his son's name was Sir Winston Churchill.

 # 3: One night, three thieves stole a lot of money from a rich man's house. They put the money in a bag and went to the forest. They felt very hungry. So, one of them went to a nearby village to buy food. The other two remained in the forest to take care of the bag of money. The thief who went for food had an evil idea. He ate his food at a hotel. Then he bought food for his two mates in the forest. He mixed a strong poison with the food. He thought, "Those two will eat this poisoned food and die. Then I will get all the money for myself." Meanwhile, the two wicked men in the forest decided to kill their mate in return. They thought that they would divide the money between the two of them. All three wicked men carried out their cruel plans. The thief who wanted all the money for himself came to the forest with the poisoned food. The two men in the forest hit him and killed him. Then they ate the poisoned food and died. Thus, these evil people met with an evil end.

 # 4: A tenant who was financially not so healthy got a small outhouse rented. They worked a lot and even had to leave the 6-year-old child alone. One day the landlord told their tenants to leave the house. She had already taken advance for a month, ₹10, 000 which is a big amount for any family who is working so hard day and night. The tenant wanted the landlord to give the advance back. She denied it and forced them to leave. After one week this happened to her car of the landlord. A big, well-grown tree fell on top of their car and no one was hurt but they got what they deserved. No rain, no wind. The sky was clear on that day.

 # 5: (A collected story) Naman and Shyam were close friends at University. When they graduated, both were invited for placement interviews in a company. During the interview, all was going well until they told Naman that they had interviewed Shyam just before him and they knew both studied together." Since you, both have an Honours degree and similar experience, can you tell us why we should recruit you and not him?"

Naman had an immediate answer as he knew that Shyam needed this job more than Naman. There should not be tough competition against each other after having studied all the time together. Naman answered the truth: *"You should employ him. He has a brilliant mind; he is hard working and passionate about software engineering."* Suddenly the recruiters started telling how dumb he is and that one has to be competitive in the job market and anyway Shyam had done a good job at disparaging me for being too emotional. *"You won't go far with such an attitude."* Naman was appalled and just wanted to go out. They insisted: *"Don't be afraid, we won't tell him, please tell us at least one of his weaknesses."*

Naman stood up and left the room. A couple of hours later they called Naman back. "We want you to know that we have followed your advice and we are offering the job to Shyam. To you, we are offering the position of team leader."

Shyam never forgave me for getting a better position than him. He was convinced that Naman had put him down to get there. Shyam always thought he might have felt secretly guilty for talking badly about Naman. Both have missed the friendship and wonder if still they would be friends.

 # 6: I saw my biological father begging (a collected story)

My parents underwent a nasty divorce when I was still inside my mom's womb. It was nasty because my father abused my mother physically. He tried to force Mom to abort me. He never wanted me. 'Girl children are useless', he lamented once.

My dad was rich and owned a huge house, some properties, and a successful business line. Also, he inherited a large sum of wealth from my grandpa. Girls threw themselves at my father. At least that's what he said. He was a spendthrift, throwing money at prostitutes, gambling, and expensive wine. He treated Mom like his doormat. At one point, Mom felt violated and left. She left the marriage and raised me alone. Dad never begged her to stay either.

My grandparents helped us. We struggled, a lot. Over the process, Mom took up many jobs and shifted around till we finally settled in a quiet neighbourhood. Mom became a lecturer, and I was about to graduate from high school. One fine day, on my way home from school, I saw a middle-aged man, probably in his early 40s curled up near the edge of the pond fast asleep. He wore dirty clothes, a long beard partially covering his face, and a filthy appearance. Yes, it was my father, who seems to be a homeless man now. I looked closer. It can't be. I reached home and looked at my mother's marriage album. I had a thousand questions running through my mind. What happened?

The next day, I went to the park again. The middle-aged man sat at the entrance near the park, wide awake this time. He had a small silver cup filled with some coins beside him. I approached him. He held the cup in front of me, shaking it. It rattled with coins and pain. I felt water in my eyes. He doesn't recognize me. Then again, why would he? I wasn't born yet when he rejected my existence took my purse out and emptied all my money inside it. His eyes were wide with excitement. I'm sorry you have to go through this, Dad, I thought. I said nothing. I asked nothing.

'Buy some nice food' I said to Dad. I went there daily, for the next two months, without telling Mom. For two months, his useless girl child brought him food and some money. Then one day, he was not there. He had left the place. I found the silver cup abandoned near the lake. I took the cup home along with those memories of my father. I still have the cup with me. I guess not all things in life can be justified or explained. His karma caught up with him, sooner than I expected. I feel bad for the man who fathered me. I love my mother but that doesn't mean that I hate my father.

7: My ex-girlfriend is today my professor in my college (a collected story).

Karma punishes everyone and today Dinesh is at the receiving end. In the year 2019, Dinesh was a final year mechanical engineering student and his girlfriend just joined the college as an Assistant professor.

Dinesh's ex-Shymalee joined the class at school in the 9th grade. She was also preparing for JEE right from the beginning and had joined a coaching institute parallel. They came into a friendship early. She was very serious about her studies while he hardly used to study and paid a heavy price for that. Dinesh failed exams, while she secured 93% marks. She also secured a good rank in the JEE appearing year.

Dinesh was responsible for the breakup and the only reason was the inferiority complex within. She was better than him in everything. Dinesh always wanted to dominate but never succeeded. Once he slapped her in front of everyone because she laughed at his poor grades. That was the end of the relationship. After that, she completely deleted Dinesh from her life. It hurtled her and then Dinesh spread terrible things about her for the next couple of months. But she never paid any heed.

Later, Dinesh could not pass and joined a private engineering college. Here too he got a year back because of so many backlogs. He should have completed B Tech in 2013 but is still in his final year. On the 20th of July, the new session started and on the very first day, Dinesh got one of the biggest shocks in their life. She came into the class to take the lecture. He saw her and couldn't believe the eyes and immediately she also noticed him. Both were shocked like never before. Dinesh was completely red from shame and embarrassment and was trying to hide his face.

After a few minutes, she took out the attendance sheet and started calling the names of the students. When his turn came, he replied as usual "Present, madam" like others and there was a sarcastic smile on her face while he was embarrassed like never before. Throughout the lecture, she was looking at him sarcastically and Dinesh was feeling humiliated and trying to hide his face.

After the lecture was over, he was eager to talk to her alone but was feeling ashamed to go in front of her. He didn't attend her class for the next 4 days because of shame. But can't do this throughout the semester because 75% attendance is compulsory and she will also take the practical classes on Refrigeration and Air conditioning.

The above has given us enough teachings on the various types of karma viz., Sakarma, Vikarma, and Akarma. These are good, bad, and spiritual karmas.

In India, we have the Himalayas, where we may come across many great sages, who are continuously in prayer positions. Many higher-level saints live in snow-clad caves in the deep Himalayas and are not easily traceable and approachable. They rarely appear in public. Some of them come to the Kumbha mela that takes place once in 12 years at Haridwar, where the sacred River Ganga leaves the Himalayan hills and comes down to the plains.

When we get an opportunity to meet the great sadhus, immediately we feel that they have great powers of miracles. True. But when you study deep into their miracles you can find that their knowledge of science is much higher than we do not know. Their knowledge of science on the conversion of one type of matter to another is something we cannot understand at our present level. It may take decades or even centuries to come to their level of scientific knowledge. Our science is at best 200 years old, while Vedic science is thousands of years old.

The same is the case with the people living on the exoplanets, sometimes we call them aliens, whose science is very much advanced as it is believed that the science they practice is thousands of years old. Therefore, Stephen Hopkins once said that our scientific knowledge is so poor that we know nothing. Probably he had the knowledge of the development of science in outer space (probably by aliens) in comparison to our knowledge and therefore remarked. He apprehended more fear from outer space than from within.

I have travelled the great Himalayas crisscrossing from Srinagar to the great and the most sacred mountain Kailash and

- to the holy lake of Manasarover. I have seen the great saints. Some of the experiences are given here, the list is very large. We have no scope to verify the facts it is only to be believed.

Nothing is Mine in This World

It was the summer of 1981. I had just joined the government service and was returning to my home town Berhampur from Baripada in Odisha via Bhubaneswar by state transport bus. In my front seat was seated an old man who had a molded plastic VIP brand suitcase. With great difficulty, he pushed his suitcase in between the space of his seat and his front seat, to the greatest disadvantage of the co-passengers of the 3 seated rows.

The bus started in the post-dinner time and reached Cuttack in the early hours of the morning and then to Bhubaneswar. Almost all got down except the old man. The conductor of the bus shouted for passengers to get down, but this gentleman did not. When the conductor came to this passenger to inform him of his arrival at the destination station, he noticed that the man was no longer alive. I was 21 years old and had many dreams in life. This incident changed my thoughts about life. The "valued suitcase", which was so close to the man and to which he was very possessive is no more of his item. In those days there were no cell phones and I wondered if his dead body could have reached his family. And what happened to the valued suitcase, the man had? This gave me a great lesson at the age of 21 and a turning point in my life. You had come alone with nothing and you shall carry back nothing except the karma that you had earned in this life.

An Indication of Prayers is Answered

The covid-19 has given me at least one good thing; I got the habit of getting up in the early morning hours what is called the Brahma Muhurta. This has brought about many changes in me. I started reading many books on Himalayan masters and other biographies that encouraged me to write this book. One day a small incident happened that is difficult to forget. As usual, when we get up early in the morning, we pray to our lord for the good of self and also for others who are dear. While meditating in the chilly winter of 2022, in December I prayed to my spiritual teacher to give some indication that my prayers are herded, be it directly or indirectly. This request has been coming to my mind almost daily for the past week. As I prayed, suddenly I heard that something had fallen and bounced in my front and rolled down. I sensed that it bounced twice before rolling down. I opened my eyes and found that it was an onion. I had no clue from where it came and how it had fallen from a height. It was a very cold morning at 4 AM at NIT campus Rourkela.

I thanked my Guru and God for hearing my prayer and showing me his presence with a significant indication that my voice reached him. After that, I had full faith in him.

The Camera Exposure

When one travels across the caves in the great Himalayas, one comes across sadhus, seated in small groups beside the burning fire (dhuni). They have the typical dress code of saffron cloths hardly covering part of their body from the waist down words. Mostly their body has a coating of the sacred ash that they collect from the residual of the fire. Once, someone tried to take a photograph of these great masters. To the utter surprise, the photo had the image of the full zone the camera could capture except the images of the saints. Initially, there was doubt about the lens or the quality of the camera. It was tested again and again but with no gain. The camera could not capture the images of the sadhus. Then someone asked the sadhu the reason, for this miracle.

The reply was very simple. They asked whether they had taken prior permission for their photography. If not, then why should they allow their body to be photographed? They explained the principles of the camera: The camera works on the basic principle of reflection of light waves. It is reflected from the object which is captured by the camera. If the person doesn't allow the light wave to reflect but refract across the body then the camera cannot catch the image and hence no photo of the object can be recorded in the camera. Through great meditation and yogic practices, these great persons acquire so much energy that they absorb the light waves during the photography time and therefore no photo of theirs can be recorded. It is a very simple thing for them but for us a simple miracle. Isn't it? Indeed so.

The Transport

Once a friend of my landlord at BJB Nagar, Bhubaneswar visited us in the summer of 1983. The two gentlemen started a discussion on various topics regarding their experiences. I was young and therefore I was just a listener. Mr. Panigrahi, a retired Government servant from the rank of Deputy Secretary had many good stories to tell. He witnessed a happening that looked like a miracle to me at that time. It was the year 1959-1960 when the then chief secretary of Odisha called Mr. Panigrahi (I do not know his full name) and requested him to accompany him to a cave in Dhenkanal in Odisha. The place is close to his native village. They started late after lunch on that day in an Ambassador car and reached a spot close to the cave. The condition of the roads was not so good. They had to walk down for a distance to reach the cave. It was almost sunset time.

The saint was in deep meditation. After some time, he opened his eyes and they had pleasure exchanges. The discussion on spirituality and personnel issues started. The saint asked for a test. He asked the chief secretary for any small item that he loved that he left at Bhubaneswar. The chief secretary immediately said the fountain pen which he uses in his residence office at Bhubaneswar. Then he asked if he wanted to have the pen here in the cave. It surprised him and then he said yes. They closed their eyes for some seconds and the yogi asked them to open their eyes. To their surprise the pen was right across there, the same pen the chief secretary uses regularly. There was no confusion at all about its identity. The yogi said he had to spend a lot of his yogic energy transporting the pen from Bhubaneswar to the cave. The longer the distance more is spent energy and the heavier the object, the more is the spending of the energy. The yogis meditating continuously collect energy through their concentration, which is used mostly for their personal development in their spiritual path or for the welfare of society. However, some of them miss utilizing the power and fall as they have used the power for their personnel and financial gains. Misuse of Siddhi is the downfall of yoga.

Science of Conversion of Matters

One day the master of the young swami Rama (Ref Book: Living with Himalayan Masters) asked him to close his life in the caves, go back to the world, and become a high Government official. He advised Rama to lead a comfortable life in society than leading a painful life in the caves as a young yogi. Then the master took the young Swami Rama to his cave and said as you love jewels, take as many jewels from this heap, I assure you that they all are genuine. It is not an illusion. These gems are for you only the yogi said. If you take them, you should be the richest man in India. Now take these and free me. I am to go up to the Himalayas for more meditation.

To this, Swami Rama was on the sharp edge of a decision for life. After a lot of self-deliberations, he decided not to take those very expensive jewels from his master. Instead, he preferred to be with his master always. He knows that it is a tough decision. The master was happy with the decision and from then onwards the young Swami Rama was always with his master. Soon after the decision, the jewels vanished from the spot. This was explained later that, the master masters knew the conversion of matter from one state to another as we convert water to ice and also to steam. In yogic practice, any material can be changed from one composition to another and here this is the conversion from ordinary stone to jewel stones. This knowledge is unknown to scientists today and we think of it as a miracle. We are incapable of understanding, but for a spiritually advanced yogi, it is a piece of simple knowledge.

Going with another happening with Swami Rama in a similar the incident, there lived Aghori Baba in a cave near Srinagar in the Uttara Khanda state of India. The word Aghor has a background in solar science and is used for healing. The babas or the masters of this science mostly behave funny. Normally people are afraid of these babas. Swami Rama requested a villager in the locality to join him for a meeting with this baba. With much persuasion a local pundit accompanied him. But a strange thing happened. The pundit tried to run away from the spot after seeing the baba as he was ferocious looking. Immediately the baba ordered him not to run away. Rather he ordered him to go to the riverside where a dead body floated in the river. He ordered me to go there, chop off some flesh from the dead body, and bring it. If he fails to obey, the baba shall kill the local village pundit immediately. The poor Brahmin pundit obeyed the order for fear of life, cut the flesh from the corpse, and brought it to the baba. But accidentally he cut two of his fingers. Baba saw it and touched the fingers which immediately cured without even a scratch in the fingers.

The next order from the baba was even more fearful. He ordered the pundit to boil the flesh in the earthen pot and cover it with a stone plate while cooking. It was frightening but had to be followed. The pundit was a pure vegetarian. Then the Aghori went inside the cave and got three small earthen bowls. He ordered them to serve the boiled human flesh to all of them. The pundit was disgusted and wanted to commit suicide. Then following Baba's order, he took out the stone cover from the boiling pot. What a surprise, there was no meat at all. The pot was full of good-smelling Rasagullas (the Indian sweet of cheese and sugar). The Aghori declared this has no meat in it, a purely vegetarian dish. The pundit was asked to take back the all remaining sweets to the village and distribute them. Swami Rama stayed back to know the answer to all that happened. The Aghor said he has a higher scientific knowledge of converting matter from one type to another. He knows science well. His external behaviour is different from his actual behaviour. This is just to avoid the public.

The next day the baba asked Rama to pick up a handful of sand from the river bank. What a surprise, it turned out to be almonds and cashews. He explained that this is another science of conversion of matter to energy and then to another matter. He further explained that as the kids do not know that water changes to ice and vapour, similarly, scientists even in the present day are like small kids to him and they do not know that any matter can be converted to any other matter through energy. Swami Rama though intellectually agreed with the explanation of the Aghori baba, did not accept it physically.

In the books and biographic documents of the great Himalayan masters, one can find hundreds of such happenings. We all think these to be the practice of magic, but it is a higher state of science that we have not pierced. It takes ages for yogis to get siddhi, but it cannot be transferred to any other person who has not attained the required siddhi. Therefore science remains close to him and is not transferred down to the next generation.

Earning Bad Karma for No Reason

It is a usual happening with most of us in our normal life that when something is not traceable at home, the owner immediately suspects someone around like a servant, who is inferior in status. They spend much of their time and energy thinking negatively about the servant relating to this small item that is lost or misplaced. By this, they earn huge negative karma. Later when they trace back the misplaced item, they feel sorry, but by then good negative karma is already added to their spiritual profile. I feel sorry for such attitudes.

Types of Karma and the Karmic Laws

- **Good karma**: This is also referred to as Sakarma. Examples of good karma are: serving the community, abiding by rules and regulations, spreading the message of peace and love, leading others the right way, and learning to forgive. There are many benefits of Good Karma and they are: it increases the power of concentration; it heals one's soul/spirit; it makes one wiser and makes you more wisdom; gives you unexpected success; helps to control his/her anger and ignorance; provides divine protection from bad luck, diseases, and others; keeps you enlightened at all times.

- **Bad karma:** This is also referred to as Vikarma. Examples of bad karma are: looking down upon others; misuse of power/ authority; oppressing the poor; forcefully taking what is not yours; cheating and hurting others; accusing other people falsely; and stealing what is not yours.
- **Spiritual karma:** *This is also named akarma :*

Starting with the description of karma in Rigveda and Brhadaranyaka Upanisad karma was known as the universal principles of cause and effect, action and reactions that are believed to control all consciousness. There are issues discussed in the context of karma, and how to reverse bad karma. Bad karma as we define is simply the bad actions and thoughts that harm your life. Many times you might feel like you have bad karma and you wish to overcome it. Below are ways in which one can resolve his/her bad karma;

1. **Apologies:** *Sometimes you feel guilty about your past actions in the act of self-judgment. You feel disturbed when it comes to your mind. In this situation try to find out the person you wronged, mistreated, or offended and apologize sincerely.*
2. **Meditate:** If you feel guilty for some of the past actions, but cannot locate him, then try to meditate or reflect on your actions. There are different ways of meditating, these include Breathing meditation, where the breathing is

controlled to increase the calmness in the mind leading to creating a sense of inner peace

Laws of karma (Karmic Laws) which include:

1. **The great law:** "What you sow, so you reap." This simply means our actions are the true reflection of what we get in return. If we want to be loved then we must first love others.
2. **The law of creation:** Always associate with yourself being part of the universe. Always be honest with yourself.
3. **The law of humility:** Says never to be negative "What you refuse to accept will continue for you".
4. **The law of growth:** It simply means control yourself, change starts with yourself "Wherever you go, there you are"
5. **The law of responsibility:** "Whenever there is something wrong in my life, there is something wrong in me".
6. **The law of connection:** always we are connected to the universe.

CHAPTER - 9

ॐ *A* ***MAnTRA*** *is a word or a set of words given to us by the great sages, when chanted properly and regularly has the power that not only takes one to a great height of meditation but provides energy and protection. It provides a compact form of prayer.*

YAnTRA *is a machine used to worship deities to gain success, wealth, and power, and to get protection from evil forces or negative energies and therefore enhance human life in various dimensions. Each deity has a specific yantra and a specific power. There are 56 kinds of yantras each representing the divinities and cosmic powers separately.*

TAnTRA *expands consciousness and is meant for the transmission of the physical power of the body (tan) from the lower planes to higher planes through the use of Tantu (nerve fibers or Nadis). In short, they can be equated with mantra = to energy, Yantra = to object, and Tantra = to plan.*

In Hinduism, the three constitute the three fundamental methods of divine worship and devotional service by which one may perform obligatory duties, practice self-purification, or achieve liberation. The mantra method is predominantly Sattvic, the Yantra is Rajasic, and the Tantra Tamasic. By combining the use of the Mantra with the Yantra we can experience true Tantra, union.

Chapter – 9

Mantra Yantra and Tantra

Mantra and its Impacts

A mantra is a syllable, a sound, a word, or a set of words found by the great sages in the deep state of their meditation. The simplest of all of them is the OM or the AUM. This simple word has the power which not only takes one to a great height of meditation through its regular chanting but also provide energy and protection. Mantra is very powerful and provides a compact form of prayer. It becomes a guide if chanted properly and regularly. If you sincerely follow the words of great masters as a promise, it is a mantra for you. If a mantra is not properly used with spiritual discipline, it may create hallucinations. Without understanding the meaning of a mantra, the proper feeling cannot be aroused and without its strong feeling, its technical repetition is not of much use.

The mantra when repeated aids concentration during meditation. It can make a lot of difference, especially if you have trouble concentrating or getting in the right frame of mind. Many people find that using a mantra can boost awareness and improve concentration. It is a sacred utterance (syllable, word, or verse) that is considered to possess mystical or spiritual efficacy. Om or Aum is the sound of the universe and the sound of creation. It's also related to the crown chakra and higher consciousness. "Om is everything and nothing, and meditating on it can help you to tap the power of the creator.

The simplest Mantra is the OM or the AUM which is the Universal Sound of Creation. This single word contains all the sounds of the entire Universe. It is usually chanted at the beginning of almost every single mantra, at the start and the end of a yoga class, and can be chanted at any time and any place and even inside your mind. In the next chapter, some of the specific mantras, their importance, and their benefits are discussed. Mantras have the power to change your life completely - a mantra chanted in the right vibration and the right atmosphere can not only purify your mind but also calm your senses. Nothing can bring you more solace than chanting a powerful mantra

Gayatri Mantra is considered one of the most universal of all Hindu mantras, invoking the universal Brahman as the principle of knowledge and the illumination of the primordial Sun. It is a form of the most powerful mantra in Hinduism. Shiva Gayatri Mantra is extremely powerful, it gives you peace of mind, and that pleases Lord Shiva. Mantra has the power to soothe anxiety and create joyous feelings. It's believed that the sound vibrations produced during mantra chanting stimulate and balance the chakras. Even more important than perfect pronunciation, you must approach mantra chanting with an intention and awareness of the mantra you are working with, not merely repeat sounds as if they have no meaning. As you think so, you become, and once the meaning of the mantra is realised through intense ideation, the practitioners attain the state of realization.

While chanting the mantra, follow certain rules to enhance its impact on you. To prepare yourself for mantra chanting, sit in a comfortable position, do some cleansing breathwork (Pranayama), and bring your hands to the prayer position at your chest before you begin. Begin chanting your mantra using as resonant a voice as possible. If you wish, you can use mala (prayer) beads during your chanting. With each recitation of the mantra, you finger a bead until you have touched all 108 beads of the mala. Once completed, start again from the first bead. You can practice as many rounds as you wish. Follow the simple procedures while chanting a mantra.

The procedure of Chanting Mantra

The purpose behind of Chanting Mantra is many. While some do it to attain spiritual significance, some do it to attain God. Some use it for meditation, while others do it to improve their concentration. No matter whatever is the reason, the important point is to do it correctly. The below pointers can help you chant a mantra correctly.

1. **Correct Pronunciation during Chanting:** Whenever you chant a mantra, make sure that you chant the mantra using coherent and correct words. The wrong pronunciation can do you more harm than good. If you are confused with difficult words, then ask an elder person in the family for help or look up the right pronunciation online. You can also start with easy mantras to get a hold of the language first.
2. **Close your eyes During Chanting the Mantra:** Even though you can chant the mantra with open eyes, it has more impact when you do it with your eyes closed. Doing so not only helps you concentrate better but will also help you feel the vibrations of that particular mantra throughout your entire body. It also helps you relax and make your body go into a trance state.

3. **Visualise:** When chanting a mantra, visualise the deity you are chanting it. For example, if you are chanting the Maha Mritunjay mantra, then make sure that you visualise the face of Lord Shiva while doing this. This will help you connect with the deity and feel his/her presence around you. This way, a mantra can be chanted anywhere and not necessarily in a temple space.
4. **Don't be too Loud:** A lot of people chant the mantra aloud, but this is not the ideal way to do it. The ideal way to chant a mantra is to slowly chant it, but it should be loud enough so that you can hear it. One should not chant the mantra mechanically and concentrate only on getting it done and over with but should feel its words and understand their meanings.
5. **Create a Space:** Although you can chant the mantra anywhere, you must assign a separate space for it in your home or anywhere else. Ideally, this place should be partially open and facing the sun, if possible. Do not change your designated space frequently, and use only that to chant your mantra every day. This builds up powerful forces in that space.
6. **Be Regular:** The good thing about chanting a mantra is that, unlike going to the temple every day or giving away charity, you do not have to physically go out anywhere to do this. Hence, do not skip chanting your mantras. You can do it even if you are sick while sitting in bed. It will help you feel better, and you do not have to make any effort for this too.
7. **Calm Mind:** There is no point in sitting down to chant a mantra if your mind is preoccupied with work or other chores of the house. For those fixed number of minutes, make sure that you concentrate your energies only on

mantra chanting and nothing else. This will be your "me time," and make sure that you make the best out of it. Avoid any sort of interference during this time.

8. **Sit at the Same Place at the Same Time and Chant:** The benefit of seating at the same location of your house and chanting is that it creates a very positive environment if one is chanting in the same room, at the same place, and in the same asana. The room is positively charged, and it benefits the chanter on early concentration. **Prepare for Chanting:** While chanting, always sit in Padma-asana or Ardha Padma-asana posture. If the age factor and other health issues do not permit you to sit in the posture for long, then you may choose any posture, such as Sukha-asana, with only the thing in mind that your backbone and head remain truly vertical.

9. **Brahma Muhurta is the best Time:** Brahma Muhurta is the time in the very early hours of the day. Each muhurta is 48 minutes, and the starting time of the Brahma Muhurta is 2 muhurta before the sun rises at the place. For example, if the sun rises at a place at 5.36 hours, then the starting time of Brahma Muhurta at the place is at 4.00 hours, which is 2 x 48 = 96 minutes or 1 hour and 36 minutes before the sun rises. This auspicious time continues up to 48 minutes after sunrise means at the same place, it is up to 5.36+48 = 6.24 hours. The good things about chanting mantras during this period are many, such as noise level is the minimum, pollution is the least, peaceful environment, good level of oxygen in the air, and minimum disturbance. However, one should keep the doors/windows open in the room to admit fresh air into the room while chanting the mantra.

Sometimes, the great sages give a mantra such as 'be cheerful always', which has the effect of a Mantra for you. If you honour the mantra, you indeed remain cheerful.

Yantra and its Usefulness

Yantra is a machine used to worship the Navagrahas, elements, gods, and goddesses in homes or at a temple. In Hinduism, each deity has a specific yantra. It is mostly used at the entrances of a house or temple floors. These yantras are used for gaining success, wealth, and power, and to get protection from evil forces and negative energies and therefore enhance human life in various dimensions. Each yantra is made for specific purposes. There are various kinds of yantra representing divinities and cosmic powers.

How to use Yantras in Meditation

Create one holy space where you can sit daily in your house. Select the yantra according to what energy you would like to get into your life. Your selected Yantra can support you to get that energy. According to your eye level, place the yantra on a table and place one candle in front of the yantra. Then, light the candle, focus your eyes on the flame for seven minutes, and try to blink your eyes. Focus all your intention and attention on gaining the energy of that yantra into your life. *This type of meditation practice is known as* **Tratika.** There are more techniques we can use when it comes to meditation. Invoking the energies of the yantras into your life aids in strengthening the aura and increases concentration and focus. This mediation practice is recommended to do for 21 days.

A Useful Discussion – How it Works

In the West, yantra has been widely popular as symbols or geometric figures. These symbols are regarded as devices that can be used to balance the mind and also help in focusing on spiritual concepts. Yantra is a Sanskrit word that is derived from the root **Yam** meaning to control or to restrain, curb or check. It is a mystical or astronomical diagram (usually a symbol, often inscribed on an amulet) said to possess mystical or magical powers.

Tantra is regarded as a cosmic weave that is composed of several energies. Human beings form an important part of this weave. *Tantra is often associated with black magic,* but the followers of Tantra believe that it has the application of cosmic science. They believe that it is a device through which knowledge is spread. The Tantra followers or preachers worship Lord Shiva and the goddess Shakti. In Hinduism, the **'Atharva Veda'** is considered to be one of the prime scriptures related to Tantra. It refers to powerful spiritual acts that are used to let ourselves free from problems and also for the enlightenment of the soul. Some Hindu and Buddhist scriptures provide detailed instructions on many Tantra-related topics, on spiritual knowledge, cosmic power, technology, and science.

Tantra expands consciousness. **Mantra** on the other hand focuses on the inner sound. The utterance of Mantras is regarded as very powerful and is supposed to create a huge impact. **Yantra** refers to the creation of a certain state by using the medium of symbols. *In short, they can be equated with mantra = to energy, yantra = to object, and tantra = to plan.*

Fundamentally, the three represent the three basic approaches available to human beings to harness the power of God and use it to perform their duties upon the earth as part of their obligatory duties. *They can be used for constructive purposes to achieve peace prosperity and liberation or for destructive ends to create chaos, cast evil spells, or inflict pain and suffering upon others.*

The method of Mantra is used to invoke divine power for positive and negative purposes through the use of mind or thought power *(man+tra)*. In Yantras, the restraining power *(yan + tra)* of the will is used for the same purpose. The Tantras are meant for the transformation and transmission of the physical (sexual) power of the body (tan) from the lower planes to higher planes through the use of Tanto (nerve fibers or Nadis). Thus, Tantra means the use of body power *(tan + tra)* the use of the nerves in the body *(tant + tra)*, or both. In that sense, Tantra means the use of the power *(Shakti)* of God for self-transformation and liberation.

In the practice of Mantras, the mind, and intelligence are active. In the practice of Tantra, the organs of actions and the organs of perception are active, whereas, in the practice of Yantra, the ego is active. From the perspective of the triple Gunas, ***the Mantra method is predominantly sattvic, the Yantra is rajasic, and the Tantra tamasic.*** In Hinduism, the three constitute the three fundamental methods of divine worship and devotional service by which one may perform obligatory duties, practice self-purification, or achieve liberation. They are also the basic and universal approaches that worshippers use in Hinduism to uphold Dharma, fulfil desires, and achieve the four aims of human life.

However, as with many other aspects of Hinduism, the distinction is rather amorphous since Mantras may be used in the practice of Yantra and Tantra and vice versa. Hence, in most Hindu forms of worship, one can see that the elements of all three are present or deeply intermingled. They are also present in the Vedic sacrificial ceremonies. Mantras are used to invoke God, Yantras to construct the sacrificial pit (Yajnastala) in specific geometric formations to impart to them certain purifying and magical powers, and Tantra to discipline the body before or during the ceremony, and to sacrifice (offer) the body and or its elements during the sacrifice. The interrelationship between the three is shown in the figure below.

Tantra is a spiritual path that embraces life to awaken consciousness. Within Tantra Yoga, various techniques are used such as Mantra, Yantra, ritual, and meditation to purify and energize our being thus bringing a deeper awareness of our spiritual existence. By combining the use of the Mantra with the Yantra we can experience true Tantra, union.

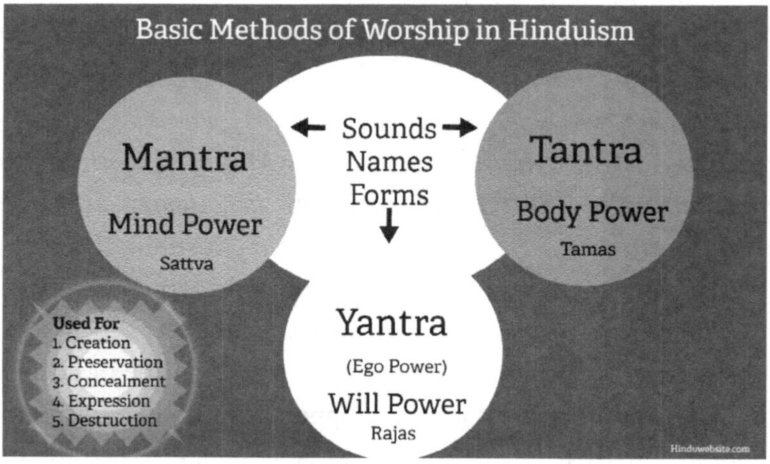

Fig. 9.1: The Interrelationship between Mantra Yantra and Tantra

Since time immemorial, the term 'Tantra' has been used for a specific process, technique, method, or system like Bhairav Tantra, Dhyaan Tantra, Paak Tantra, Kaam Tantra, and others. All healing techniques are Tantra skills. All sorts of activities such as meditation, prayer, and worship are Tantra skills. The use of a special method is called Tantra. The Tantra used with pure and selfless feeling is a 'divine Tantra" (White Magic) and the one used with ill feeling is called "Tantrikta" (Black Magic).

In India, all the symbols, designs, geometrical shapes, and statues of gods/goddesses come under the category of 'Yantra'. We also create a "Swastik" sign, which consists of four clockwise lines attached to a "+" (plus) sign. Then we write our feelings on their sides – "Shubh" (fortune) and "Laabh" (profit). It implies that good fortune and wealth may continue to flow into our Homa from all sides and cause us to always move forward and towards the future (the four clockwise lines). How does this Swastik demonstrate its value? Swastik is merely a way for us to express our emotions and ideas. Swastik by itself does not have any power embedded with it, it is one's deep feeling that gives strength to it. Strong thoughts produce strong vibrations, and weak thoughts produce weak vibrations because thoughts cause vibrations.

Yantra (symbols) assist us in strengthening and amplifying our thoughts. When Swastik is used in conjunction with a wish for prosperity and fortune, the outcomes are undoubtedly superior to those of the identical wish made without Swastik. Hence, to strengthen our thoughts and objectives, we need a sign. Any sign that has ever been deeply ingrained in our subconscious mind instantaneously elicits the corresponding emotions. Because symbols make up the language of our subconscious mind, they are therefore of utmost significance. Since then, a great number of symbols have been created. At the same time, most of the Germans hate Swastik, because a bad German dictator named Hitler had adopted the Swastik's reverse form as his symbol.

We should keep in mind that all of the symbols, Yantra, and gods and goddesses in the world were created by various individuals using various ideas. *A manufactured emblem is powerless in comparison to a human being. Even if we make symbols, gods, and Yantras for our convenience, we eventually turn into their obedient slaves. Because they are the only tools available for generating powerful thoughts, symbols, deities, and Yantras are necessary. But, we should also be cognizant of the scientific rationale underlying them and avoid blindly adhering to them.*

A mantra is a surge of a certain feeling or thought. Emotion comes from the heart, whereas thought comes from the mind. Therefore emotion is more powerful than thought. Thus, a surge from our body creates a layer in our aura whenever we experience a particular emotion. The waves of emotion that are produced when we experience this feeling repeatedly have a powerful magnetic pull on the layers of our aura. We attract waves of energy from the universe that are identical to the waves we produce through our emotions. The mantra's impact is that by repeating a feeling, we create a magnetic power in our aura and draw a similar type of effect from the universe toward ourselves. This is because it is a fundamental law of nature that attracts like, or in other sense, vibrations attract a similar type of vibrations.

Similar to how a tape recorder records our speech as well as our sound vibrations, the aura records each vibration we make as well as its unique character. Each vibration creates an Akashic record, which is kept. The akashic records include countless such vibrations that have been successfully discovered by precise tools by current scientists. These vibrations never vanish and are kept indefinitely by the universe.

In India, yantra was introduced between 11,000 and 10,000 BCE. The earliest known example of Yantra is thought to be the Baghor stone, which was discovered in the Son River valley in an upper-paleolithic environment and dates between 25,000 and 20,000 BCE. The triangular stone had religious significance and had triangle engravings on one side. The form is very similar to the Muladhara Chakra and Kali Yantra. The Sanskrit syllables found written on yantras, known as mantras, are the primary "thinking forms" that deities or cosmic forces use to influence people through sound vibrations.

Typical geometric shapes seen in yantras include triangles, rectangles, circles, hexagons, octagons as well as symbolic lotus petals. These shapes radiate concentrically from the centre. Yantras can be three-dimensional or on a flat surface. Yantras can be carved on metal, painted, or drawn on any flat surface, including paper. By using mantras that are directly related to the particular god and yantra, a priest typically consecrates and energizes occult yantras. An unenergized yantra, in the opinion of practitioners, is lifeless. Based on how they are used, they are divided into three broad types:

1. Yantras serve as the base for ceremonial objects like lamps and containers. The utensils are usually set on these plain geometric shapes.
2. Yantras, like the Sri Yantra, is utilised in regular worship. They contain geometrical diagrams, are imbued with mantras to the god, and occasionally have written mantras incorporated into the artwork.
3. Yantras are employed in particular desire-centreed rituals. These yantras are frequently created on birch bark or paper and may contain unique components like flowers, rice paste, ashes, etc.

It is believed that Tantra began to have been created on the Indian subcontinent around the middle of the first millennium. Any systematic and broad things like a theory, system, method, instrument, technique, or practice can also be referred to as tantra. Puja is one example of a non-Vedic form of worship whose conception and practices are said to be tantric. Most Hindu temples adhere to the enduring tantra.

Tantric traditions gained popularity throughout India and abroad from the eighth to the fourteenth centuries. The primary components of tantric practice were matured by the 10th century and used by the Saiva and Buddhists. Some academics have referred to this time as the *"Tantric Era"* because Tantra was so common. Many tantric texts (Agamas, Samhitas, and Tantras) were composed in the 10th century, mainly in Bengal, Kashmir, and Nepal. Tantric practices had already spread throughout South Asia by this time, and Tantric writings had also been translated into local tongues like Tamil. Moreover, the Tantra reached China, Tibet, and Indonesia.

While tantra was developed throughout the entire northern and Himalayan regions of India, Kashmir was particularly significant, where several important tantric scriptures were published.

Buddhist Tantra was adopted by the Mahayana Buddhist establishment and studied in prestigious institutions like Nalanda and Vikramashila throughout the Tantric Era. From there, it expanded to the East Asian nations of China, Korea, and Japan. The Pala Dynasty (8th–12th centuries), which financed these academic institutions, supported this new Tantric Buddhism. The Khmer kings as well as the Srivijaya state of Indonesia backed tantric Buddhism.

Both Shaiva and Buddhist tantra developed into more intellectual and liberation-focused faiths in the 10th and 11th centuries. With this change, rituals that were outward and transgressive were replaced with practices that were more yogic and aimed at gaining spiritual awareness. Tantric faiths became far less vulnerable to criticism by other groups as a result of this recasting.

The codification of tantric yogic practices, which would eventually separate into the independent movement known as Hatha Yoga, was another significant development at this time. Later, Saiva yogic traditions (Naths) accepted it and cited it in their writings.

Hindus who follow the more traditional Vedic traditions rejected the Tantras as they regarded them as needing higher understanding. At the same time, the Tantrikas incorporated Vedic concepts into their systems. While others saw the Tantras as a complement to the Vedas, some Tantrikas thought they were better. The more well-known Bhakti movements that swept through India starting in the 15th century eclipsed the Hindu tantra. They adopted these new devotional religious practices that placed a strong focus on emotional obedience to a sovereign savior deity.

Swami Vivekananda put a lot of work into reconstructing yoga, usually through a selected Vedantic reading of Patajali's Yogasutra. The initiative was largely successful, and many modern Westerners who practice yoga for health and relaxation have found success despite knowing little to nothing about its original purpose.

Hindu Tantra

Tantric Upanishads and tantric Puranas were part of the Hindu system. Besides these, there are also various types of tantric "sastras". For people who practice Vedic religion, Tantric texts and practitioners known as Tantrikas are frequently compared with "Vaidikas". Mantra-marga was the name given to this non-Vedic path. *The debate over whether tantric or Vedic techniques are preferable continues today.*

The Skull Observance *(Kapalavrata)*, which entails transporting a skull and performing worship on cremation sites, is promoted by the Mantrapha tradition. The ***Aghoris*** are a contemporary ascetic sect of the Kapalika. The scriptures of this religion emphasise rituals relating to charnel houses and sexuality, as well as worshipping goddesses, known as yogins or kins.

By the ninth century, the goddess-centric traditions, which refer to the goddesses and their Shakti tantras, may have been created. It emphasises the significance of spirit possession as well as sexual rituals and alcohol intake. It contains several regionally specific sub-traditions from India. The nath or "Split-Ear" Kanphaa tradition, which first appeared in the 12th century, is the final significant Aiva tantric lineage.

To Sum up: A mantra substantially improves the quality of our prayer when chanted properly and regularly. It is a higher state of meditation that generates enormous energy within, with the power of protection. There are 56 kinds of Yantra machines used to worship the respective deities. Tantra expands consciousness. Mantra, Yantra, and Tantra constitute the three fundamental methods of divine worship and devotional service: mantra = to energy, yantra = to object, and tantra = to plan. The Yantra is rajasic, the Tantra is tamasic, and the mantra technique is sattvic. We can experience genuine Tantra, or the union, by combining the use of the Yantra and the Mantra.

Each vibration that we generate through the utterances produces its signature in the aura and gets registered as an Akashic record. These vibrations are permanently stored in the Universe and never get destroyed. In the next chapter, some important mantras are given which are of great help to the practicing chanters for their pronunciation accuracy.

CHAPTER -10

ॐ *A mantra when chanted properly and regularly becomes a compact form of prayer that generates tremendous power within the self and provides extra energy and protection to the chanter.*

In Hinduism, there are 330 million gods and goddesses each God has one-to-many special mantras. Therefore, it is not possible to describe all the mantras here, except some important and popular ones. The power of reciting a Sanskrit Mantra lies within each letter itself, which vibrates at its unique frequency, stimulating different energy in the parts of the body. When letters are combined to mold into words, their sounds create energy that protects and heals all parts of the body. The practice of reciting this mystical chant every day is said to grant health, wealth, prosperity, and happiness.

Chapter - 10

Popular Mantras with Meanings

Om Mantra

The OM mantra is thought to be the most fundamental frequency and the sound of nothingness. The first sound, OM, is a pure manifestation of God. When we chant OM, it creates a direct connection between the chanter and the Divine. All living things are linked to the natural world and the cosmos via OM. OM can be chanted in silence or out loud. OM is a fantastic tool for drawing good things into your life. Your mind is calmed and pleasant energy is brought into your body when you chant the OM.

The most sacred syllable symbol and the mantra of Brahman, OM represents the ultimate reality, consciousness, or Aatma, which is your inner self. Also, during meditation, the syllable OM serves as the foundation for a variety of other mantras. For instance, the meaning of the mantra OM namah Shivaya is "I honour the divine inside myself." The phrase "peace be with you" is **OM** shanti. **OM** is spoken as an extended **O** sound followed by a vibrating **M,** or it can be pronounced **AH-UU-MM** by separating the **A** and **U** sounds. **OM** is displayed as ॐ. Om is mostly pronounced "a-u-m" when the vowels a and the sound of an O make the symbol ॐ.

Om chanting induces relaxation and positive changes in our automated nerve system, which controls heart rate, blood pressure, metabolism, and other physiological processes, according to a 2018 study. The limbic brain areas, which govern emotions and memories, become inactive as a result of chanting. According to additional studies, chanting the Om aloud for 30 minutes greatly boosts theta brain waves, which represent a deep state of relaxation. It alters delta waves, which are the same as what people experience during deep, dreamless sleep, according to a study in 2019. During the om chanting, researchers also noticed brain activity that was similar to that used to treat epilepsy and depression.

Unknown as to its origin of ॐ, the symbol's three curves are considered to represent the three stages of consciousness — waking, dreaming, and deep sleep, with the dot in the symbol standing in for the fourth state of awareness.

In a different way of thinking the three curves of ॐ symbol can stand for various things (three worlds: earth, atmosphere, and heaven; three Hindu Gods: Brahma, Vishnu, and Siva; three sacred Vedas: Rig, Yajur, and Sama; or even thought: speech, and action). They can also stand for the three qualities of matter (goodness, passion, and darkness), as well as the past, present, and future. In the Vedas, Om initially appeared between 1500 and 1200 BCE. The Vedas, Upanishads, and Yoga Sutras are where the fundamental teaching on Om originates.

"Om is the prime mantra of the Higher Self or Aatma. It is the sound of the creator, preserver, and destroyer of the universe. It reflects both the manifest and un-manifest Brahman, sustaining the vibration of being, life, and consciousness in all worlds and all creatures."

Choose a relaxed seat, close your eyes, and breathe deeply as you recite the mantra. Slowly exhale while making the Om sound. Repeat the Om inhalation and recitation after pausing.

Relax the thoughts and concentrate on the sound's vibrations. Go on chanting for another 20 to 30 minutes.

Gayatri Mantra - A Universal Prayer

Om Bhur Bhuvaḥ SuvahaTat-savitur Vareñyaṃ Bhargo Devasya DheemahiDhiyo Yonaḥ Prachodayāt

-Rigveda 3.62.10

General Meaning: *We contemplate the Creator; the most revered Supreme Lord, whose effulgence (divine light) illuminates all realms (physical, mental, and spiritual). May this divine light illumine our intellect* (sathyasai.ca).

Word meaning:

Om: The primeval sound;

Bhur: The physical body/physical realm;

Bhuvah: The life force/the mental realm

Suvah: The soul/spiritual realm;

Tat: That (God);

Savitur: The Sun, Creator (source of all life);

Vareñyam: adore;

Bhargo: effulgence (divine light);

Devasya: supreme Lord;

Dheemahi: meditate;

Dhiyo: the intellect;

Yo: May this light;

Nah: our;

Prachodayāt: Illumine/inspire

One must adhere to a specific procedure to receive the benefits of chanting the Gayatri mantra. One should constantly close his eyes when chanting and make an effort to focus on each syllable and comprehend its meaning. It is important to pronounce each word and sound exactly as it should be. While the mantra can be chanted at any time of day, it is advised that the best times are, first in the morning and the second just before going to bed. The mantra is an act of thanksgiving to God.

Reciting a mantra is to focus on the mind and body. The power of reciting a Sanskrit Mantra lies within each letter itself, which vibrates at its unique frequency, stimulating a different part of the body. When letters are combined to mold into words, their sounds create healing energy that protects and heals all parts of the individual's body upon hearing it. The practice of reciting this mystical chant every day is said to grant health, wealth, prosperity, and happiness. This beautiful mantra consists of 24 syllables as salutations to the divine and primeval force, believed to be responsible for the creation of the universe. It is known to remove the effects of past and present karma and bring about positive changes in one's life. It also helps bring peace as it is thought to purify one's consciousness, thus, allowing people to experience reality as it is in actuality.

Goddess Gayatri has been given great importance in the religious scriptures of Sanatan culture. It is believed by the scriptures that by simply understanding the Gayatri Mantra, one attains knowledge of the four Vedas. For this reason, the Gayatri Mantra is also considered the essence of the Vedas. It is believed that the virtuous fruit that a human gets after acquiring the knowledge of the four Vedas; they get also by understanding the Gayatri Mantra alone.

It is believed that Goddess Gayatri is the mother of four Vedas, Shastras, and Shrutis. She is also called Vedmata, the mother of Vedas. She is also considered to be an adored goddess of Tridev Brahma, Vishnu, and Mahesh. Worshipping Goddess Gayatri is believed to fulfil all wishes and help attain salvation. To get the best results, the Gayatri Mantra should be recited in a soft and calm voice, with a relaxed mind, in peaceful surroundings. It is recommended to chant this mantra after Pranayama while facing the sun. The most important part about reciting the Gayatri Mantra is knowing the meaning of each word and pronouncing it correctly. It is best to meditate on the mantra in a secluded spot without any distractions such as cell phones and gadgets. By meditating on the Gayatri Mantra, you may feel united with the entire cosmos and feel a perfect alignment between your mind, body, and soul.

The best time to chant the Gayatri Mantra is around 4:00 to 5:30 a.m. However, one can chant it at any time. Furthermore, chanting this mantra on Fridays has significance and religious benefits. Besides this, it is generally advised to repeat the mantra at least three times a day.

Vishnu Mantras

1. Mukti or the Liberation Mantra (ॐ नमो भगवते वासुदेवाय॥) (Om Namo Bhagavate Vasudevaya॥)

"I bow to the Lord who resides in the hearts of everyone," is how the Vishnu mantra is translated. This mantra encourages compassion since it serves as a reminder that in every living being there is the presence of godly existence. Chanting this mantra releases feelings of love that assist in removing obstacles from one's life.

2. Vishnu Shantakaram Mantra

॥ विष्णु शान्ता कारंमंत्र ॥

शान्ताकारं भुजंगशयनं पद्मनाभं सुरेशं
विश्वाधारं गगनसदृशं मेघवर्ण शुभांगम्।
लक्ष्मीकांत कमलनयनं योगिभि ध्र्यानगम्यं
वन्दे विष्णु भवभयहरं सर्वलौकेक नाथम्॥

Shantakaram Bhujagashayanam Padmanabham Suresham
Vishvadharam Gaganasadrisham Meghavarnam Shubhangam।
Lakshmikantam Kamalanayanam Yogibhir dhyana gamyam
Vande Vishnum Bhavabhayaharam Sarvalokaika natham॥

The mantra translates to, "*I bow to Lord Vishnu who preserves and protects the universe, who is pacific, who lies on the divine serpent, from whose navel arises the Lotus with the power of creation, who is the Supreme Being, who holds the entire universe, who is all-pervading as the sky, who is dark like clouds and has a magnificent form, Lakshmi's lord, one with lotus eye, who is perceived through meditation by the Yogis, I salute you, Lord Vishnu, who removes the fear of worldly existence and who is the Lord of all worlds". Regular recitation of this mantra makes one brave because it is intended to free one from anxieties and unreal worldly concerns.*

3. Shri Vishnu Mantra

त्वमेव माता च पिता त्वमेव त्वमेव बन्धुश्च सखात्वमेव।
त्वमेव विद्या द्रविण म्त्वमेव त्वमेव सर्व म्मम देवदेव॥

Tvameva Maataa Cha Pitaa Tvameva Tvameva Bandhush-Cha Sakhaa Tvam-Eva
Tvameva Viidyaa Dravinnam Tvam-Eva Tvameva Sarvam Mama Deva Deva॥

When facing a challenge or seeking guidance, it is good to recite this mantra. The sages believe that repeating this particular mantra aids in focus and Lord Vishnu's guidance is provided in every sector of life. The translation of this mantra reads, *"O Lord you are my father and mother, you are also my friend and brother, your wealth and education itself, I see my hopes and Salvation in you".*

4. Moola Vishnu Mantra (ॐ नमो नारायण॥) Om Namo Narayanaya॥

The mantra, which means *"I kneel before the Almighty,"* is a homage to Lord Vishnu. One is said to travel to Vaikuntha via the mantra and live a pleasant afterlife there. Vaikuntha refers to the state of wanting less; by using this mantra, one might become liberated from materialistic attachment and anxiety.

However, the following six mantras are not used by people at large

5. Vishnu Mangalam Mantra

मङ्गलम्भ गवानविष्णु:, मङ्गल म्गारुणध्वज:।
मङ्गल म्पुण्डरी काक्ष:, मङ्गलाय तनो हरि:॥

Mangalam Bhagwan Vishnuh, Mangalam Garunadhwajah।
Mangalam Pundari Kakshah, Mangalaya Tano Harih॥

Hindus frequently chant Ganesha's mantra and appeal to him before beginning new projects. The same mantra is available for Vishnu to perform auspicious tasks like pooja, marriage, aarti, and other similar activities. To reap the full benefits of the Mangalam mantra, it should be chanted on auspicious occasions. The mantra reads, "All auspiciousness to Lord Vishnu, all auspiciousness to one who has Garuda as His flag. All auspiciousness to one, who has eyes like the lotus flowers, and auspiciousness to Hari.

6. Vishnu Gayatri Mantra

ॐ श्री विष्णवे च विद्महे वासुदेवाय धीमहि। तन्नो विष्णुः चोदयात्॥

Om Shri Vishnave Cha Vidmahe Vasudevaya Dhimahi।
Tanno Vishnuh Prachodayat॥

This Vishnu mantra means, "Om, Let me meditate on Lord Vishnu, Oh, Lord Vasudeva, give me higher intellect, And let Lord Vishnu illuminate my mind".

The Vishnu Gayatri Mantra like every other Gayatri Mantra has the effect of removing fear and bringing one to reality.

Shiva Mantras

1. Maha Mrityunjaya Mantra

Maha Mrityunjaya Mantra, by definition, protects us from our deepest fear - the fear of death. From the day we are born, we fear many things. Fear may be divided into 3 core categories, fear of death, fear of losing things/people that are dear to us, and fear of failure. These mantras have been powerful tools for human beings to overcome fear. Maha Mrityunjaya Mantra, is written as:

ॐ त्र्यम्बकं यजामहे सुगन्धिं पुष्टिवर्धनम् ।
उर्वारुकमिव बन्धना न्मृत्योर्मुक्षीय मामृतात्

oṃ tryambakaṃ yajāmahe sugandhiṃ puṣṭivardhanam।
urvārukamiva bandhanān mṛtyormukṣīya māmṛtāt ॥

I worship that fragrant Shiva of three eyes, the one who nourishes all living entities. [Source: Maha Mrityunjaya Mantra,

- Rigved 7.59.12.]. Maha Mrityunjaya Mantra was given to us by Rishi Markandeya. It was a secret mantra, and Rishi Markandeya gave the Mantra to Sati - Daksha's daughter for the Moon. This is how this mantra became known. **It is also called the Rudra mantra, and also as Mrita-Sanjivini mantra.** In the Vedas it finds its place in three texts – (a) the Rig Veda VII.59.12, (b) the Yajur Veda III.60, and (c) the Atharva Veda XIV.1.17.

There are many mythological facts and stories related to this Mantra. The mantra means that we offer our prayers to the three-eyed Lord Shiva, who nurtures all living beings. May we get liberated from the eternal cycle of life and death and achieve immortality. May Lord Shiva give us the strength to detach ourselves from the physical and material forces of the universe. Mahamrityunjaya Mantra holds special significance along with various other powerful Mantras.

While the most chanted Gayatri Mantra is meant for spiritual progression, the Mahamrityunjaya Mantra is meant for seeking immortality. The Tryambakam Mantra, when chanted with complete devotion leads to liberation or moksha. It cures illness, bestows longevity, and wards off evil forces. The right pronunciation of each syllable during the chant is very important as these sound vibrations generate a flow of energy in the body. It reverberates our inner self helping us to achieve a meditative mind. It is believed that the recitation of the Mahamrityunjaya Mantra consumes the negativism. The mantra is known for its divine healing powers. It leads us toward the path of enlightenment and self-revelation. Chanting the Mahamrityunjaya Mantra during Brahma Muhurta or the early morning time before sunrise is said to be beneficial but the devotees can reap the benefits of the Mantra by chanting it any time of the day with complete devotion.

If you are chanting to get rid of fear-chant this mantra 1100 times. If you want to improve health and get rid of diseases, then chant it 11000 times. For the protection of family from sudden death and all-around development chant the mantra 125000 times. During the Mahamrityunjaya mantra in chanting, place the **Maha Mrityunjaya yantra** at pooja place to get most of the benefits. After placing the yantra, one should have to do the Shodashopachara pooja of this yantra.

2. **Shiva Moola Mantra: ॐ नमः शिवाय॥ Om Namah Shivaya॥**

This mantra is said to be the heart of all the Vedas and Tantras. Om Namah Shivaya is found, quite literally, in the middle of the Vedas. It is difficult to give a clear meaning to the mantra. The easy exposition of it would be *"Om, I bow to Shiva"*. But this interpretation does not do it justice. Shiva means Auspicious, so it could be said that the *Om Namah Shivaya mantra means bowing to auspiciousness.* Shiva however should be understood in a fuller context, and not in the overly simplistic picture that is typically given in books and websites as a god of destruction.

Hey! Lord Shiva, I bow to you. I bow to the peaceful one who is the embodiment of the entire universe. It is also called the 'Panchakshari Shiva Strota' and is the most common and mool (basic) mantra of Lord Shiva, who is the supreme god. This mantra is used for protection and security. Being the simplest one, this mantra can be chanted anytime and anywhere, while performing Rudrabhishek or any other ritual related to Lord Siva.

3. Shiva Gayatri Mantra

ॐ तत्पुरुषाय विद्महे महादेवाय धीमहि तन्नो रुद्रः प्रचोदयात्!

**Om Tatpurushaya Vidmahe Mahadevaya Dhimahi,
Tanno Rudrah Prachodayat**

Meaning of the Mantra: I pray to the mightiest of the Gods, the ideal *Purusha, Mahadev.* I pray to God to bless me with intellect and illuminate my path with the light of knowledge. The Shiva Gayatri Mantra is believed to be very powerful. This sacred mantra can be chanted daily in the morning time. This mantra pleases Lord Shiva and is believed to have the power to fulfil all your wishes and give you peace of mind.

4. Rudra Mantra: ॐ नमो भगवते रुद्राय Om Namo Bhagavate Rudraya

Meaning of Mantra: I bow to the holy one, to the Rudra LordShiva. Rudra is one of the ancient forms of Lord Shiva. The word "Rudra' comes from the Sanskrit language and means 'the wild one'. Lord Shiva in his Rudra form was the God of the storm and had a fiery face. The Rudra Gayatri mantra is very useful and powerful in fulfiling your desires. Mantra is the best way to please Lord Shiva and get his blessings. By chanting this mantra, you get Rudra's blessing.

5. Shiva Yajur Mantra

कर्पूर गौरं करुणावतारं, संसार सार म्भुजगेन्द्र हारम्।
सदा वसन्तं हृदयारविन्दे भवं भवानी सहितं नमामि॥

Karpur Gauram Karunavataram,
Sansara Saram Bhujagendra Haram |
Sada Vasantam Hridayaaravinde,
Bhavam Bhavani Sahitam Namami | |

Meaning of the Mantra: Hey Lord Shiva, I bow to you. You are the essence of the world and are pure like the 'sheet Kapoor or the white camphor. You are the epitome of compassion in this universe. Within you, you have the essence of existence and you wear the King of serpents as a garland. You always reside in the heart that's like a lotus. I bow to you and your consort Bhavani (Maan Parvati), who always accompanies you. This mantra is chanted at the end of every ritual, at the time of aarti. It hails Lord Shiva as the Supreme Being and describes his looks and qualities.

Hanuman Mantra

Amongst the Hindu Gods, the great favorite with devotees is Hanuman, the powerful deity who is the greatest devotee of Sri Ram. What many may not know is that Hanuman is the incarnation of the mighty Lord Shiva. Lord Hanuman is the epitome of ultimate devotion manifested with its full glory - unparalleled and unchallenged in all times and places. By the very power of his devotion to Lord Sita Rama, he has easily achieved the supreme status of oneness with Paramatma – the spiritual resonance. Lord Hanuman is the link between devotees and god, for on the Lord's behalf he serves, inspires, and protects his Lord's servants, and by worshipping him devotees are blessed with all kinds of power, valor, and prosperity.

Ghosts, devils, and spirits never trouble a person who regularly recites the Hanuman Mantra. Its recitation infuses one with unlimited energy and Prana. Hanuman Mantra also helps in overcoming the malefic effects of Saturn. It also helps small children to get rid of scary and fearful thoughts. Regular chanting of the Hanuman Mantra increases a person's resilience and he emerges victorious in every challenging situation. The Hanuman mantra helps to overcome the difficulties or problems one might encounter in getting a wish fulfilled. Hanuman Mantra is also used for attaining physical strength, stamina, and power. Hanuman Mantra helps to quickly solve the problems of life such as problems in married life, debt problems, mental disturbances, and agony. It blesses one with the qualities of courage and confidence, thwarts the efforts of one's enemies and ensures success, strengthens the immune system, and blesses one with a long life. By chanting the Hanuman Mantra daily, one becomes active and energetic and doesn't experience laziness in doing any work.

1. **Hanuman Mantra for getting physical strength, stamina, and power: ॐ हनुमते नमः Om Hanumate Namah**

Recite this Hanuman Mantra 21000 times to eradicate diseases, evil spirits, and other types of disturbances in life.The following two more Hanuman Mantra are also popular

ॐ नमो भगवते आंजनेयाय महाबलाय स्वाहा |

Om Namo Bhagvate AanjaneyaayMahaabalaay Swaahaa

ॐ ऐं ह्रीं हनुमते रामदूताय लंकाविध्वंसनाय अंजनी गर्भ संभूताय शाकिनी डाकिनी डाकिनी विध्वंसनाय किलि किलि बुबुकारेण विभिषणाय हनुमद्देवाय ॐ ह्रीं श्रीं हौं हाँ फट्स्वाहा।।

Om Aing Hring Hanumate Ramdutay Lankavidhvansnay Anjani Garbh Sambhutay Shakini Dakini Dakini Vidhvanssnay Kilikili Bubukaren Vibhishanay Hanumaddevay Om Hring Shring Haung Ha Phat Swaha ||

2. Hanuman Chalisa

Lord Hanuman is known for his devotion to Lord Ram and is considered to be the *embodiment of faith, surrender, and devotion. 'Hanuman Chalisa' is composed by Saint Goswami Tulsidas, the author of the Tulsi Ramayana (Ramacharitamanasa). It is believed that an ailing Tulsidas composed the Hanuman Chalisa. Composing and singing the praises of Lord Hanuman, helped Tulsidas regain his health. The 40 verses in 'Hanuman Chalisa' are filled with praises for Lord Hanuman* (Internet Source: www.speakingtree.in).

Sri Guru Charan Saroj Raj, nij Mann Mukuru Sudhaari.
Barnaun Raghuvar Bimal Jasu, Jo Daayaku Phal Chaari.

Having polished the mirror of my heart with the dust of my Guru's lotus feet, I recite the divine fame of the greatest king of the Raghukul dynasty, which bestows us with the fruit of all four efforts.

Buddhiheen Tanu Janike, Sumiraun Pawan-Kumar.
Bal Buddhi Vidya Dehu Mohi, Harahu Kalesh Bikaar.

Knowing that this mind of mine has less intelligence, I remember the 'Son of Wind' who, granting me strength, wisdom, and all kinds of knowledge, removes all my suffering and shortcomings.

Jai Hanuman Gyan Gunn Sagar.
Jai Kapees Tihun Lok Ujaagar.

Ramdoot Atulit Baldhama.
Anjani-Putra Pawansut Naama.

Victory to Lord Hanuman, the ocean of wisdom and virtue. Victory to the Lord who is supreme among the monkeys, illuminator of the three worlds. You are Lord Rama's emissary, the abode of matchless power, Mother Anjani's son, and also popular as the 'Son of the Wind'.

"Mahaveer Vikram Bajrangi. Kumati Nivaar Sumati Ke Sangi.
Kanchan Baran Biraj Subesa. Kaanan Kundal Kunchit Kesa."

Great hero, You are as mighty as a thunderbolt. You remove evil intellect and are the companion of those having good ones. Your skin is golden in colour and You are adorned with beautiful clothes. You have adorning earrings in Your ears and Your hair is curly and thick.

Haath Braj Au Dhwaja Biraaje. Kaandhe Moonj Janeu Saaje.
Shankar Suvan Kesarinandan. Tej Prataap Maha Jag Bandan.

In Your hands, shine a mace and a flag of righteousness. A sacred thread adorns Your right shoulder. You are the embodiment of Lord Shiva and Vanar-raj Kesari's son. There is no limit or end to Your glory, Your magnificence. The whole Universe worships You.

Vidyavaan Guni Ati Chaatur. Ram Kaaj Karibe Ko Aatur. Prabhu Charitra Sunibe Ko Rasiya. Ram Lakhan Sita Mann Basiya.

You are the wisest of the wise, virtuous, and (morally) clever. You are always eager to do Lord Rama's works. You feel extremely delighted in listening to Lord Rama's doings and conduct. Lord Rama, Mother Sita, and Lord Laxmana dwell forever in Your heart.

Sukshma Roop Dhari Siyanhi Dikhawa.
Bikat Roop Dhari Lanka Jarawa.
Bheem Roop Dhari Asura Sanghare.
Ramchandra Ke Kaaj Sanware.

Taking the subtle form, You appeared in front of Mother Sita. And, taking the formidable form, You burnt Lanka (Ravana's kingdom). Taking the massive form (like that of Bheema), You slaughtered the demons. This is how, You completed Lord Rama's tasks, successfully.

Laaye Sanjeevan Lakhana Jiyaaye. Sri Raghuveer Harashi Urr LaHaye. Raghupati Keenhi Bahut Badai. Tum Mum Priya, Bhartahi Sum Bhai.

Bringing the magic herb (Sanjivani), You revived Lord Laxmana. Raghupati, Lord Rama praised You greatly and overflowing in gratitude, said that You are a dear brother to Him just as Bharat is.

Sahas Badan Tumharo Jas Gaave.
Asa Kahi Sripati Kanth Lagaave.
Sankaadik Brahmadi Munisa. narad Sarad Sahit Aheesa.

Saying this, Lord Rama drew You to Himself and embraced You. Sages like Sanaka, Gods like Brahma, and sages like Narada and even the thousand-mouthed serpent sing Your fame! Sanak, Sanandan, and the other Rishis and great saints; Brahma - the god, Narada, Saraswati - the Mother Divine and the King of serpents sing Your glory.

Jam Kuber Digpal Jahan Te. Kabi Kobid Kahi Sake Kahan Te. Tum Upkaar Sugreevahi Keenha. Ram Milaaye Raj-Pad Deenha.

Yama, Kubera, and the guardians of the four quarters; poets and scholars - none can express Your glory. You helped Sugriva by introducing Him to Lord Rama and regaining his crown. Therefore, You gave Him the Kingship (the dignity of being called a king).

Tumharo Mantra Bibhishan Maana. Lankeshwar Bhaye Sab Jag Jaana. Yug Sahastra Jojan Par Bhanu. Leelyo Taahi Madhur Phal Jaanu.

Likewise, complying with Your preaching, even Vibhishana became the King of Lanka. You swallowed the sun, located thousands of miles away, mistaking it to be a sweet, red fruit!

Prabhu Mudrika Meli Mukh Maahi.
Jaladhi Laandhi Gaye Achraj naahi.

Durgam Kaaj Jagat Ke Jete.
Sugam Anugrah Tumhare Tete.

Keeping the ring in Your mouth, which was given to You by Lord Rama, you crossed over the Ocean, to no astonishment, whatsoever.

All difficult tasks of this world become easy, with Your grace.

Ram Duaare Tum Rakhvare.
Hott na Aagya Binu Paisare.
Sab Sukh Lahe Tumhari Sarna.
Tum Rakshak Kahu Ko Dar Na.

You are the guardian at Lord Rama's door. Nobody can move forward without Your permission which means that Lord Rama's darshans (to get the sight of) are possible only with Your blessings. Those who take refuge in You, find all the comforts and happiness. When we have a protector like You, we do not need to get scared of anybody or anything.

Aapan Tej Samharo Aape.
Teeno Lok Haank Te Kaampe.
Bhoot Pishaach nikat nahi Aavein.
Mahaveer Jab naam Sunaave."

You alone can withstand Your magnificence. All the three worlds start trembling at one roar of Yours. O Mahaveer! No ghosts or evil spirits come near the ones who remember Your name. Therefore, just remembering Your name does everything!

naase Rog Hare Sab Peera.
Japat nirantar Hanumat Beera.
Sankat Te Hanuman Churave.
Mann Kram Vachan Dhyaan Jo Laave.

O Hanuman! All diseases and all kinds of pain get eradicated when one recites or chant Your name. Therefore, chanting Your name regularly is considered to be very significant. Whoever meditates upon or worships You with thought, word, and deed, gets freedom from all kinds of crisis and affliction.

Sab Par Ram Tapasvi Raja. Tin Ke Kaaj Sakal Tum Saaja. Aur Manorath Jo Koi Laave.
Soi Amit Jivan Phal Paave.

Lord Rama is the greatest Ascetic among all the Kings. But, it's only You who carried out all the tasks of Lord Sri Rama. One who comes to You with any longing or a sincere desire obtains the abundance of the manifested fruit, which remains undying throughout life.

Chaaron Yug Partap Tumhara.
Hai Parsidh Jagat Ujiyara.
Saadhu-Sant Ke Tum Rakhvare.
Asur nikandan Ram Dulaare."

Your splendor fills all the Four Ages. And, Your glory is renowned throughout the world. You are the guardian of saints and sages; the destroyer of demons and adored by Lord Rama.

Ashta Siddhi nau nidhi Ke Daata. As Var Deen Janaki Mata. Ram Rasayan Tumhare Paasa. Sadaa Raho Raghupati Ke Daasa.

You have been blessed by Mother Janaki to give boon further, to the deserving ones, wherein You can grant the siddhis (eight different powers) and the nidhis (nine kinds of wealth). *You have the essence of* Ram *bhakti, may you always remain the humble and devoted servant of* Raghupati.

Tumhare Bhajan Ram Ko Paave. Janam Janam Ke Dukh Bisraave. Antkaal Raghuvar Pur Jaayi. Jahan Janam Hari-Bhakt Kahayi.

When one sings Your praise, Your name, He gets to meet Lord Rama and finds relief from the sorrows of many lifetimes. By your grace, one will go to the immortal abode of Lord Rama after death and remain devoted to Him.

Aur Devta Chitta na Dharai.Hanumat Sei Sarva Sukh Karai. Sankat Kate, Mite Sab Peera. Jo Sumire Hanumat Balbeera.

It is not needed to serve any other Deity or God. Service to Lord Hanuman gives all the comforts. All troubles cease for the one who remembers the powerful lord, Lord Hanuman, and all his pains also come to an end.

Jai Jai Jai Hanuman Gosain.
Krupa Karahu Gurudev Ki naai.
Jo Sat Baar Paath Kar Koi.
Chutahi Bandhi Maha Sukh Hoyi.

O Lord Hanuman! Praise and glory to you O mighty Lord, please bestow your grace as our Supreme Guru. One who recites this Chalisa a hundred times is released from all bondages and will attain great bliss.

Jo Yeh Padhe Hanuman Chalisa,
Hoye Siddhi Saakhi Gaurisa.
Tulsidas Sada Hari Chera,
Keeje Nath Hriday Mah Dera.

One who reads and recites this Hanuman Chalisa, all his work gets accomplished. Lord Shiva, Himself, is the witness to it. O Lord Hanuman, May I always remain a servant, a devotee to Lord Sri Ram, says Tulsidas. And, May You always reside in my heart.

Pawan Tanay Sankat Haran, Mangal Murti Roop.
Ram Lakhan Sita Sahit, Hriday Basahu Sur Bhoop.

O the Son of Wind, You are the destroyer of all sorrows. You are the embodiment of fortune and prosperity. With Lord Rama, Laxmana, and Mother Sita, dwell in my heart, always.

Ganesh Mantra

This sacred mantra for wealth is dedicated to Lord Ganesha, and his two wives Riddhi and Siddhi representing the Hindu Goddess of prosperity and spiritual enlightenment respectively.

"Vakratunda Maha-Kaaya Surya-Kotti Samaprabha
Nirvighnam Kuru Me Deva Sarva-Kaaryeshu
Sarvadaa||"

Vakra – means one that is not straight.

Vakratunda – means curved trunk.

Mahakaya – means large body, in a more divine sense it means most powerful.

Suryakoti – means 'Surya' or sun and koti means crore. **Samprabha** – means 'Prabha – aura, grandeur', 'sama- like'. **Suryakoti Samprabha** – means whose aura is like the light of crores of sun put together.

Nirvgnam – obstacle-free.

Kurume – give me. **Deva –** means God. **Sarva –** means all. **Karyeshu -**work.

Sarvada -always.

Full meaning: "Oh God, may you remove all obstacles from my works forever. Your enormous, curved body and aura are like the light of a million suns. Benefit: By reciting this mantra, one calls Lord Ganesha, who will remove all barriers to happiness and prosperity and grant them wealth, knowledge, good fortune, prosperity, and success in all their activities.

Basic Ganpati Mantra: "Om Gan Ganpataye Namah"

Meaning: It entails submitting to the All-Powerful Ganpati with our entire being and accepting all of his admirable qualities in ourselves. Benefit: Before starting any work, it banishes all negativity from one's life. By repeating this phrase, one can be sure to be successful in any new endeavors they desire to start.

Om Gan Ganpataye Namo Namah
Shree Siddhi Vinayak Namo Namah
Ashtavinayak Namo Namah Mangal Murti Moraya

Devi Stuti

"Ya devi sarva bhuteshu, shanti rupena sangsthita
Ya devi sarva bhuteshu, shakti rupena sangsthita
Ya devi sarva bhuteshu, matri rupena sangsthita
Yaa devi sarva bhuteshu, buddhi rupena sangsthita
Namastasyai, namastasyai, namastasyai, namo namaha"

Reference: (Internet Source - www.templepurohit.com) **Meaning:** The goddess who is omnipresent as the universal mother, as the embodiment of power, as the symbol of peace, Oh Goddess (Devi) who resides everywhere in all living beings as intelligence and beauty, I bow to her, I bow to her, I bow to her again and again. Benefit: Regular utterances of this universal mantra bless one with power, prosperity, and positive energy. The inner power of the chant is enhanced.

Goddess Durga in Hinduism is believed to be the principal form of the Mother and is the root cause of creation, sustenance, and annihilation. The name 'Durga' in Sanskrit means 'unconquerable'. Goddess Durga has the collective strength of all divine forces and is said to have manifested when evil forces called "Aasurs" threatened the very existence of the Gods. To destroy these demons, all Gods offered their radiance to her creation and each formed different parts of Durga's body. She also obtained very powerful weapons, such as the Chakra from Lord Vishnu and the Trishul (trident) from Lord Shiva.

Lakshmi Narayan Mantra - for material wealth and abundance

Lakshmi Narayana is the manifestation of Lord Vishnu as Narayana and Goddess Lakshmi. Goddess Lakshmi is the consort of Lord Vishnu. Lord Vishnu is known as Narayana while he is resting with his consort, Lakshmi. This mantra helps invoke material wealth and abundance. Goddess Lakshmi is the consort of Lord Vishnu (Narayana), and both can bestow their devotees with wealth and prosperity. Lakshmi and Narayana are for wealth, prosperity, and success. Chanting this mantra is highly beneficial for those seekers who are interested in acquiring financial prosperity as well as materialistic success. The mantra is bound to relieve all kinds of issues related to career and finances when chanted regularly.

Lakshmi Narayan Mantra:

ॐ श्री लक्ष्मी नारायणा यनमः

| | OM SHREE LAKSHMI-NARAYANAY NAMAH | |

Dhanalakshmi Mantra

Goddess Dhana Lakshmi is worshipped for money, wealth, and property by many Hindus. Below is the Dhanalakshmi mantra in English. The mantra is chanted daily 108 times. It is also the ideal mantra to chat on Thursdays. People chanting the mantra should wear a yellow colour dress. It is said that people who chant the mantra with devotion will win the lottery and learn about treasure. It is also chanted to find a solution to financial problems...

Namastestu Mahamaye,
Sri Peede Sura Pujite Shankha Chakra
Gada Haste Mahalakshmi Namostute.

Saraswati Mantra Shri Saraswati Chalisa (English)

Reference: www.pandit.com (Internet Source)

!! Janak Janani Padam Raj, Nij Mastak Par Dhari, Bandau Matu Saraswati, Buddhi Bal De Datari, Purn Jagat Mein Veapt Tav, Mahima Amit Anantu, dushtjano Ke Paap Ko, Matu Tuhi Ab Hantu !!

!! Jai Shri Sakal Budhi Balrasi, Jai Sarvage Amar Avinasi, Jai Jai Jai Venakar Dhari, Karti Sada Suhans Savari, Roop Chaturbhujdhari Mata, Sakal Vishv Andar Vikhata, Jag Mein Paap Budhi Jab Hoti, tab Dharm Ki Phiki Jyoti !!

!!Tab hi Matu ka Nij Avtari, Paap Heen Karti Mahitari, Balmiki Ji The hatyara Gyani, Tav Prsad Jane Sansara, Ramchrit Jo Rache Banai, Aadi Kavi Ki Padvi Pai, Kalidas Jo Bhae Vikhata, Teri Kripa Drishti Se Mata !!

!! Tulsi Sur Aadi Vidvana, Bhaye Aur Jo Gyani Nana, Tinhe Na Aur Raheu Avlamba, Kev Kripa Aapki Amba, Krhu Kripa Soi Matu Bhavani, Dukhit Din Nij Dsahi Jani, Putra Krai Apradh Bahuta, Tehi Na dhari Chitt Mata !!

!! Rakhu Laj Janani Ab Meri, Vine Karu Bahu Bhanti bhu teri, Mein Anath Teri Avlamba, Kripa Karu Jai Jai Jagdamba, Madhu Kaitabh Jo Ati Balvana, Bahuyudh Vishnu Te Thana, Samar Hajar Panch Mein Ghora, Phir Bhi Mukh Unse Nahi Moda !!

!! Matu Sahae Bhai Tehi Kala, Budhi Viprit Kari Khalhala, Tehi Mritu Bhai Khal Keri, Purvahu Matu Manorath Meri Chand Mund Jo The Vikhyata, Chan Mahu Saharu Tehi Mata, Raktabij Se Samrath Papi, Sur-Muni Hride Dhara Sab Kampi!!

!! Kateu Sir Jimi Kadli Khamba, Baar Baar Binvau Jagdamba, Jag Prasidh Jo Shumbh Nishumbha, Chhin Me Badhe Tahi Tu Amba, Bharat-Matu Budhi Phereu Jayi, Ramachandra Banvas Karai, Ehi Vidhi Ravan Vadh Tum Kina, Sur Nar Muni Sabko Sukh Dina !!

!! Ko Samrath Tav Yash Gun Gana, Nigam Anadi Anant Bakhana, Vishnu Rudra jas kahi Na Mari, Jinki Ho Tum Rakshakari, Rakt Dantika Aur Shatakshi, Naam Apaar Hai Danav Bhakshi, Durgam Kaj Dhara Par Kina, Durga Naam Sakal Jag Lina !!

!! Durg Aadi Harani Tu Mata, Kripa Krhu Jab Jab Sukhdata, Nrip Kopit Jo Maran Chahi, Kanan Mein Ghere Mrig Nahi, Sagar Madhy Pot Ke Bhange, Ati Tofan Nahi Kou Sange, Bhoot Pret Badha Yaa Dukh Mein, Ho Daridra Athava Sankat Mein !!

!! Naam Jape Mangal Sab Koi, Sanshay Isame Karai Na Koi, Putrahin Jo Aatur Bhai, Sabi Chandi Puje Ehi, Karai Path Nit Yah Chalisa, Hoy Putra Sundar Gun Isa, Dhupadik Naivedy Chadhavei, Sankat Rahit Avashy Ho Javi !!

!! Bhakti Matu Ki Kari Hamesha, Nikat Na Aavi Tahi Kalesha, Bandi Path Kare Shat Bara, Bandi Pash Door Ho Sara, Krhu Kripa Bhavamukti Bhavani, Mo Kahn Daas Sada Nij Jani !!

!! Mata Soraj Kanti Tav, Andhakar Mam Roop, Doban Te Raksha Krhu, Paru Na Mein Bhav-Koop, Bal Buddhi Vidya Dehu Mohi, Sunhu Sarasvati Matu, Adham Ram sagar adam, ko Aashrae detaru !!

Hare Krishna Mahamantra

This mantra has a syllable and is known as the tarak brahma mantra. Hare Krishna Mahamantra is mentioned in the Bhagavad Gita and Padma Puranaas the most sacred and powerful for the people in Kali Yuga. The mantra is chanted as:

Hare Krishna Hare Krishna Krishna Krishna Hare Hare Hare Rama Hare Rama Rama Rama Hare Hare

The great God incarnate Sri Chaitanya Mahaprabhu preached this maha-mantra some 500 years ago. On the instructions of his Guru Maharaj Srila Bhaktisiddhanta Saraswati Thakur, the founder of ISKCON and the Hare Krishna Movement Sri Srila Prabhupada went to the USA at the age of 70 to generate the love of Godhead to the world in the form of this Hare Krishna Mahamantra. In the recent few years, very highly qualified people have chanted this maha-mantra almost regularly in search of their inner peace and the meaning of life.

A mantra when chanted properly and regularly becomes a compact form of prayer that generates tremendous power, extra energy, and protection for the chanter. In Hinduism, each God/Goddess has one-to-many specific influencing powers on us and therefore has a specific mantra dedicated to the purpose. It is not possible to incorporate all of them. However, the important and popular ones are given with the purpose of correct pronunciation and accuracy. The reason is that wrong pronunciation is more dangerous. The practice of reciting this mystical chant every day is said to grant health, wealth, prosperity, and happiness.

CHAPTER - 11

ॐ *"**Puja** is a form of ritual prayer showing reverence to the Gods. Puja fulfils human desires, wants, freedom from suffering, good of the family, marriage, rise in status and position, health, wealth, and other desires. **Japa** is the recital of a Mantra or the Name of the Lord while **Dhyana** is the meditation on the form of the Lord with His attributes.*

***Dharna** is the start of meditation; **Dhyana** is mid-way into meditation and **Samadhi** is when you reach the climax of your meditation. **Tapasya is** the concentration of the will to get the results of sadhana and conquer the lower nature. **Aradhana** is the worship of the Divine, with our love and self-surrender.*

Chapter - 11

Puja Dhyana Japa Tapa and Samadhi

Understanding Puja

Puja is a form of ritual prayer showing reverence to the Gods to offer devotional homage to Him. It is mostly followed by Hindus, Buddhists, and Jains. The Sanskrit word "puja" denotes respect, esteem, tribute, devotion, and worship. Puja is one of the most important Hindu rituals that involves the loving gift of light, flowers, water, and food to the divine. The majority of practicing Hindus perform Puja at least twice daily and also on all significant festivals. Puja can be performed either singly or in groups; in silence or with chants and voiced prayers. Through invocations, prayers, songs, and rituals, one expresses their profound reverence for a deity, a spirit, or another aspect of the divine. Making a spiritual connection with the divine is a crucial component of puja for the Hindu devotee.

It is believed that puja became popular during the years 300-750 during which the building of temples gained momentum. Later the Vedic sacrifice Yajna was incorporated into the puja system, which became the main ritual of the time

Regular puja at home generates positive thoughts and spiritual energy throughout the house. These spiritual energies try to remove the bad effects from our lives and assist us in surrounding ourselves with good energy, which can bring us mental peace. This increases our material well-being and makes it easier for us to connect with the Divine, which is the essence of life. Further, the benefit of worshipping God at home is that when we worship, we are in a /conversation with our Lord and Savior which results in joy. God responds to our, chants, devotional songs, and hearts of gratitude by giving us back, the bread of life, the breath of his spirit, healing, and all else we are entitled to. Puja creates spiritual vibrations and positive sentiments within us. These heavenly powers operate to keep us with positive energy that can provide serenity and prosperity in us and drive out any bad influences from our lives. Pujas are historically conducted with God's idols and yantras at temples and houses.

Puja might be more beneficial if we engage in spiritual practices. We attempt to cleanse ourselves through practices like meditation, fasting, prayer, and mantra chanting so that more spiritual energy can be invoked in us. When we are engaged in worship, we always think of God, which is part of the rituals. Rituals bring order to life by enhancing our good habits. By doing puja regularly with a **positive** idea or goal in mind, success is achieved subject to the worthiness of his karmic actions. *Puja brings the satisfaction that enhances fulfiling our desires, wants, marriage, rise in status and position, health, wealth, and other desires including relieving us from suffering.* By not doing Puja daily, we are harming ourselves.

The Greeks, who started their sphere of influence on the Indian subcontinent, may have brought the Puja rite to India. They honoured their deities as well as some Indian deities including Skanda, Siva, and Vishnu. With time the system of puja has also gained momentum and people started doing puja to various Hindu Gods and Goddesses. Thus, for specific Hindu deities separate systems and procedures of puja and the specific mantras that need to be chanted during the process were developed.

Japa and Dhyan

Japa is the recital of a Mantra or the Name of the Lord. **Dhyana** is the meditation on the form of the Lord with His attributes. Japa may be practiced both while meditating and without. Japa can be practiced in a group during formal worship or when standing or sitting in a meditative position while engaging in other activities. The mantra or the name of the Lord may be spoken aloud or quietly. It may also be whispered enough for the practitioner to hear it. The Sanskrit word Japa means *"to utter in a low voice, repeat internally or mutter"*. Patanjali defined it as the process of destroying birth, death, and reincarnation, as a means to destroy one's sins.

Tapasya is the concentrated effort to achieve the goals of Sadhana. **Aradhana** entails invoking the name of the Divine, praying, and worshipping the Divine with love and self-surrender. **Dhyana** refers to inner meditation, consciousness focus, and entering **Samadhi.** Japa can be repeated in four different ways: *Vaikhari (loud audible), Upamshu (whispering), Manasika (mental), and Lakhita (written).*

Any meditation practice can include the use of a mantra. However, Transcendental and Metta meditations are the two forms that have historically used mantras. Transcendental meditation involves sitting quietly for 20 minutes twice daily while closing your eyes and repeating a mantra to yourself. Buddhist meditation practices include metta meditation. Metta is the Sanskrit word for compassion and uplifting energy and is referred to as "loving-kindness meditation." Keeping the mind tranquil improves focus, memory, clarity of thinking, and willpower. Proper rest is essential to refresh the whole body and mind. For self-conduct oneself the following guidelines need to be followed.

a. **Yoga Asanas- postures for strength, flexibility, and stamina** Pranayama- breath control for emotional and mental stability;

b. **Pratyahara-** restraining of the senses;

c. **Dharana-** means concentration; and

d. **Dhyana-**means meditation.

Manasika japa is the most *powerful* which is recited in the mind. Practitioners scale it up and say that Manasika japa is 1000 times more effective than Upamshu Japa and therefore 100 000 times more effective than Vaikhari japa.

Upamsu is a Sanskrit term that refers to murmuring or repeating the mantra while moving the lips and generating a faint sound or whisper. By focusing on the meaning of each syllable and meditating on the mantra's whole conceptualization without moving the tongue or lips or creating any sound, Manasika (mental or meditative) japa is performed. **Vaikhari japa** is spoken loud enough so that nearby people can hear the most powerful meditation technique to restore the body and mind yoga Nidra.

Samadhi (**समाधि**) is a state of meditative consciousness which is the highest stage of meditation. In Buddhism, it is the last of the eight elements of the "Noble Eightfold Path".

A feeling of increased awareness is an indication that you're practicing meditation properly. You become more conscious of your environment, as well as of your thoughts and feelings. You start paying attention to things that you are never concerned about, or that you'll notice things for the first time. Ten minutes should be good enough if you're just starting and want to de-stress. However, up to 30 minutes may be preferable if you want to concentrate more on serenity and improved attention because you'll have time for some mild stretching and breathing exercises during that period.

In simple terms, Dharna is the start of meditation, Dhyan is mid-way into meditation and Samadhi is when you reach the climax of your meditation. It might be difficult to understand how dharana and dhyana vary from one another. **Dharana** is the cautious attention and concentration on a single thing. **Dhyana** is a mental state in which one's attention is sustained or engrossed in the object of attention. Dhyana is when the thing is motionless and the camera's focus is fixed on it, while dharana is like concentrating the lens of a camera on a moving object.

Dharana in Sanskrit means concentration focus singularly. "Dha" means "holding, carrying, or maintaining", and "ana" means "other or something else." It's the first step towards achieving a state of meditation. The practice of continuous concentrated attention on a single object is known as Dharana. Usually, this focus is the breath, but it can also be a mantra being repeated, a deity being visualised, or a profound truth being thought about. With this complete attention, it aims to calm the mind. These phases of growth are experienced by every Yogi before reaching total nirvana. The path of knowledge starts at the low level of awareness towards **Samadhi,** the highest level of knowledge. *Samadhi is the state in which one is free from suffering and at the same time experiences the state of one's bliss.* This is stage one, while the 2nd stage Moksha known as permanent Moksha is attained only after death.

Yoga Nidra, often known as yogic slumber, is a potent meditation method that encourages profound relaxation. One begins by lying down in savasana (the corpse posture), after which they are led into a state of conscious meditation. In the samadhi state, the person is in touch with the Aatma within and rests in pure awareness. The three levels of Samadhi are Level 1: *Savikalpa Samadhi, Level 2: Nirvikalpa Samadhi,* and Level 3: *Dharmamegha Samadhi. Nirvikar-Samādhi is the highest form of cognitive ecstasy.* Another definition of Samadhi in Hinduism and Buddhism is the highest state of mental concentration that people can achieve while still bound to the body and which unites them with the highest reality.

Deep meditation, or tapasya, is a self-realization endeavor. Tapasya, a Sanskrit term, denotes the "generation of heat and energy." Deep meditation, self-control, austerity, and an attempt to realise oneself are all part of this practical spiritual practice. A continuous practice of Yoga is the Sadhana, while full *concentration of the will to get the results of* ***sadhana is Tapasya. Aradhana*** *is the worship of the Divine, love, self-surrender, and prayer to God.*

Samadhi and its Types

The word *samadhi* can be broken down into two terms, "*sama*" meaning equal, and "*adhi*" meaning to adhere. By combining them, it results in equal states of consciousness, joining the physical, spiritual, mental, and emotional aspects. It is the state of supreme bliss, super consciousness, and enlightenment. In Samadhi the mind is completely absorbed in the object occupying the space to which it is confined. At this stage, the process, the object, and the mind all become a single entity.

Samadhi is the highest state of mental concentration that one can achieve while still in the physical body. It unites you with God. During **Savikalpa samadhi** the yogi's consciousness is temporarily absorbed into the Brahman. In the yogic tradition, Savikalpa is the second highest level of Samadhi, while **Nirvikalpa samādhi** is the highest state of complete absorption. In this state, the body, mind, and object of meditation become one, and your connection to the material world ceases to exist.

Mantra Sadhana and Moksha

Moksha is achieved through meditation. It detaches from the material world and elevates to attain divinity. It liberates the soul from the endless cycle of rebirth and frees the soul from the pain of the material world. Hindus consider six ways to achieve Moksha of which the jnana way, or Jnana Marga, is the way to achieve moksha through knowledge and study, while bhakti is through devotion and karma through actions. After attaining moksha, one senses a feeling of oneness with a higher power and can elevate from the process of life and rebirth. It is the major goal of most practicing Hindus.

Mantras normally start working once you complete 100 rosaries in a particular time. You can start reciting 1 rosary or Mala which is 108 beads, every day. It is proved that, when a mantra is chanted in rhythm, it creates a neuro-linguistic effect, even if the meaning of the mantra is not known. *It is believed that it takes 40 days for a seeker to get used to a transformation by practicing either a mantra or tantra.* Around 20 days of practice is required to break old habits and another 20 days to form new ones. For example, a way to do an extended practice of the mantra "*Om Namah Shivaya*" is to repeat it at least 108 times per day and do that for 40 days. A 40-day Meditative Mind in Sadhana is an opportunity to dedicate ourselves to practicing meditation. Besides its potential to change the conscious mind, chanting the mantra itself calms down the body and mind. The reasons why one should practice Sadhana are:

- Daily mantra practice calms our minds. It brings the stress down. The vibrations of these ancient mantras by utterances bring positive vibes in and around us, even if the meanings are unknown.
- In meditating through these mantras, our understanding of ourselves and our lives becomes deeper. We become more connected with our true selves.
- Practicing consistently every day for 40 days brings in a substantial change in habits, relationships, and the self attitude.
- Minimum 40-day meditation practice brings self-discipline into life. To get the full benefits, continuous 40 days of practice is a must to receive its full benefits.
- Meditation for 40 days makes it possible to break the jinx to bring structure to our lives. Many a time we feel out of balance because we are either too much into one thing or we are fully absorbed by the day-to-day tasks and projects.

Previous experience in meditation is not necessary. Even if you never learned a Mantra is okay. If you do not believe in God it is fine. It has nothing to do with your religion or the country or caste or your belonging. All you need is a commitment to yourself that you want to transform yourself.

1. **Commitment:** Be committed for 40 Days. With closed eyes, take a deep breath, and ask yourself the changes you want to bring in yourself and why you need these changes.

2. **Time and Place:** Fix a definite time slot of 45 minutes to 1 hour for this practice of chanting mantras. It might be difficult at first but later you start loving the schedule.

3. **Journal:** After each meditation, journal your experience. Write down in your special journal that reflects on the changes you see within yourself after 40 days.

One mantra needs to be chanted 108 times. When a mantra is chanted **1001** or **1008** times, it is symbolic of having done it an infinite number of times. A quick Google search shows an overwhelming number of explanations for the significance of the number **108** in the practice of Japa – the mental repetition (or loud for beginners) of the mantra as a meditative practice. Some explain that **1** stands for the highest truth, **0** for the **completeness** of spiritual practice, and **8** for infinity. Another says that the diameter of the Sun is **108** times that of the Earth and many other good logic prove the sacredness of 108. Others feel that the power of the mantra siddhi comes after 125,000 repetitions of a mantra which is about 1200 rounds of a mala.

Moksha

Method 1: Attaining the First 3 Purusharths

(Internet Source: www.wikihow.com)

(i) It is essential to first fulfil all the desires (kama). Enjoy the various pleasures that life has to offer virtuously. These pleasures can include enjoying good food, appreciating music or art, or having a fulfiling sex life. Your pleasure should not harm others, but rather benefit them such as by performing music, parting education to others, creating art, or cooking delicious food for someone else.

(ii) Earn wealth as much as you need but, it is important to achieve success and wealth through honest, ethical means. Fulfil all the material desires from the wealth you have earned. Fulfil a successful career and establish a stable and successful household and family. The objective is to earn wealth for your family and to share the wealth you obtain with others

(iii) Behave virtuously throughout your life to achieve dharma. The path to achieving dharma includes the following:

- Practicing humble devotion to God (yagna)
- Be charitable to others (daan)
- Maintain physical, mental, and verbal discipline (tapas)
- Meditate on what is right
- Set a good example of yourself through regular spiritual practice

Prepare for moksha that can take a lifetime to achieve. Moksha does not mean renouncing your place in society after living a full life enriched by simple enjoyment, family and material success, and spiritual devotion. However, the following are wrong practices.

- Some people seek moksha by cutting ties with society and their personal life after their first grandchild is born.
- Others become a sannyasin at a young age and live an ascetic lifestyle, detached from society and material things

Method 2: Following the Main of Moksha

- The most important component of achieving moksha is letting go of the things that tie you to your life in the physical world. This is part of the reason that most people renounce society and live a simple, ascetic lifestyle once they are ready to achieve Moksha. Practice selfless acts of service, such as helping the sick or needy. Doing any kind of task, from cooking a meal to meditating, can be considered an act of service as long as you do it intending to help others without expecting any reward in return. Of course, wishing to achieve moksha is a desire in itself, but many Hindus consider the desire for moksha to be necessary for letting go of all other desires.
- Everyone has ignorance and this should be conquered through study and meditation. This is a great obstacle to moksha. Try to meditate for enlightenment.
- If you get the correct teacher, you should practice jnana yoga which focuses on the study and experience of spiritual knowledge.
- One should have high self-control in physical, mental, and emotional aspects. One should always remain calm and peaceful under any circumstances. Every word uttered should help others rather than disturb or harm them. One should always remain away from negative things.

Method 3: Choosing Your Path to Moksha

(i) The easiest and the best way of achieving enlightenment is through working with a suitable guru (spiritual teacher). Finding and working with an enlightened spiritual teacher is considered vital. The correct teacher helps you to let off your ego, desires, and attachments. In Hinduism, it is believed that one may not find a guru by actively seeking him, rather the teacher shall search for you and find you if you are suitable and prepared – have patience.

- Choose a yoga path that is the most suited for you. Practicing yoga is a popular path toward attaining moksha. Traditional yoga not only focuses on physical exercise, but also on meditation, spiritual study, and acts of service to others. To achieve moksha through yoga, consider taking up any one of the six yoga practices (Bhakti yoga, Jnana yoga, Raja yoga, Karma yoga, Hatha yoga, and Tantra yoga)

(ii) Tapa is a good path for moksha which by itself is self-disciplined. While practicing tapa, one must stay alone, and lead a simple life with a focus on calmness. Focus on meditating, studying, and reciting spiritual texts, with self-disciplinary practices involving fasting and remaining in silence for certain periods.

The signs of moksha are compassion for the world, a feeling of purposefulness and peace of mind, and a love for the Supreme Being as being the Source of it all.

Start right now to get rid of the freedom of desire. When one practices meditation regularly, his thought process changes and desires become a way for spirituality. Desires for materialistic needs fade away with the replacement of the desires that are good for him. A perfect balance between the physical, mental, and emotional ways is established and thus one always remains cheerful and happy.

Signs and Symptoms of Spiritual Awakening

Sign # 1: Feeling Love for all

Everyone is loved by you. This is not sexual or romantic, but that's not always precluded. On several levels, you can sense the affection. Regardless of how bad someone may be to you and others in the world, you love them all.

Sign # 2: A Deep Sense of Calm, Peace, or Serenity

A profound sense of calmness is another sign of a spiritual awakening. With complete surrendering of the ego, the calmness in us grows manyfold. We do not move back and forth from this calmness. When something gives rise to agitation again, the control of it becomes easier. With this, the inner peace expands. When one is in peace, clarity of mind is enhanced. With love, peace, and clarity, one can understand the depth of errors that increase talent. These changes within the self are a must when one advances toward spiritual awakening.

Sign # 3: A Profound Sense of Clarity

Once you are on a spiritual path and the awakening has started, there is no more confusion in the mind. Everything becomes crystal clear. Typically, it's in a spiritual opening where everything is only love and cherry blossoms. There's also a lot of pain and suffering in the world, and opening to reality means seeing that suffering too. But before you go on a crusade to save everyone, start by dealing with the suffering you notice in yourself.

Sign # 4: Loss of the Desire/Sense of Wholeness or Oneness

Everyone leads a luxurious life with the possession of good materialistic items that make him feel good. But when he progresses toward spirituality, suddenly he requires nothing. Some people suddenly decide to give away lots of stuff because suddenly they realise how these things burden and choke their lives. This may initially be strange to your near ones, but it simply makes you feel good.

Sign # 5: Abiding Awareness

How to define spiritual awakening that is abiding 24/7. Ultimately, the path of awakening leads to spiritual freedom and reality. In freedom, we are now free from ego projections and false beliefs that inhibit how we interact with reality. This makes our actions wiser, usually more loving, and in an interesting way. It's efficient because we no longer waste time and energy trying to make reality fit our illusions. And of course, we no longer suffer from the conflicts we create within ourselves and with others by trying to make reality and ourselves something we're not. My experiences of spiritual awakenings are the follows:

1. You improve the coolness of your mind and remain cool
2. You become honest with yourself and with the society.
3. You remain away from power, position, and property (3 Ps)
4. You speak less and always try to speak the truth
5. You start praying to God sincerely and regularly
6. Your voice changes and becomes more thrilling
7. Your radiance of the body becomes more positive
8. You lose your ego.
9. You always sit straight with your backbone upright.

10. You try only vegetarian food.
11. You become fearless
12. You think positive, do positive, and be positive
13. You love one and all
14. You always try to help others
15. You remain always happy and satisfied

Dharana, Dhyana, and Samadhi are the core of the meditation practice. In **Dharana,** *we concentrate by holding or fixing the attention of the mind onto one object.* **Dhyana** *in which we do meditation through sustained concentration, whereby the attention continues to hold or repeat the same object or place, and finally the* **Samadhi** *where we go to deep absorption or the state of the essence of the object. Through* **Puja,** *we essentially make a spiritual connection with the divine, while through Moskya, we are liberated from the bondage of rebirth.*

CHAPTER - 12

ॐ *'The Veda (वेद ◌: knowledge) is the earliest literary record of Indo-Aryan civilization and the most sacred book of Bharat. They are the original scriptures of Hindu teachings, containing spiritual knowledge from all aspects of life. There are four types of Vedas {Rig Veda, Samaveda, Yajurveda, and Atharvaveda} and each of them has four subdivisions: (a) Samhitas (mantras), (b) Aranyakas (text on rituals, ceremonies, sacrifices, and symbolic- sacrifices), (c) Brahmanas (commentaries on rituals, ceremonies, and sacrifices), and (d) Upanishads (texts discussing meditation, philosophy, and spiritual knowledge). The Upanishads form the concluding portions of the Veda and are therefore called the "Vedanta" or the end of the Veda.*

Puranas are the vast encyclopedia of Indian literature covering a wide range of topics particularly myths, legends, and other traditional stories. Some post-Vedic texts, including the Mahabharata, and certain Puranas, refer to themselves as the "fifth Veda".

Chapter - 12

Veda and Upanisad

Veda and its Types

The Vedas (वेद: knowledge) is considered the earliest literary record of Indo-Aryan civilization and the most sacred books of Bharat. They are the original scriptures of Hindu teachings, containing spiritual knowledge encompassing all aspects of life. Vedic literature has stood the test of time. The word Veda means wisdom, knowledge, or vision, and it serves to manifest the language of the gods in human speech. The laws of the Vedas have regulated the social, legal, domestic, and religious customs of Hindus up to the present day. All the obligatory duties of Hindus at birth, marriage, death, etc. are guided by Vedic rituals.

There are four types of Vedas:

(i) Rig Veda - It is the earliest form of Veda,

(ii) Samaveda - The earliest reference for singing,

(iii) Yajurveda - It is also called the book of prayers, and

(iv) Atharvaveda - The book of magic and charms.

The oldest Veda is the Rigveda and its features are given in the table below

Features of Rigveda
The oldest form of Veda and the oldest known Vedic Sanskrit text(1800–1100 BCE)
The meaning of the word 'Rigveda' is Praise of Knowledge

It has 10600 verses
Out of 10 books or mandalas, book number 1 and 10 are the youngest ones as they were written later than books 2 to 9
Rigvedic books 2-9 deal with cosmology and deities
Rigvedic books 1 and 10 deal with philosophical questions and also talk about various virtues including charity in the society
Rigvedic books 2-7 are the oldest and shortest also called family books
1028 hymns deal with deities including Agni, Indra and are attributed and dedicated to a sage rishi
The ninth Rigvedic book/mandala is solely dedicated to Soma
The meters used to form hymns are Gayatri, Anushtubh, Trishtubh, and Jagati (Trishtubh and Gayatri are most important)

The Rig Veda (The Book of Mantra): The Rig Veda is a collection of inspired songs or hymns and is a main source of information on the Rig Vedic civilization. It is the oldest book in any Indo-European language and contains the earliest form of all Sanskrit mantras, dating back to 1800 BCE- 1100 BCE, some scholars date it back to 12000 BCE - 4000 BCE. The Rig- Vedic 'Samhita' or collection of mantras consists of 1,017 (some say 1028) hymns or 'suttas', covering about 10,600 stanzas, divided into eight 'stakes,' each having eight 'Adhayayas' or chapters, which are sub-divided into various groups. The hymns are the work of many authors or seers, called 'rishis,' namely Atri, Kanwa, Vashistha, Vishwamitra, Jamadagni, Gotama, and Bharadwaja. The Rig Veda accounts in detail for the social, religious, political, and economic background of the Rig-Vedic civilization. The Sama Veda, Yajur Veda, and Atharva Veda were compiled after the age of the Rig Veda and are ascribed to the Vedic period.

Samaveda: Known as the Veda of melodies and chants, Samaveda dates back to 1200-800 BCE. This Veda is related to public worship. The key features of Samaveda are given in the table below:

Features of Samaveda
There are 1549 verses (except 75 verses, all have been taken from Rigveda)
There are two Upanishads embedded in Samaveda – Chandogya Upanishad and Kena Upanishad
The Samaveda is considered the root of Indian classical music and dance
It is considered the storehouse of the melodious chants
Though it has fewer verses than Rigveda, however, its texts are larger
There are three recensions of the text of the Samaveda – Kauthuma, Raṇayaniya, and Jaimaniya
Samaveda is categorized into two parts – Part I includes melodies called Gana and Part II includes three verses book called Archika.
Samaveda Samhita is not meant to be read as a text, it is like a musical score sheet that must be heard

The Sama Veda (The Book of Song): Sama Veda is purely a liturgical collection of melodies ('saman'). The hymns in the Sama Veda were used as musical notes that were almost completely drawn from the Rig Veda. Hence, its text is a reduced version of the Rig Veda. Therefore it can be said that Rig Veda is the word, Sama Veda is the song or the meaning; if Rig Veda is the knowledge, Sama Veda is its realization; if Rig Veda is the wife, Sama Veda is her husband.

Yajurveda: Stands to mean 'Worship Knowledge', Yajurveda dates back to 1100-800 BCE. It compiles ritual-offering mantras/chants. These chants were offered by the priest alongside a person who used to perform a ritual. Key features of Yajurveda are given below:

Features of Yajurveda
It has two types – Krishna (Black/Dark) and Shukla (White/Bright)
Krishna Yajurveda has an un-arranged, unclear, motley collection of verses
Shukla Yajurveda has arranged clear verses
The oldest layer of Yajurveda has 1875 verses mostly taken up from Rigveda
The middle layer of the Veda has Satapatha Brahmana which is a commentary of Shukla Yajurveda
The youngest layer of Yajurveda consists of various Upanishads – Brihadaranyaka Upanishad, the Isha Upanishad, the Taittiriya Upanishad, the Katha Upanishad, the Shvetashvatara Upanishad, and the Maitri Upanishad
Vajasaneyi Samhita is the Samhita in the Shukla Yajurveda
There are four surviving recensions of the Krishna Yajurveda – Taittiriya saṃhita, Maitrayani saṃhita, Kaṭha saṃhita, and Kapisthala saṃhita

The Yajur Veda (The Book of Ritual): The Yajur Veda was made to meet the demands of a ceremonial religion.

The Yajur Veda served as a practical guidebook for the priests who executed sacrificial acts while muttering simultaneously the prose prayers and the sacrificial formulae ('yajus'). It is similar to ancient Egypt's "Book of the Dead."

Atharvaveda: Stands to mean a tatpurusha compound of Atharvan, an ancient sage, and knowledge (Atharvan + knowledge), it dates back to 1000-800 BCE. Key features of Atharvaveda are given table.

Features of Atharvaveda
The daily procedures of life are very well enumerated in this Veda
It has 730 hymns/Suktas, 6000 mantras, and 20 books
Paippalada and the Saunakiya are two surviving recensions of Atharvaveda
Called a Veda of magical formulas, it includes three primary Upanishads – the Mundaka Upanishad, the Mandukya Upanishad, and the Prashna Upanishad
The 20 books are arranged by the length of the hymns they contain
Unlike Samaveda where hymns are borrowed from Rigveda, hymns of Atharvaveda are unique
This Veda contains hymns many of which were charms and magic spells that are meant to be pronounced by the person who seeks some benefit.

The Atharva Veda (The Book of Spell): The last of the Vedas, This is completely different from the other three Vedas and is next in importance to the Rig Veda about history and sociology. A different spirit pervades this Veda. Its hymns are more diverse than the Rig Veda and are also simpler in language. Many scholars do not consider it part of the Vedas at all. The Atharva Veda consists of spells and charms prevalent at its time and portrays a clearer picture of the Vedic society.

Origin, Author, and Structure of Veda (Origin of the Vedas): It is difficult to say when the earliest portions of the Vedas came into existence. As the ancient Hindus seldom kept any historical record of their religious, literary, and political realization, it is difficult to determine the origin period of the Vedas with precision. Historians provide us with many guesses but none are guaranteed to be precise. It is thought, though, that the earliest Vegas may date back to roughly 1700 BCE which is the late Bronze Age. Who Wrote the Vedas?: Tradition has it that humans did not compose the revered compositions of the Vedas, but that God taught the Vedic hymns to the sages, who then handed them down through generations by word of mouth. Another tradition suggests that the hymns were "revealed," to the sages. The formal documentation of Vedas was done mainly by Vyasa Krishna Dwaipayana around the time of Lord Krishna (c. 1500 BC).

Each of the four Vedas has four subdivisions:

(a) ***Samhitas*** (mantras and benedictions),

(b) ***Aranyakas*** (text on rituals, ceremonies, sacrifices, and symbolic sacrifices),

(c) ***Brahmanas*** ((commentaries on rituals, ceremonies, and sacrifices), and

(d) ***Upanishads*** (texts discussing meditation, philosophy, and spiritual knowledge).

Vedas are śruti (what is heard), distinguishing them from other religious texts, which are called ***smṛti*** (what is remembered). Vedas have been orally transmitted since the

2nd millennium BCE with the help of elaborate mnemonic techniques.

Structure of Vedas: The collection of mantras or hymns is called the Samhita. The Brahmanas are ritualistic texts that include precepts and religious duties. Each Veda has several Brahmanas attached to it. The Aranyakas (forest texts) intend to serve as objects of meditation for ascetics who live in forests and deal with mysticism and symbolism. *The Upanishads form the concluding portions of the Veda and are therefore called the "Vedanta" or the end of the Veda. The Upanishads contain the essence of Vedic teachings.*

Veda is the Mother of all Scriptures: Although the Vedas are seldom read or understood today, they no doubt form the bedrock of the universal religion or "Sanatana Dharma" that all Hindus follow. The Upanishads, however, are read by serious students of religious tradition and spirituality in all cultures and are regarded as principal texts within the body of mankind's wisdom traditions. Vedas have guided our religious direction for ages and will continue to do so for generations to come. And they will forever remain the most comprehensive and universal of all ancient Hindu scriptures.

Sub-divisions of Vedas

Samhitas (collection) are collections of mantras. In some contexts, the term Veda is used to refer only to these Samhitas. These oldest Vedic texts were composed between circa 1500–900 BCE (Rig Veda). The Samhitas contain invocations to deities like Indra and Agni. All the Vedic mantras consist of some 89,000 padas (metrical feet), of which 72,000 occur in the four Samhitas. The Brahmanas are prose texts each of which is associated with one of the Samhitas. The Brahmanas were completed in 700 BCE. The Brahmanas may either form separate texts or can be partly integrated into the text of the Samhitas. They may also include the Aranyakas and Upanishads.

The *Aranyakas,* "forest treaties", were composed of people who meditated in the woods as recluses and are the third part of the Vedas. The texts contain discussions and interpretations of ceremonies, from ritualistic to symbolic views. It is frequently read in the secondary literature.

Upanishads composed between 800 BCE and the end of the Vedic period are largely philosophical works, some in dialogue form. They are the foundation of Hindu philosophical thought and its diverse traditions. They alone are widely known, and the central ideas of the Upanishads are still influencing Hinduism.

The Brahmanas, Aranyakas, and Upanishads, among other things, interpret and discuss the Samhitas in philosophical and metaphorical ways to explore abstract concepts such as the Absolute (Brahman), and the soul or the self (Aatma), introducing Vedanta philosophy.

Vedas are śruti ("what is heard"), distinguishing them from other religious texts, which are called smṛti ("what is remembered"). Among the widely known śrutis include the Vedas and their embedded texts - the Samhitas, the Upanishads, the Brahmanas, and the Aranyakas. Some of the well-known smṛtis include Bhagavad Gita, BhagavataPurana, and the epics Ramayana and Mahabharata

In the Hindu Epic Mahabharata, the creation of Vedas is credited to Brahma. The Vedic hymns themselves assert that they were skilfully created by Rishis (sages), after inspired creativity, just as a carpenter builds a chariot. The oldest part of the Rig Veda

Samhita was orally composed in north-western India (Punjab) between c. 1500 and 1200 BCE, while book 10 of the Rig Veda and the other Samhitas were composed between 1200 and 900 BCE more eastward, between the Yamuna and the Ganges rivers, the heartland of Aryavarta and the Kuru Kingdom (c. 1200 – c. 900 BCE). *Vyasa is the compiler of the Vedas, who arranged the four kinds of mantras into four Samhitas (Collections). The Vedic period spanned from the middle of the 2nd to mid-1st millennium BCE, or the Late Bronze Age and the Iron Age.*

The Vedas were orally transmitted since their composition in the Vedic period for several millennia from father to son or from the teacher (Guru) to the student (Shishya), believed to be initiated by the Vedic rishis who heard the primordial sounds. Only this tradition, embodied by a living teacher, can teach the correct pronunciation of the sounds and explain hidden meanings. In the transmission of the Samhitas, the emphasis is on the phonology of the sounds (śabda) and not on the meaning (artha) of the mantras. At the end of the Vedic period, the original meaning had become obscure for ordinary people. The words of the mantras are by themselves sacred and do not constitute linguistic utterances. By reciting mantras the cosmos is regenerated. As long as the purity of the sounds is preserved, the recitation of the mantras will be efficacious, irrespective of whether their discursive meaning is understood by human beings.

The *Vedas,* Vedic rituals, and its ancillary sciences were part of the curriculum at the ancient universities of Taxila, Nalanda, and Vikramashila. Veda can be interpreted in three ways, giving the truth about God, dharma, and para brahman. The pūrva-kāṇda (karma-kanda), part of the Veda dealing with ritual, gives knowledge of dharma that brings satisfaction. The Uttarakanda (or jnana-kanda) part of the Veda dealing with the knowledge of the absolute, gives knowledge of Parabrahma, which fulfils all of our desires.

In *Vedic* learning, priority has been given to recitation over the interpretation of the Samhitas. Vedic knowledge was first perceived by the rishis and munis. Only the perfect language of the Vedas, in contrast to ordinary speech, can reveal these truths, which were preserved by committing them to memory. Realization of Truth and the knowledge of paramatman as revealed to the rishis are the real aim of Vedic learning, and not the mere recitation of texts.

The four Vedas were transmitted in various śākhās (branches, schools) with each school representing an ancient community of a particular area, or kingdom. Some of these texts have survived, but most of them are lost and are yet to be found. Rigveda which survives in modern times, for example, is in only one extremely well-preserved school of Śåkalya, from a region called Videha, in modern north Bihar. Each of the four Vedas was shared by numerous schools, but revised, interpolated, and adapted locally, in and after the Vedic period. Some texts were revised into the modern era, raising a significant debate on parts of the text that are believed to have been corrupted at a later date.

The Indian culture ensured that these texts were transmitted from generation to generation with inordinate fidelity. The texts were subsequently "proofread" by comparing the different recited versions. The Vedas were orally transmitted by memorization for many generations and were written down for the first time around 1200 BCE. However, all printed editions of the Vedas that survive in modern times are likely the versions existing in about the 16th century CE.

In the Rigveda Samhita hymns are dedicated to deities. The books were composed by poets from different priestly groups over several centuries. Rigveda is structured based on clear principles that begin with a small book addressed to Agni, Indra, Soma, and other gods decreasing the total number of hymns in each deity collection. The Samaveda Samhita consists of 1549 stanzas and is taken almost entirely from the Rigveda.

The *Yajurveda Samhita* (c.1200-800 BCE) consists of prose mantras. It is a compilation of ritual offering formulas that were said by a priest while an individual performed ritual actions such as those before the yajna fire. The core text of the Yajurveda falls within the classical Mantra period of Vedic Sanskrit at the end of the 2nd millennium BCE, younger than Rigveda, and roughly contemporary with the Atharvaveda. The earliest and most ancient layer of the Yajurveda Samhita includes 1,875 verses. Unlike Samaveda which is almost entirely based on Rigveda mantras and structured as songs, the Yajurveda samhitas are in prose, and they are different from earlier Vedic texts. The Yajur Veda has been the primary source of information about sacrifices during Vedic times and associated rituals.

The *Artharvaveda* Samhita has 760 hymns, out of which 160 hymns are in common with the Rigveda. Most of the verses are metrical, but some sections are in prose. Atharvaveda was not considered a Veda in the Vedic era and was accepted as a Veda in the late 1st millennium BCE. It was compiled probably around 900 BCE, although some of its material may go back to the time of the Rigveda. The Atharvaveda is sometimes called the "Veda of magical formulas". The Atharva Veda has been a primary source for information about Vedic culture, the customs, and beliefs, the aspirations and frustrations of everyday Vedic life, as well as those associated with kings and governance. The text also includes hymns dealing with the major rituals of marriage and cremation.

The *Brahmanas* are commentaries, explanations of proper methods, and meanings of Vedic Samhita rituals in the four Vedas. They also incorporate myths, legends, and in some cases philosophy. Each regional Vedic shakha (school) has its operating manual like Brahmana text, most of which has been lost. Now 19 Brahmana texts have survived, two associated with the Rigveda, six with the Yajurveda, ten with Samaveda, and one with Atharavaveda (between 900 BCE to 700 BCE).

The *Aranayakas* layer of the Vedas includes rituals and discussions of symbolic meta-rituals. Some include chapters of Upanishads within them. With regards to the origin of the word Aranyakas, one theory holds that these texts were meant to be studied in a forest, while the other holds that the name came from those in the Vanaprastha (retired, forest-dwelling) stage of their life, according to the historic age-based Ashrama system of human life.

The Upanishads reflect the last composed layer of texts in the Vedas. They are commonly referred to as Vedānta, interpreted to mean either the "last chapters, parts of the Vedas" or "the object, the highest purpose of the Veda". The central concern of the Upanishads is the connections "between parts of the human organism and cosmic realities." The Upanishads intend to create a hierarchy of connected and dependent realities, evoking a sense of unity of "the separate elements of the world and human experience compressing them into a single form." The concepts of Brahman, the Ultimate Reality from which everything arises, and Ātman, the essence of the individual, are central ideas in the Upanishads and knowing the correspondence between Ātman and

Brahman as "the fundamental principle which shapes the world" permits the creation of an integrative vision of the whole. The Upanishads are the foundation of Hindu philosophical thought and its diverse traditions, and of the Vedic corpus. They alone are widely known, and the central ideas of the Upanishads have influenced the diverse traditions of Hinduism.

Aranyakas are sometimes identified as Karma-Kanda (ritualistic section), while the Upanishads are identified as Jnana-Kanda (spirituality section). In an alternate classification, the early part of Vedas is called Samhitas and the commentary is called the Brahmanas which together are identified as the ceremonial karma-kanda, while Aranyakas and Upanishads are referred to as the jnana-kanda.

The *Vedang* was developed towards the end of the Vedic period, around or after the middle of the 1st millennium BCE. These auxiliary fields of Vedic studies emerged because the language of the Vedas, composed centuries earlier, became too archaic to the people of that time. The Vedangas were sciences that focused on helping understand and interpret the Vedas that had been composed many centuries earlier. Vedangas developed as ancillary studies for the Vedas, but its insights into meters, the structure of sound and language, grammar, linguistic analysis, and other subjects influenced post-Vedic studies, arts, culture, and various schools of Hindu philosophy.

The term Upaveda (applied knowledge) is used in traditional literature to designate the subjects of certain technical works. There are four Upavedas: (i) Archery (Dhanurveda), associated with the Yajurveda, (ii) Architecture (Sthapatyaveda), associated with the Rigveda, (iii) Music and sacred dance (Gāndharvaveda), associated with the Samaveda and (iv) Medicine (Āyurveda), associated with the Atharvaveda.

The Puranas

The Puranas is a vast encyclopedia of Indian literature covering a wide range of topics, particularly myths, legends, and other traditional stories. Several of these texts are named after major Hindu deities such as Vishnu, Shiva, and Devi. There are 18 Maha-Puranas (Great Puranas) and 18 Upa-Puranas (Minor Puranas), with over 400,000 verses. Puranas have influenced the Hindu culture. Bhagavata Purana is among the most celebrated and popular texts in the Puranic genre and is non-dualistic. Puranic literature generated the Bhakti movement in India.

Many religious Hindus implicitly acknowledge the authority of the Vedas. Hindu reform movements such as Arya Samaj and BrahmoSamaj accepted the authority of Vedas. Some post-Vedic texts, including the Mahabharata, and certain Puranas, refer to themselves as the "fifth Veda". The earliest reference to such a "fifth Veda" is found in the Chandogya Upanishad in hymn 7.1.2.

According to scholars, the Upanishads may be regarded as the end of the Vedas in different senses:

- Vedanta is the pursuit of knowledge into Brahman and the Ātman).
- The Upaniṣads, Bhagavadgītā, and the Brahma Sūtras constitute the basis of Vedanta.
- Scripture is the main reliable source of knowledge (Pramana).
- Brahman - Ishvara (God) exists as the unchanging material cause and instrumental cause of the world.
- The self (Ātman) or Jiva) is the agent of its acts (karma) and the recipient of the consequences of these actions.

- It believes in rebirth (samsara) and the desirability of release from the cycle of rebirths (moksha) is the essence.

The contents of the Vedas are in the form of a collection of mantras. The word Mantra means 'that which protects when repeated and reflected upon'. The Rig Veda mantras are called 'Rik' meaning hymns or stanzas of verses metrically set to convey a definite meaning. The Sama Veda mantras are called 'Saman' meaning chants while Yajur Veda mantras are called 'Yajus' meaning sacrificial sentences. These collections are called Samhitas. They bring out the purpose of a Veda in the shape of mantras, methodically arranged. Samhita means that which is collected and arranged. The flow of thought from the Samhitas to Brahmanas to Aranyakas to Upanishads is the indication of the process of evolution of Hindu religion over the centuries".

Many times we come across terms like Sooktas, Sootras, and Shakhas that need to be understood, before going forward.

Sooktas, Sootras, and Shakhas
(Internet Source: www.esamskriti.com)

Sookta: Verses (Rik or hymns) are composed to create the whole of the Rig Veda Samhita. These verses are the praising stanzas of different Devatas. Later, these verses were known as Slokas. Each verse is a mantra, while several of these constitute a Sookta (e.g. Narayana Sooktam, Sri Sooktam, and others).

Sootra: Generally a sutra means the use of minimum words to project a maximum dimension of thought. A sutra is like a short formula that means a lot without any ambiguity. The best examples are the famous Patanjali Yoga Sootra, Narada Bhakti Sootra, Shandilya Bhakti Sootra, Brahma Sutra

(Vedanta or Sariraka Sootra) that has the mystifying way of spelling out in the Upanishads.

Shakha: The Vedic traditions started branching off due to the vast geographical location of the country, adopting the diverse cultural heritage of the priests, ritual specialization, languages, and traditional disputes. Each of the principal sages with several disciples started editing the Vedic mantras to suit the rites that they needed to perform, keeping in mind the influence of the local culture. The vastness of the subject to be covered by a student for achieving his spiritual goal may be another reason for the division of Vedas into many Shakhas.

The process of Vedic learning starts with (i) First studying and recitation of the hymns (Samhita), (ii) Followed by a performance of Yajnas (Brahmana), then (iii)An inquiry into the rationale behind the performance of these Yajnas (Aranyaka), and (iv) Finally, an inquiry into 'Paramatma Tattwa' and attaining its experience (Upanishad).

Mastering these tasks was almost impossible for any student. Then it was simplified in which it was required to learn only an optimum number for each purpose. Each Shakha thus contains many mantras under each category of Samhita, Brahmana, Aranyaka, and Upanishad as would enable a seeker to accomplish liberation."

Vedas and Upanishads – Similarities and Dissimilarities Similarities between Vedas and Upanishads:

Upanishads are part of the Vedas, therefore an Upanishad can be a Veda, but a Veda cannot be an Upanishad.

Difference between Vedas and Upanishads: Never confuse that Vedas and Upanishads are the same. To avoid confusion the following major differences are worth knowing.

1. The Vedas were composed from 1200 to 400 BCE, through different stages of development. Upanishads were written between 700 to 400 BCE.
2. Upanishads are a sub-category of any of the four Vedas and are the last section of any of them.
3. The Samhita, Brahmana, and the Aranyaka are the three other parts contained in the Vedas that deal with the ritualistic aspects of life such as the conduct of rituals and sacrifice, and the strictness of personal conduct. While Upanishads, as the fourth part, deal with what is considered the highest knowledge and is philosophical.
4. Vedas were written to preserve the details of different traditions, sacrificial uses, ritualistic practices, ceremonies, and philosophical thoughts. It was meant to teach and be referred to in external practices. Upanishads are the written form of philosophical thoughts from a variety of men and women, focused mainly on spiritual enlightenment, and disavowing the individual's identification with the physical body.
5. Each Veda has its Upanishad section. Amongst these sections 12 Upanishads are attributed with great authority; however, there have been more than 200 Upanishads discovered to date. Each Upanishad is associated with a certain Veda.

Veda is our earliest literary record and is the most sacred book of Hindus. It is also the original scriptures of Hindu teachings, containing spiritual knowledge from all aspects of life. Since it is the oldest record of any civilisation, we ought to know it. Veda discusses the universal truth and therefore it is as relevant today as it was millenniums before. The Upanishads are the concluding portions of each Veda and are therefore called the "Vedanta". Puranas are the vast encyclopedia of Indian literature covering a wide range of topics, such as myths, legends, and other traditional stories. Some post-Vedic texts, including Ramayana *and the Mahabharata, along with other Puranas, refer to themselves as the "fifth Veda".*

The inclusion of this chapter on Veda here is just to impart a thin knowledge about the topic to the readers with discussion on its broad structures so that we do not feel sorry for not knowing anything about Veda. It is beyond my/our capacity to understand Veda.

CHAPTER - 13

ॐ *Earth is our temporary home, where both good and evil souls stay together. The number of evil souls on Earth is far higher than the limited good ones and therefore Earth is a perfect place for testing and training and to quickly shedding off karma. Souls in the astral and causal world have still some residual karma. Since all the souls in these realms are good, it takes a very long time for these dwellers to shed off the karma in those realms. To shorten the journey time to go to higher realms, many souls from the astral and causal world also prefer to take birth on earth to do good karma and thus quicken the time of their progress to higher realms. However, many of them fall as they are greatly influenced by the materialistic attraction once born on earth.*

To help the earth dwellers for their spiritual progress, some Great souls from the higher realms take birth in this world for spreading, God's messages of peace and influence people for their spiritual growth. They have very high spiritual powers. Out of the list of 235 great masters who have taken birth here and contributed significantly to the spiritual growth of mankind the works of nine great masters are discussed in brief in the next chapter. However, I believe that there are uncountable saints-masters, who have taken birth on earth and gone unnoticed. My highest reverence to all these great masters.

Chapter - 13

The Great Masters

Purpose of Sacred Souls Born on Earth

When the world is controlled by tyrant rulers or the evil people and their bad actions outweigh good actions, then some great masters from higher realms or other higher exoplanets take birth on earth to protect the people with the direction of the supreme force, 'the God.' That is why time and again, great souls such as Christ, Prophets, Lord Rama, Krishna, Buddha, Mahaveer, and others have come to earth to spread peace and protect the people. Besides, the earth is never free from great saints. There are many great saints, who live in the caves of the mighty Himalayas and lead simple life with very high spiritual potential. They do not like public appearances and have limited disciples.

This chapter, introduction to some of the great masters and elevated souls are presented out of the thousands of such great souls who have gone unnoticed as they have maintained a low profile. They have probably crossed the cycle of rebirths by now due to their very high stage of spiritual elevation. If someone is interested to know the list the following links are helpful.

A guru is characterized as a "teacher, spiritual adviser, godman," by author David Smith. A conventional initiation procedure known as diksha is required to gain the title of guru, during which the participant is given a Mantra or sacred Sanskrit phrase.

Mahavatar Babaji

The ageless, formless, and eternally young Mahavatar Babaji is respectfully addressed by various names by their endless disciples. Facts about his birth, identity, and life are still unknown. He is the primal, and immortal without the bounds of time and space. He is the unparallel among all saints and sages and is the supreme one. He proposes himself as a compassionate, beautiful, and luminous form guiding the people along the path of God.

Babaji Maharaj mostly remains in deep meditation in the dense forests and caves of the Himalayas, while keeping a watchful observation on earnest seekers on their paths to God. His appearances and disappearances are miraculous which are described by his disciples Lahiri Mahashaya, Swami Pranavananda, Swami Shri Yukteswar, and Hamsa Swami Kevalananda. Paramahamsa Yogananda, and Paramahamsa Hariharananda. He has uniquely guided them to his disciples on the path of divinity.

Lahiri Mahashaya learned the liberating techniques of Kriya Yoga from Mahavatar Babaji and was blessed with limitless divine power by which he entered the deepest level of the Nirvikalpa samadhi. For seven days he remained the deathless realm of Brahma Loka.

Fig 13.1 : Mahavatar Babaji

Following the instruction of Babaji Maharaj, Lahiri Mahasaya returned to the world and performed his worldly duties as an ideal yogi householder. He demonstrated that liberation for worldly people and sannyasis are alike if one earnestly tries for God-realization. Babaji taught that liberation was no longer the monopoly of a few select sannyasis. People leading a normal family life could attain Godhood without abandoning their duties. One should assiduously seek God at every moment and during all activities to achieve enlightenment.

Once an American devotee was searching for Babaji along the inaccessible areas of the Himalayan mountains. Upon seeing Babaji, the foreign devotee was extremely happy. The devotee requested Babaji Maharaj to accept him as his disciple, but Babaji Maharaj immediately declined. The American devotee suddenly jumped from the mountain. Seeing this, Babaji Maharaj instructed his disciples to collect the dead body. With Babaji's divine touch, the American devotee came back to life. Later he was accorded the rare privilege of being Babaji Maharaj's disciple.

Babaji once in Kumbha mela addressed Swami Shri Yukteswar, the dear and close disciple of Lahiri Mahashaya, as "Swamiji." He then instructed Yukteswar to write a book on the essence of Indian metaphysics with that of the West. He promised to meet him again on the day the manuscript of the book was ready. Indeed, Babaji Maharaj visited him on the day the assigned work was completed. There are ample examples of Babaji suddenly appearing to his devotees and asking for their services for the betterment of mankind.

Kriya Yoga had spread to the West through the efforts of Paramahamsa Yogananda and Paramahamsa Hariharananda, under the direction of their Guru Swami Shri Yukteswar. It helped many with their spiritual grooming. Babaji appeared before Paramahamsa Yogananda before Yogananda Ji started his journey to the West. Babaji also appeared before Brahmachari Paramahamsa Hariharananda in Puri Karar Ashram in 1949, in his earnest prayer for a glimpse of him. He was pleased with Paramahamsa Hariharanandaji's high spiritual attainment which inspired him to visit the West to propagate the Kriya Yoga.

Early Life and Astonishing Facts: It is said that he was born in Parangipettai, in Tamil Nadu. Most people believe that he was born around 203 AD. In his book, "The Second Coming of Christ", Yogananda mentions that Christ visited India once, and met Mahavatar Baba; this makes his age around 1800 years believing that he is still alive.

Even today, Mahavatar Baba looks like a young person of 24- 25 years, snowy white complexion, long shoulder-length hair, and sharp facial features. It is said that when he sits in "padmasana", he is about 5 feet tall. Usually, he spends his maximum time in "Samadhi" and the rest of his time giving guidance to his followers and other sadhus.

Govindan stated in his book that Babaji's father was the temple priest in his village. Sometime later he was kidnapped and sold as a slave. But the person who bought him was a very kindhearted man, and he set Nagaraj (Babaji's childhood name) free. After his freedom from slavery, Babaji at the young age of 15 years joined a group of wandering sadhus.

Meeting and Learning from Agastya Muni: Govindan mentions in his book that Nagaraj made a tough journey to Sri Lanka and met Siddha Bhogarnath. On the advice of Bhogarnath, he met Agastya Muni with much dedication. He learned the secrets of Kriya Kundalini Pranayam. After spending 18 months on the pilgrimage at Badrinath, practicing yogic kriya taught to him by Agastya and Bhogarnathji; Babaji finally attained Self- realisation. It is believed that these instances were revealed by Babaji himself.

Rajnikanth Became His Disciple: Rajnikanth, a famous film actor of India, claims that he became familiar with the Babaji after reading Yoganandas 'An Autobiography of a Yogi'. As he was reading the book a light emanated from the picture of Babaji in the book and told him to sit in a particular position. After he sat in the said position and started reading the book, a spark of light entered his body. He became an ardent follower of Babaji and began following the practice of Kriya Yoga. Rajnikant says this had a very positive effect on his life.

The Present-Day Belief: In Sri M's autobiography, he mentioned that Babaji was Lord Shiva, who mentions that Babaji changed his form to Lord Shiva.

Babaji has the powers of eternal life. Yogananda states in his autobiography that "Babaji is roaming for hundreds of years in the remote Himalayan regions in India through the powers of his Kriya Yoga; but can only be seen in person by a very small number of people."

He has been bestowed with the Honours such as "Deathless Guru", MahaYogi, Shiva Baba, and so on. He is ever-present and eternal. According to Lahiri Mahasaya, "Whenever anyone utters with reverence the name of Babaji, that devotee attracts an instant spiritual blessing." Babaji lives in the Himalayas with a few highly advanced students. He is the first in this line of gurus, of unknown age. In his Autobiography of a Yogi, Yogananda gives the following description of "the deathless guru".

Fig 13.2: Babaji and his chain of disciples

The deathless guru looks to be no older than a twenty-five-year-old and has no signs of aging on his physique. Babaji is a tall, fair-skinned man with a medium frame. His attractive, powerful body emits a noticeable radiance. His long, glossy hair is copper in colour, and he has dark, serene, and sensitive eyes. The master rarely eats since his body is undecaying and does not need food. Sometimes he takes fruits or rice cooked in milk as a social courtesy to visiting disciples.

In a vision in 1920, Paramhansa Yogananda received the order to represent the Kriya Yoga teachings in the West. Yogananda decided to fervently pray to God to gain God's confirmation and blessing for his next mission. In answer,

Yogananda saw Babaji personally, who bestowed his blessings and assured him of complete safety. "You are the one I have chosen to spread the message of Kriya Yoga in the West. Long ago I met your guru Yukteswar at a Kumbha Mela; I told him then I would send you to him for training... Kriya Yoga, the scientific technique of God-realization, will ultimately spread in all lands, and aid in harmonizing the nations through man's personal, transcendental perception of the Infinite Father."

Lahiri Mahasaya – The Disciple Follower (30/9/1828-26/9/1895)

Lahiri Mahasaya was a great yogi and disciple of Mahavatar Babaji. Many claim that he was the only disciple of Babaji, the rest being just the followers of Nagaraj Baba. He was selected by Babaji in 1861 to revive the Kriya Yoga science to the people.

A distinct man among the holy gurus of India, he was a householder, taking due care of his family; and also working as an accountant for the government. Unlike other hermits and saints who lived in temples or monasteries, he lived with his family at his home in Varanasi.

For his exceptional way of living as a householder Yogi, he became a spiritual inspirational master of numerous followers. Because of his advanced teachings of Kriya, he made many disciples, to name a few Panchanan Bhattacharya and Swami Sri Yukteswar Giri.

Early Life: Lahiri Mahasaya was born in a remote village in the Nadia district near Krishnagar, Bengal on September 30, 1828. His childhood name was Shyama Charan. He frequently appeared seated in the yogi position beneath the sands, with his entire body concealed except his head. Every one of his friends adored Shyama Charan because he was a nice, compassionate, and courageous young man. The nearby Jalangi River changed its course in 1833 and merged with the Ganges thus destroying the Lahiri estate. The father Gaur Mohan Lahiri immediately built a Shiva temple in Benares, the family moved there from Nadia. He ran his household according to the principles of Vedic discipline, with regular ritual worship, charitable deeds, and biblical study.

He was fair and open-minded, yet he did not dismiss the positive trend of contemporary thought. Srimati Kashi Moni and Shyama Charan Lahiri were wed in 1846. Kashi Moni, a role model for Indian housewives, enthusiastically performed her household responsibilities as well as her duty to help visitors and the underprivileged. Tincouri and Ducouri, two pious sons, were from their blessings of the union.

Lahiri Mahasaya joined the English government's Military Engineering Department in 1851 at the age of 23, taking a position as an accountant. Throughout his service, he obtained numerous promotions. He was thus successful in the small human drama where he played his assigned duty as an office worker in the world, in addition to being a master in God's eyes.

Lahiri Mahasaya witnessed the accomplishment of the reason for which he had been reincarnated on earth in his thirty-third year. Around Ranikhet, he encountered his wonderful master, Babaji, and received his Kriya Yoga initiation from him. It was a heavenly reunion of two people who had known each other in previous lives.

Fig 13.3: Sri Lahiri Mahasaya

Lahiri Mahasaya experienced an awakened blessing that caused him to become enveloped in a spiritual aura of divine understanding that would never leave him. This lucky occurrence didn't just benefit him; it was also fortune for the entire human race, many of whom later had the opportunity to benefit from Kriya's soul-awakening powers. To do this task, Lahiri Mahasaya returned to his house in Banaras. He was the first to transmit the long-forgotten Kriya science and created the groundwork for the modern Indian yoga revival, which started in the latter half of the nineteenth century and is still going strong today.

Paramahansa Yogananda wrote in Autobiography of a Yogi: *"As the fragrance of flowers cannot be suppressed, so Lahiri Mahasaya, quietly living as an ideal householder, could not hide his innate glory. Devotee-bees from every part of India began to seek the divine nectar of the liberated master. He harmoniously balanced the life of the great householder-guru and became the inspiration of thousands of men and women."* He is reverenced as a Yogavatar or incarnation of Yoga.

Paramahansa Yogananda's parents were disciples of Lahiri Mahasaya and blessed "Little mother, thy son will be a yogi. As a spiritual engine, he will carry many souls to God's kingdom." Lahiri Mahasaya predicted: "About fifty years after my passing, an account of my life will be written because of a deep interest in Yoga that will arise in the West. The message of Yoga will encircle the globe. It will aid in establishing the brotherhood of man: unity based on humanity's direct perception of the one Father."

People from many origins, such as Christians, Muslims, and members of lower castes, were initiated by Lahiri Mahasaya. He was open to everyone seeking spiritual direction. He had a family, was married, and worked as an accountant. Lahiri authored several spiritual writings, such as commentary on the Bhagavad Gita. It is said that before he died, Lahiri gathered his disciples and told them, "I am going home, be comforted; I shall rise again." On September 26, 1895, in Banaras, he attained enlightenment. He intentionally left his body to enter Maha Samadhi. In America, fifty years later, his prophecy came true when Paramahansa Yogananda's book Autobiography of a Yogi, which includes a lovely portrayal of Lahiri Mahasaya's life, was inspired by the growing popularity of yoga in the West. *"You have been chosen to bring spiritual solace through Kriya Yoga to numerous earnest seekers. The millions who are encumbered by family ties and heavy worldly duties will take new heart from you, a householder like themselves. You must guide them to see that the highest yogic attainments are not barred to the family man… From your balanced life, they will understand that liberation is dependent on inner, rather than outer, renunciations."*

Sri Yukteswar Giri (10 May 1855 – 9 March 1936)

Known as Priya Nath Karar in early school days, the great Indian yogi was the guru of Paramahansa Yogananda and

Swami Satyananda Giri. Sri Yukteswar was born in Serampore, West Bengal on 10th May 1855. He was a great scholar of the Bhagavad Gita. He had mastered the Upanishads. He was also known as Kriya Yogi, a Vedic astrologer, an educator, an author, and an astronomer. He was a pupil of Varanasi's Lahiri Mahasaya. He was a great guru and had two ashrams, one in Serampore and the other in Puri, Odisha, where he altered his residence regularly while instructing students.

Priya Nath managed his family's land holdings to a large extent after the early death of his father. As a talented student, he joined Srirampur Christian Missionary College and began reading the Bible, which subsequently assisted him in writing the book "The Holy Science," which explores the relationship between the scientific concepts behind yoga and the Bible. He went to Calcutta Medical College as well. Priya Nath married after graduating from college, and they had a daughter. A few years after their wedding, his wife passed away.

In the 19th century, Sri Yukteswar was a progressive person. He established a "Satsang Sabha," the spiritual study group, held religious festivals throughout the year, and updated his analysis of the Vedic astrological yugas. His Kriya yoga pupils looked up to him throughout the Kolkata area because of his sharp mind and profound knowledge. He also frequently invited people from various social backgrounds to his ashrams to talk and share views on a variety of issues.

Satyananda and Yogananda were finally prepared for the demanding humanitarian work in India and America by rigorous training. Sri Yukteswar was considered by Yogananda as a Jnanavatar, or *"Incarnation of Wisdom."*

Priya Nath met Lahiri Mahasaya in 1884, who later served as his teacher and initiated him into the Kriya Yoga discipline. The following few years saw Sri Yukteswar spending a lot of time with his master. Sri Yukteswar met Mahavatar Babaji, the Guru of Lahiri Mahasaya, in 1894 while taking part in the Kumbha Mela in Allahabad. Babaji requested that Sri Yukteswar produce a book contrasting Hindu text and the Christian Bible. At that encounter, Sri Yukteswar was also given the title of "Swami" by Mahavatar Babaji. The required book was finished by Sri Yukteswar in 1894, and it was given the title *Kaivalya Darsanam*, or 'The Holy Science'.

At Serampore, Sri Yukteswar converted his sizable, two-story family home into an ashram called "Priyadham," where he lived alongside followers and students. Moreover, he founded the "Karar Ashram" in 1903 in the seashore city of Puri. Sri Yukteswar established Sadhu Sabha and trained students from these two ashrams.

Indian astrology (Jyotish) was one of Yukteswar's specialties, and he prescribed his students, advice on various astrological bangles and gemstones. He had a deep interest in science and astronomy as seen by the formulation of his Yuga theory in the book "The Holy Science."

Sri Mukunda Lal Ghosh, who would later become Sri Yukteswar's well-known student in 1910 and eventually propagated the Kriya Yoga teachings over the world as Paramahansa Yogananda, was one of the few long-term disciples he ever had.

Fig 13.4: Sri Sri Yogananda with his spiritual Guru Yukteswar

He first saw Lahiri Mahasaya Sri Shyamacharan at Kashi, Banaras, in 1884, who would become his Guru and received Kriya Yoga initiation from him. He continued to follow his Guru ever since and gave himself completely to meditation and Kriya practice while being close to and with Lahiri Mahasaya. He captured Lahiri Mahasaya's heart and thoughts, and as a sign of his exceptional regard, Lahiri Mahasaya referred to him as Priya (a loved one).

He went to the Kumbha Mela at Allahabad in 1894. On the way back, he first came across the famous Mahavatar Babaji, the Guru of Lahiri Mahasaya, who requested Sri Yukteswar to produce a book contrasting Hindu text with the Bible. On this occasion, Mahavatar Babaji also bestows the title of Swami on Sri Yukteswar.

The required book, Kaivalya Darsanam or The Holy Science, was finished by Sri Yukteswar in 1894. In it, he presented his interpretation of the Yuga theory. He demonstrated in the book that the world was ascending to the Dwapar Yuga (Electrical Era of Energy) based on astrological and biblical perspectives.

Mahavatar Babaji, as promised, favoured Sri Yukteswar and appeared before him as he emerged from his bath in the Ganga after meditating all night. Babaji refused to come to the ashram despite fervent requests by Sri Yukteswar. With joy, he rushed to the ashram and returned with milk and fruit to offer. But Babaji in the meanwhile vanished. When he could no longer find Babaji, Sri Yukteswar was disappointed and threw his offerings.

Sri Yukteswar translated the (i) Brahmacharya (celibacy), (ii) Grihastha (father of a family), (iii) Vanaprastha (life of solitude), and (iv) Sannyasa (renunciation) with the insight of four Purusarthas: dharma, artha, kama, and moksha in an illustrious, complete, and perfect way. The ancient sages practiced these four stages of Hindu life Scriptures.

Swami Sri Yukteswar entered Maha Samadhi on March 9, 1936, in his Karar Ashram in the holy town of Puri in eastern India. Swami Sri Yukteswar Giri himself indicated his departure in advance to his disciple Narayan. At this time, he was sitting in Shambhavi posture on Padmasana as usual. He ordered his disciple Narayan to support him. Sri Yukteswar Giri went into a state of the deepest Samadhi. He was calm and stable. He then consciously freed himself from his body. His disciple Narayan felt a slight pulsation from the chest of his Guru's body to the Brahmarandhra and also heard a very slow sound that resembled the sound OM. His disciple Narayan kept massaging his calm body for a long time.

As narrated by Yogananda, his resurrection before him in a Mumbai hotel after his mahasamadhi, recounting his stay in Hiranyaloka and repeatedly appearing before Paramahamsa Hariharananda and other disciples, fills the devotees with spiritual vibrations.

Teachings and Quotes of Sri Yukteswar Giri: (As available on the Internet Source: vedicfeed.com)

"Man's desire for material things is eternal; man is never fully satisfied and is following one goal after another. A man wants to achieve everything, and God can only provide him the lasting joy. External cravings take us away from our inner happiness and our inner heaven; they only give us false happiness. The lost inner heaven can be quickly returned by divine meditation."

Regarding the importance of the Guru/Teacher in our life. he said to Paramahansa Yogananda, "I will be your friend internally now whether your mental state is very good or not. If you make a mistake, I will still be your friend. At that point, you will need my friendship the most. Gurus are always with us (not physically but mentally and spiritually). The Gurus always extend a helping hand to us. He gives his disciples opportunities to progress by letting them ask questions."

"Just as hunger has a real purpose, but not gluttony, in the same way, nature has created the tendency of sensual passion only for the promotion of species, not to awaken lust. Destroy your wrong desires right now; otherwise, they will stick with you in your soul and subtle form even after leaving this physical body. It may not be easy to control the desires of your body, but your mind should regularly keep on opposing."

"If temptation invades you, then use your will, make it unbeatable, and analyse the temptation with your will. Be like a vast ocean in which all the rivers of your senses will quietly disappear. The lusts will awaken with new power each day and drown your inner peace with it. These lusts are like the holes in the reservoir that drain your life and soul into a desert of sensuality. The powerful impulse of these lusts is the greatest enemy of your happiness. Develop inner peace through your strong will and self-control."

"In 1894 Sri Yukteswar anticipated that the 20th century would be the period of great discoveries for humanity, during which we would understand that everything rests on one thing: energy. This was stated about 11 years before Einstein presented the famous formula $E = mc^2$ to the world. Sri Yukteswar believed that such discoveries would result from the influence of the energies of the Dwapar Yuga, knowing that at the beginning of each new Yuga, the human mentality changes radically."

Paramahansa Yogananda (Mukunda Lal Ghosh; 5/1/1893 – 7/3/ 1952)

His organisation, Self-Realization Fellowship (SRF)/Yogoda Satsanga Society (YSS) of India, introduced millions of people to the teachings of meditation and Kriya Yoga. He was a prominent Indian Hindu monk, yogi, and guru. He spent most of his final 32 years in America, bringing the art and science of Kriya Yoga to the West. He was dispatched to demonstrate the compatibility between the Eastern and Western religions and to teach a balance between Western material advancement and Indian spirituality as the foremost student of the Bengali yoga master Swami Sri Yukteswar Giri. Yoga experts refer to him as the "Father of Yoga in the West" because of his longstanding effect on the American yoga movement, particularly in the yoga culture of Los Angeles.

Yogananda arrived in Boston in 1920 and began a successful speaking tour before settling in Los Angeles in 1925. He was the first significant Indian teacher to immigrate to the United States and the first prominent Indian to be hosted in the White House (by President Calvin Coolidge in 1927). He established a monastic order, taught followers, went on teaching tours, purchased properties for his organisation in various California locations, and initiated thousands of people into Kriya Yoga over the following 25 years. SRF had centres over 100 locations in the US and India by 1952, and they still have organisations in almost all major US cities today. His "plain living and high thinking" principles attracted people from all backgrounds.

His book Autobiography of a Yogi, which has been listed as one of the "100 best spiritual books of the 20th Century," was initially published in 1946 and has since sold over four million copies. For his memorial, former Apple CEO Steve Jobs ordered 500 copies of the book, one for each guest. The book, which has seen numerous printings, is referred to as "the book that changed the lives of millions. "Awake: The Life of Yogananda", a documentary about him produced by the SRF, was made public in 2014. He is still a key player in Western spirituality today and is the most well-known and adored of all the Indian spiritual gurus who have immigrated to the West.

Yogananda was born into a Hindu Bengali Kayastha household in Gorakhpur, Uttar Pradesh, India. He was the second of four boys and the fourth of eight children born to Gyan Prabha Devi and Bhagwati Charan Ghosh, Vice president of the Bengal - Nagpur Railway. His mother passed away when he was only eleven years old, soon before his oldest brother Ananta was married. He made every attempt to locate an illuminated instructor who could lead him on his spiritual journey, but to no avail.

He first met Swami Sri Yukteswar Giri when he was 17 years old. Yogananda was informed by Sri Yukteswar that the great guru in their lineage, Mahavatar Babaji, had sent him to Yogananda with the specific global goal of spreading yoga. He received a Bachelor of Arts, or B.A., from Serampore College in 1915 after clearing his Intermediate Examination in Arts from the Scottish Church College, Calcutta. In 1917, Yogananda established a boys-only school at Dihika, West Bengal, fusing contemporary academic methods with yoga instruction and spiritual goals. The school moved to Ranchi a year later.

He was permitted by the American Unitarian Association to represent India in the Boston-based International Conference of Religious Liberals in 1920. Sri Yukteswar counselled him to go. He was in serious prayer when Mahavatar Babaji, the lineage's Great Guru, unexpectedly dropped by and informed him that he had been chosen to bring Kriya Yoga to the West. Confident and inspired, Yogananda quickly accepted the invitation to travel to Boston.

He left for the United States in August 1920 on a ship that arrived in the Boston area by the end of September. Early in October, after giving a well-received speech at the World Congress, he established the Self-Realization Fellowship (SRF) to spread his teachings on India's age-old yoga traditions and philosophy around the world. In the following four years, Yogananda lived in Boston. The spiritual and organisational focus of his expanding activity was the International Self-Realization Fellowship Centre that he founded in Los Angeles,

California, in 1925. He spent his whole life in the United States, from 1920 to 1952, except for a lengthy journey overseas in 1935–1936.

Together with two of his Western disciples, he travelled back to India in 1935 to see his master Sri Yukteswar Giri, and to aid in the founding of his Yogoda Satsanga Society of India. He experienced a touching reunion with his spiritual mentor Sri Yukteswar at Serampore. He also met with other individuals who piqued his interest, including C V Raman, the renowned physicist, Mahatma Gandhi, Anandamayi Ma, Giri Bala, an elderly yogi woman who survived without food, and several followers of Sri Yukteswar's mentor Lahiri Mahasaya.

While in India, Sri Yukteswar officially replaced Yogananda's former title of "swami" with the monastic title of Paramahansa, which means "supreme swan" and denotes the highest level of spiritual development. At his Puri hermitage in March 1936, Sri Yukteswar reached Maha Samadhi. Yogananda continued to teach, give interviews, and hang out with friends for a while after performing his guru's burial rituals before making plans to fly back to the US in the middle of 1936.

His book claims that in June 1936, following a vision of Krishna, he had a paranormal experience with the Spirit of his master Sri Yukteswar, who had appeared before him when he was in a room at the Regent Hotel in Mumbai. During the meeting, Yogananda physically held onto his guru's solid form. Sri Yukteswar revealed that "he now served as a spiritual guide on a high-astral planet and explained truths in great detail about the astral realm, astral planets, and the afterlife; the lives, skills, and varying degrees of freedom of astral beings; the workings of karma; man's various super physical bodies and how he works through them; (Yogananda with his autobiography, 1950)."

Yogananda petitioned for citizenship in 1946, taking advantage of reform in immigration regulations. In 1949, once his application was approved, he was naturalised as a citizen of the United States.

Fig 13.5 : Sri Yogananda

He attended a dinner hosted by the Indian Ambassador to the United States, Binay Ranjan Sen, and his wife on March 7, 1952, at the Biltmore Hotel in Los Angeles. Yogananda concluded his remarks by reading from his poem My India and adding the following: "Where Ganges, woods, Himalayan caves, and men dream God - I am hallowed; my body touched that sod." Daya Mata stated that "as he uttered these words, he lifted his eyes to the Kutastha centre, and his body slumped to the floor." Many people attended his funeral service, which was conducted at the SRF office on Mount Washington in Los Angeles.

The book Divine Interventions: True Stories of Mysteries and Miracles That Changes Lives states that Yogananda's body "showed no indications of physical degradation" for three weeks following his death. His unchanged face is the greatest signature of divine attainment and blessings. A notarized letter from Harry T. Rowe, the mortuary director, added: *"The absence of any visual signs of decay … offers the most extraordinary case in our experience. This state of perfect preservation of a body is, so far as we know from mortuary annals, an unparalleled one. Yogananda's body was apparently in a phenomenal state of immutability. No odour of decay emanated from his body at any time. For these reasons, we state again that the case of Paramahansa Yogananda is unique in our experience."*

Rowe wrote that Yogananda's body was embalmed about twenty-four hours after he passed away. Yogananda's nose had a slight desiccation on March 26; on March 27, Rowe observed that Yogananda's body appeared fresh and unspoiled by deterioration. Yogananda's bones are buried in the Grand Mausoleum at Forest Lawn Memorial Park.

To help people come to this realisation, which he called self-realization, he taught Kriya Yoga and other meditation techniques. This understanding is essentially the realisation that we are one with God's omnipresence, that we do not need to pray for it to come to us, that we are not just near it at all times, but that God's omnipresence is our omnipresence, and that we are just as much a part of Him now as we ever will be. All we need to do is get more knowledge of Him.

Anybody can talk with God, according to the author of the book *How You Can Talk with God*, if one persists in one's sincere plea with devotion. He claims that God had spoken to him numerous times. He also had many miracle experiences in his life. In the book, he claims, "We may in a vision see a face of some divine/saintly being, or we may hear a Divine voice talking to us and will know that it is God. When our heart call is intense, and we do not give up, God will come. We must remove from our mind any slightest doubt that God will answer."

In his autobiography, Yogananda provided a general description of Kriya Yoga. A Kriya Yogi will mentally guide his life force in an upward and downward motion revolving around the six spinal centres that correspond to the 12 astral signs of the zodiac, or the Cosmic Man. A subtle advancement in a person's evolution can be seen every half-minute of energy revolving around his sensitive spinal cord, which is equal to one year of natural spiritual development. He propounded a great equation of a half-minute of Kriya equivalent to one year of spiritual work.

Yogananda's 1946 publication Autobiography of a Yogi has been translated into 45 other languages. A group of spiritual writers in 1999 named it one of the "100 Most Significant Spiritual Books of the 20th Century". Steve Jobs, George Harrison, and Ravi Shankar are just a few of the luminaries who have cited the Autobiography as an inspiration.

In celebration of the official publication of the Hindi translation of Yogananda's book "God Talks with Arjuna: The Bhagavad Gita," Ram Nath Kovind, the President of India, paid a visit to the Ranchi Ashram of the Yogoda Satsanga Society of India on November 15, 2017, coinciding the organization's 100th anniversary. On March 7, 2017, Indian Prime Minister Narendra Modi issued a new commemorative postage stamp in celebration of the Yogoda Satsanga Society of India's 100th anniversary. At Vigyan Bhawan in New Delhi, Prime Minister Modi expressed his gratitude to Yogananda for promoting Indian spirituality abroad. Yogananda, he claimed, stayed tied to India even after he departed its borders to promote his message.

Anandamayi Ma (Nirmala Sundari: 30 April, 1896 – 27 August 1982)

(Internet Sources: godbless-u.ning.com, mrinalinieroole1.hubpages.com, soulnpeace.com)

Sri Sivananda Saraswati of the Divine Life Society described Maa Anandamayi as an Indian saint and the great yoga guru, the most perfect flower the Indian soil has ever produced. She had the astonishing powers of miracles as seen by her followers. She was always in a perpetual state of divine joy.

The Father of Anandamayi Ma, Bipin Behari Bhattacharya, was an ardent singer of Vaishnava songs. Often people had seen him fully engrossed in the devotional songs. He would rise at 3 AM and sing songs and was seen wandering. His wife would go searching for him and bring him back home. Once, during a storm, the roof of his house blew off, but he continued singing in the rain. Anandamayi's mother, Moksada Sundari Devi, was also known for her states of religious emotion. While pregnant with Nirmala (Anandamayi's given name), she would see visions of sages and statues of deities that would appear and disappear.

Nirmala, as a child, was very sensitive to religious rituals. The sound of religious chanting would bring about jubilant feelings in her. She had the illusion of visions of religious figures emerging from statues in the temples and re-entering them. Often, she was seen gazing into space for long hours. Nirmala had very limited education and, therefore, minimum writing skills.

At the age of 13, she was married to Ramani Mohan Chakrabarti or Bholanath and spent a few years in her brother-in-law's house. From childhood, she was not at all focused on household chores. After the death of her brother-in-law, she was shifted to live with her husband at the age of 18 years.

Her marriage with Bholanath was not by their choices; it was a family-arranged marriage. Anandamayi would faint, and she used to become dead-like whenever thoughts of sexuality occurred to Bholanath. After sustained efforts of chanting mantras, she used to come back to normal consciousness. Sometimes, in such situations, her body would become distorted or it would become stiff. Whenever Bholanath tried to touch her with the wrong intention, her husband used to get spontaneous electrical shocks. This situation had become a permanent feature. Even though persuaded by the family, her husband did not go for remarriage. Finally, Bholanath accepted Anandamayi as his Guru.

People around her recognized her spiritual qualities from the very childhood. Whenever there was the sound of religious chanting, she would behave differently. Her body would become stiff and sometimes fall to the ground in a faint, with a deformed body during these events. The body would shrink, or its limbs would take up impossible structural positions. For long periods, she would hold difficult yogic positions (asanas) and also some complex tantric hand positions (mudras).

Due to her illness, she moved back to her parent's home in Vadyakuta, and after two years, in 1918, she and her husband moved to Bajitpur. She had a future vision of what actions to perform and which images to visualise during the spiritual practices. She had spontaneous yogic practices (Kriyas) that were like a manufacturing factory working in perfect harmony and sequence of production.

Her behaviour was sometimes abnormal, like shedding profuse tears to laughing for hours. Again, she was seen talking fast in a different language that people could not understand.

She was unusual with actions like rolling in the dust and dancing for long periods. Sometimes, she would be fasting for long periods, while during other times, she would consume enough food beyond the imagination of the people around her.

It was difficult to understand how Anandamayi could change her bodily structure so often and with extreme diversity. Sometimes, she was seen sweating, fainting, crying, changing in skin colour, hair standing on end, and so on, which indicates her strong religious state of things.

Anandamayi loved to travel to various pilgrimage places in India. En route, she was staying in ashrams. Attending religious festivals was her favourite option. The devotees built a temple for her in Dacca but she left the day it was completed. Once at Dehradun, she lived in an abandoned Shiva temple for almost a year without money. She, too, lived there in cold winter without blankets.

Anandamayi had tremendous yogic powers through which she could read the thoughts of her devotees just by looking at them at a distance. Through her tremendous power of ***siddhi,*** she could make her body shrink and expand at will. She could cure the sick persons who were visiting her. A lady disciple claimed to have said, "She was saved from death after a car accident when Anandamayi grasped her 'life substance' and brought it back into her dead body."

She was also very sensitive to environmental influences. Once, while passing through a Muslim tomb, she immediately recited portions of the Quran and performed Namaz. She often considered her body as an object and described her actions in phases like *"this body did this"* or *"this body went there"*. Her disciples and she believed that her erratic actions were the result of the divine will. She had almost no sense of pleasure or pain. She was stated to have said, "Sometimes He draws me outside, and sometimes He takes me inside, and I am completely withdrawn. I am nobody; all of my actions are done by Him and not by me."

Sometimes, she was so high in her spiritual ecstasy that she was feeling empty with no sense of individuality. After losing herself in the great void *(Mahasunya),* the actions that emerged from this void were often in chaos and incoherent. She also heard stating that her actions and expressions were the play of the Lord acting through her body.

She always downplayed individual identity and considered it a kind of "spiritual disease or bhava roga, or the disease of feeling". The upsurge of individual identity brings in the ego leading to looking him up as a "separate individual."

Anandamayi Ma was never formally initiated by any guru. Suddenly in an evening, she performed her initiation spontaneously. visualizing both the ritual scene and movements. Simultaneously, she heard the chanting of initiatory sacred words (**mantras**) inwardly.

Fig. 13.7 Ma Anandamayi in Samadhi State

Fig. 13.6 Ma Anandmayi

According to her: "There were four stages in her spiritual evolution. First, the mind was 'dried' of desire and passion. It could catch the fire of spiritual knowledge easily. Next, the body became still, and the mind was drawn inward, as religious emotion flowed in the heart like a stream. Third, her identity was absorbed by an individual deity, but some distinction between form and formlessness remained. Lastly, there was a melting away of all duality. Here, the mind was completely free from the movement of thought. There was also full consciousness even in what is normally characterized as the dream state."

She could be quoted as saying in the spiritual gatherings that "Her spiritual identity had not changed since early childhood. She claimed that all the outer changes in her life were for the benefit of her disciples."

Once Paramahansa Yogananda met Anandamayi Ma and wanted to know about her life. Her answer was simple as quoted here: "*Father, there is little to tell, my consciousness has never associated itself with this temporary body. Before I came on this earth, Father,* ***'I was the same.' As a little girl, 'I was the same.' I grew into womanhood*** *but still 'I was the same.' When the family in which I had been born made arrangements to have this body married, 'I was the same.' ... And, Father, in front of you now, 'I am the same.' Even afterwards, though the dance of creation change[s] around me in the hall of eternity, 'I shall be the same.'*"

Whatever Anandamayi Ma was doing before others was a simple act that was directed to teach a lesson to one of the people present in the audience. These actions were coming to her automatically without any preplanning. For hours and days, she remained in ecstatic states which proved her as a holy woman. She never had any formal religious training or initiation. Also, Anandamayi Ma never had any religious teacher or guru. All she did was from her inner voices that resonated from what voices she heard that told her what religious and meditative practices to perform. The importance of detachment from the world was her main modus of attainment. She also emphasized religious devotion. She preached that service to mankind is the service to God. She was an extensive traveller.

Many were inspired by Anandamayi Ma's special abilities and message of love. She had made a perfect analysis of dance, which she considered as a representation of the relationship between individuals and God. This impressed Uday Shankar, a well-known Indian dancer. She lived in the same era as well-known Hindu saints, including Paramahansa Yogananda, Swami Ramdas, Ramana Maharshi, Neem Karoli Baba, and Udiya Baba.

Ma passed away in Dehradun on August 27, 1982. Later, in the courtyard of her Kankhal ashram in Haridwar, devotees erected a Samadhi (shrine) in honour of her. One of her sayings is, *"Regard everyone as equal to your own body, just as you cherish your own body".*

Depending on their innate nature, any person can progress. She embraced and engaged in conversation with followers of various paths and faiths, including Shaivite, Vaishnavite, and Tantric, as well as followers of Islam, Christianity, Judaism, Sikhism, and Buddhism. She welcomed everyone and was at ease while offering advice to followers of all religions. The Muslim community of Kheora continues to refer to her as "our own Ma", even today. She was mentioned by Sri Yogananda in his book "Autobiography of a Yogi." She describes her origins and their meeting in the chapter titled "The Bengali 'Joy-Permeated Mother'".

Swami Vivekananda (12 January 1863 – 4 July 1902)

He was one of the finest Indian Hindu monks, a philosopher, author, religious teacher, and the most important follower of the Indian mystic Ramakrishna. He was also known as Narendranath Datta. He promoted interfaith understanding and elevated Hinduism to the position of an important international religion. Due to his efforts, Vedanta and Yoga became popular in the Western world.

After delivering his well-known address at the 1893 Parliament of Religions in Chicago and introducing Hinduism to Americans with the words "Sisters and brothers of America," Vivekananda became a very popular spiritual figure. He made such an impact at the Parliament that he was called "an orator by divine right and unquestionably the greatest figure at the Parliament" by an American publication. After having great success at the Parliament, Vivekananda went on to give hundreds of lectures on Hindu philosophy throughout the United States, England, and Europe in the years that followed. He also founded the Vedanta Societies of New York and San Francisco, which later became the basis for Vedanta Societies in the West.

When he discovered Ramakrishna, he became a monk. Vivekananda travelled widely around the Indian subcontinent after Ramakrishna passed away to gain firsthand information on the conditions of life of Indians in British India. He was moved by their predicament and decided to aid his compatriots. He then managed to get to the United States and became quite successful there. Vivekananda established the Ramakrishna Mission in India to carry out charitable, social, and educational endeavours, as well as the Ramakrishna Math, which offers spiritual instruction to monks and devotees.

On January 12, 1863, in a Bengali family in Kolkata, Vivekananda was born as Narendranath Datta, one of the nine siblings. Vishwanath Datta, his father, worked as a lawyer at the Calcutta High Court. Bhuvaneswari Devi, his mother, was a devoted housewife. As a young child, Narendra was naughty and restless, and his parents frequently struggled to keep him under control. His mother once said Shiva sent one of his demons to his mother when she pleaded to him for a son, she claimed.

At the age of eight, in 1871, he attended school. William Hastie (principal of Christian College, Calcutta, from where Narendra graduated) wrote, "Narendra is a genius. I have travelled far and wide but I have never come across a lad of his talents and possibilities, even in German universities, among philosophical students. He is bound to make his mark in life."

Narendra was renowned for having an incredibly strong memory and the capacity for rapid reading. Examples of many instances can be quoted. One instance is an argument he had with a Swede in which he brought up some historical facts about Sweden, which the Swede originally denied but eventually admitted. In a different event, Vivekananda was reviewing some poetical writing with Dr. Paul Deussen in Kiel, Germany, and he did not respond when the professor spoke to him. Afterwards, he expressed regret to Dr. Deussen, explaining that he had been too preoccupied with reading to hear him. This explanation did not satisfy the professor, but Vivekananda quoted and explained verses from the scripture, leaving the professor speechless at his memory trick. He once issued some books of Sir John Lubbock from the library to be returned on the following day and claimed to have read them. The librarian did not believe it. Before being persuaded that Vivekananda was telling the truth, he cross-examined about the book's contents. Narendra has been described in these instances as having an extraordinary memory.

He questioned several well-known Kolkata citizens about their experiences, "face to face with God," but none of their responses satisfied him. Ramakrishna provided a real response to Narendra's query when he said, "Yes, I see Him as I see you, but in an immensely vivid manner." After the passing of his father in 1884, Narendra met Ramakrishna, who eventually became his spiritual inspiration. Narendra visited Dakshineswar in late 1881 or early 1882 with two pals and met Ramakrishna there. It turned out that this encounter was a turning moment in his life. He originally resisted Ramakrishna as his teacher and disagreed with several of his teachings, but after becoming attracted to him, he started to frequently visit him in Dakshineswar. Ramakrishna was put to the test by Narendra, who listened to his arguments carefully and responded, "Try to perceive the truth from all aspects."

The family became insolvent with the sudden death of Narendra's father in 1884. Once the son of a wealthy family, Narendra now ranks among the poorest college students. Narendra once asked Ramakrishna to offer prayers to Kali, the Hindu goddess of wealth, on his behalf. Ramakrishna recommended that he go to the temple himself and pray there instead. He visited the temple three times on the advice of Ramakrishna, but instead of praying for any material needs, he instead prayed to the goddess for true wisdom and devotion. Ramakrishna was moved to a garden home in Cossipore after being diagnosed with throat cancer in 1885 and treated in Calcutta.

He attained Nirvikalpa samadhi in Cossipore. In turn, Ramakrishna asked his disciples to regard Narendra as their leader and requested him to take care of the other monastic pupils. In the early hours of August 16, 1886, in Cossipore, Ramakrishna passed away. Following Ramakrishna's passing, his followers and admirers ceased helping them. Every day, Narendra and his followers would spend many hours engaging in religious fasting and meditation. They didn't even consider whether the world was real or not.

For five years, Narendra travelled widely around India, visiting educational institutions and getting to know various religious and social customs. Ajit Singh of Khetri's suggestion that Narendra be given the name "Vivekananda"—a combination of the Sanskrit terms Viveka and Ananda—which means "the delight of discerning wisdom" was well accepted. With this new name, he left Bombay for Chicago on May 31, 1893. Beginning his voyage to the West on May 31, 1893, Vivekananda stopped in several towns before arriving in Chicago on July 30, 1893, the location of the "Parliament of Religions" in September of that year.

Vivekananda was eager to participate but was dismayed to find that no delegates without credentials from legitimate organisations would be admitted. Professor John Henry Wright of Harvard University and P C Mozoomdar of the Brahmo Samaj, both members of the selection committee for the Parliament, were approached by Vivekananda. They identified Swami as a representative of the Hindu monastic order, and permission to speak was granted.

Though nervous at the beginning, he bowed to Saraswati (the Hindu goddess of learning) and began his speech with the words "*Sisters and brothers of America*". At these words, Vivekananda received a two-minute standing ovation from the crowd of 7 thousand. Vivekananda quoted, "As the different streams having their sources in different places all mingle their water in the sea, so, O Lord, the different paths which men take, through different tendencies, various though they appear, crooked or straight, all lead to Thee!" and "Whosoever comes to Me, through whatsoever form, I reach him; all men are struggling through paths that in the end lead to Me."

Parliament President John Henry Barrows said, "India, the mother of religions, was represented by Swami Vivekananda, the Orange monk who exercised the most wonderful influence over his auditors." Vivekananda attracted widespread attention in the press, which called him the "cyclonic monk from India". The New York Critique wrote, "He is an orator by divine right, and his strong, intelligent face in its picturesque setting of yellow and orange was hardly less interesting than those earnest words, and the rich, rhythmical utterance he gave them." The New York Herald noted, "Vivekananda is undoubtedly the greatest figure in the Parliament of Religions. After hearing him, we feel how foolish it is to send missionaries to this learned nation." American newspapers reported Vivekananda as "the greatest figure in the parliament of religions" and "the most popular and influential man in the parliament". He soon became known as a "handsome oriental" and made a huge impression as an orator.

He toured many parts of the US as a guest after the Parliament of Religions. His popularity opened up new views for expanding on "life and religion to thousands".

Throughout the eastern and central United States, particularly in Chicago, Detroit, Boston, and New York, Vivekananda gave lectures for over two years. In 1894, he established the Vedanta Society of New York. By the spring of 1895, his health had been impacted by his demanding schedule. He met an Irish woman in November 1895 named Margaret Elizabeth Noble, who would later become Sister Nivedita. Vivekananda met Max Müller, from Oxford University, who had written Ramakrishna's first biography in the West. A meeting took place during his second trip to the UK in May 1896. A chair in Eastern philosophy at Harvard University and a position of a similar nature at Columbia University were offered to Vivekananda; however, he turned them both down since they would contradict his vows as a monk. His published book on Raja Yoga in 1896 became an instant success. It was highly influential in the Western understanding of yoga.

Throughout the US and Europe Vivekananda attracted supporters and admirers. Vivekananda established the Ramakrishna Mission for social service on May 1st, 1897 in Calcutta. It is based on Karma Yoga's principles. The trustees of the Ramakrishna Math make up its governing body (which conducts religious work). Ramakrishna Math and Ramakrishna Mission share Belur Math as their administrative centre. In January 1898, Vivekananda visited Calcutta once more. He left for the West again in June 1899 despite his deteriorating condition, and he eventually made it back to Calcutta on December 9, 1900. Vivekananda made Belur Math his home.

Vivekananda got up early on July 4, 1902 (the day of his death), went to the monastery at Belur Math, and meditated there for three hours. Vivekananda went to his room at 7:00 p.m. and asked that no one bother him; he passed away at 9:20 p.m. while meditating. Vivekananda attained maha samadhi, as recorded by his followers; a blood vessel burst in his brain was suggested as a potential cause of death. His followers said that the rupture was caused by the piercing of his Brahmarandhra, an aperture in the crown of his head when he attained maha samadhi.

"The holy, the absolute, dwells within all human beings regardless of social rank," he advocated. Any soul can be heavenly. The objective is to control both internal and exterior nature to make this Divine within the manifest. Do this through your work, your devotion, your mental discipline, your philosophy, or any combination of these, and you will be free. This is the entirety of the religion.

Nationalism was a prominent theme with Vivekananda. India observes "National Youth Day" on his birthday, 12 January, and "World Brotherhood Day "on the 11th of September, commemorating the day he delivered his masterful speech at the Parliament of Religions. Some Indian film directors have made documentary and feature films depicting the life of Swami Vivekananda.

Sai Baba of Shirdi (1838 - 15 October 1918)

He was a revered Hindu and Muslim follower during and after his lifetime. He was a prominent Indian spiritual guru, fakir, and saint. Sai Baba advocated the necessity of "realization of the self" and denounced "love for perishable things". His moral teachings emphasize love, forgiveness, service to others, charity, contentment, inner tranquillity, and loyalty to God and the Guru.

Discrimination based on caste or religion was condemned by Sai Baba. It is still unknown if he was a Muslim or a Hindu. His teachings incorporated aspects of both Hinduism and Islam, and he practised both Hindu and Muslim rites in addition to using words and imagery from both religions to convey his lessons. He is believed to be an avatar of the Hindu god Dattatreya by his followers.

The majority of information about Shirdi Sai Baba is found in a book called Shri Sai Satcharitra, which was authored in Marathi by a disciple named Hemadpant in 1922. The book is a collection based on reports from numerous disciples and firsthand experiences dating back to 1910. Sri Narasimha Swamy, another follower, penned the book Life of Sai Baba.

Although Shirdi Sai Baba's birthplace and year are uncertain, it is believed that he was born to a boatman named Ganga Bhavadia and his wife Devagiriamma in the Maharashtrian village of Pathri. Others claim that his parents were Vaishnavdevi and Abdul Sattar from Tamil Nadu.

He spent 12 years as a pupil of his Hindu guru, Venkusa of Selu. According to legend, Baba travelled to the Shirdi hamlet when he was sixteen years old and lived there for three years.

After going missing for a year, he reappeared permanently in 1858. There are some hints that he encountered several fakirs and saints around this period. He lived a hermit's lifestyle, meditating while seated in an asana under a neem tree. The villagers were astounded to see a little boy performing a difficult penance while disregarding the heat or cold. His regular visitors included Mhalsapati, Appa Jogle, and Kashinatha, three of the village's more devout residents.

The real name of Sai Baba is still unknown. When he returned to Shirdi in 1858, the temple priest Mhalsapati gave him the name Sai. The name Sai Baba indicates "holy father or saintly father" because Sai is a religious mendicant but can also represent God, and Baba is an honorific that denotes grandfather, father, old man, or sir.

Almost for five years, he lived under a neem tree and undertook long periods of meditation. Often, he was seen wandering for long periods in the jungle around Shirdi. He took up residence in an old and dilapidated mosque, where he lived a solitary life, surviving by begging for alms and receiving Hindu or Muslim visitors. He maintained a sacred fire **(dhuni)** and gave sacred ash from the fire to guests on their departure.

The ash was believed to have healing and protective powers. By 1910, Sai Baba's fame began to spread in Mumbai. He was regarded as a saint with the power of performing miracles and even as an avatar, many people came to visit him. They built his first temple at Bhivpuri, Karjat.

Fig. 13.8 Sri Sai Baba with his Followers

In August 1918, Shirdi Sai Baba told some of his devotees that he would soon be "leaving his mortal body". By the end of September, he had a high fever and stopped eating. As his condition deteriorated, he asked his disciples to recite holy texts to him, although he also continued to meet visitors. He died on 15 October 1918. The place of his remains in Shirdi later became a place of worship that is known today as Shree Samadhi Mandir or Shirdi Sai Baba Temple.

Fig. 13.9 A rare photo of Sai Baba

Sai Baba instructed his devotees and followers to lead a moral life, help others, love every living being without any discrimination, and develop two important features of character: faith **(Shraddha)** and patience **(Saburi).** Sai Baba emphasized the importance of performing one's duties without attachment to earthly matters and of being content regardless of the situation. All the spiritual paths, viz. the Bhakti Yoga, Jnana Yoga, and Karma Yoga, influenced his teachings. Sai Baba encouraged charity and stressed the importance of sharing.

If a man or creature comes to you for help, do not discourteously drive them away, but receive them well and treat them with due respect. SriHari (God) will certainly be pleased if you give water to the thirsty, bread to the hungry, clothes to the naked, and your veranda to strangers for sitting and resting. If anybody wants any money from you and you are not inclined to give, do not give, but do not bark at him like a dog."

Mhalsapati Nagre, a native Khandoba priest, was Sai Baba's first follower. Due to Sai Baba, Shirdi, which only had a small number of devotees in the 19th century, has grown to an important location in India.

The first Sai Baba temple was constructed in 1922 in Kudal, Sindhudurg. On average, lakhs of visitors visit the Sai Baba Temple in Shirdi each day, with peak attendance occurring during religious holidays.

The outside cone and the temple's interior are both coated in gold. The statue of Sai Baba within the temple is made of Italian marble and is dressed in a royal robe, a gold crown, and fresh flower garlands. The Shri Sai Baba Sansthan Trust is in charge of running the temple. The Shirdi Sai Baba movement started in the 19th century, and it has recently extended to most nations.

Fig. 13.10 The Present Statue of Sai Baba at Shirdi

Despite demands, Shirdi Sai Baba did not bestow formal initiation (diksha), a spiritual heir, or even a disciple. He was also respected by Muslims and Hindus equally, as well as by the Nath-Panchayat, a group of Shaivic yogis. He is regarded as a Sadguru or saint and an avatar of the "Supreme Truth" (Brahman or God). In Hinduism, where there is no overarching ideology or cosmology but rather a foundation in personal faith and spirituality, this is not unusual. Abdul Baba, a devoted follower of Sai Baba, looked after the shrine from 1918 to 1922.

Prominent Zoroastrians like Homi Bhabha and N Palkhivala adored Saibaba. Zoroastrian Meher Baba met Sai Baba in December 1915, and this is regarded as a pivotal moment in Meher Baba's life.

Attaining a state of Samadhi, lighting lamps with water, healing the terminally ill, and seeming to beat when another is beaten and many such events were common features in Saibaba's ashram.

Depending on the level of followers' trust, he appeared to them as Shiva, Vithoba, Sri Rama, and other gods like Krishna and Vithoba. He visited them in their dreams and offered guidance. His followers have written about their encounters. Both in India and the majority of other nations, there are numerous Shirdi Sai Baba shrines.

Neem Karoli Baba (1900 – 11 September, 1973) (Internet Source: www.indiatvnews.com, clamorworld.com)

He was a great guru and a follower of the Hindu god Hanuman. His devotees called him Maharaj-ji. One group of Americans who visited India in the 1960s and 1970s included him as their most well-known spiritual guide. He established ashrams in Vrindavan, Kainchi, Rishikesh, and Shimla. Neem Karoli Baba had the childhood name Lakshman Narayan Sharma was born to a rich Brahmin family around the year 1900 in a village called Akbarpur in the Indian state of Uttar Pradesh. His parents forced him into marriage when he was just 11 years old. After marriage, he left home to become a wandering sadhu. At his father's request, he later went back home to start a stable married life. He had a daughter and two sons.

In 1958, Neem Karoli Baba left his house. According to Ram Dass, Baba was forced to get off the train as he boarded it without a ticket in the village station of Neem Karoli, located in the Farrukhabad district (U.P).

The train would not start when the conductor forcibly removed Baba. After numerous failed attempts to start the train, someone proposed to the conductor that they let the sadhu back on the train. Neem Karoli consented to ride the train under certain conditions. After the officials had agreed, Neem Karoli Baba boarded the train and joked, "What? Is it up to me to start trains?" The train started after he boarded it, but the drivers would not move until the sadhu gave his blessing. With Baba's blessing, the train departed. The village of Neem Karoli afterwards saw the construction of a train station. For a while, Baba resided in the Neem Karoli village.

He then spent a lot of time wandering around Northern India. He went by various names, some of which were Lakshman Das, Handi Wallah Baba, and Tikonia Walla Baba.

Fig. 13.11 Neem Karoli Baba

He went by the name Tallaiya Baba while performing tapasya and sadhana at Vavania Morbi in Gujarat. At Vrindavan, he was referred to as Chamatkari Baba by locals (miracle baba). At Kainchi and Vrindavan, two main ashrams were constructed during his lifetime. Afterwards almost 100 temples were eventually built in his honor. The Kainchi Dham ashram, built in 1964, features a Hanuman temple, and that is where he spent the last ten years of his life.

The temple, which is located on the Nainital-Almora Road 17 kilometres from Nainital, is a popular destination for pilgrims from all over the world as well as locals. The Kainchi Dham Bhandara, which commemorates the opening of the temple, is held annually on June 15 and normally draws over one lakh worshippers.

On September 11, 1973, early in the morning, Neem Karoli Baba passed away at a hospital in Vrindavan, India. He was in a diabetic coma, but the medical team reported that his pulse was normal. Then, after saying "Jaya Jagadish Hare" multiple times, he displayed a very calm expression, and all indications of agony vanished. The Vrindavan ashram complex, where his samadhi shrine is located, also houses some of his personal effects. Being a lifetime practitioner of bhakti yoga, Neem Karoli Baba promoted service to others as the pinnacle of unconditional devotion to God. Anjani writes the following account in the book, "Miracle of Love", which was compiled by Ram Das.

He had no biography. There are more stories than facts. In several regions of India, he appears to have gone by various names and appeared and vanished over time. In recent years, his non-Indian followers primarily referred to him as "Maharajji," but also knew him as Neem Karoli Baba. He didn't give speeches; instead, his teachings consisted of the shortest, most simple stories. He typically sat or lay on a wooden bench with a few followers sitting around him, covered in a plaid blanket. He occasionally sat in silence, lost in another universe that we were unable to follow, but joy and tranquillity descended upon us.

According to Baba, the greatest obstacles to realizing God are attachment and ego, and "a knowledgeable man and an idiot are similar as long as there is attachment and ego in the physical body," He would counsel individuals to submit to God's will above everything else to grow in love and trust and so be free from needless worries in life.

Ram Dass, Bhagavan Das, novelist and meditation teacher Lama Surya Das, and musicians Jai Uttal and Krishna Das are just a few of Neem Karoli Baba's well-known students. Humanitarian Larry Brilliant and his wife Girija, Dada Mukerjee, academic and author Yvette Rosser, American spiritual leader Ma Jaya Sati Bhagavati, director John Bush, and Daniel Goleman are a few other well-known admirers. Baba Hari Dass (Haridas) oversaw several structures and maintained the ashrams in the Nainital region (1954–1968) before moving to the US and starting to teach spirituality in California at the beginning of 1971.

Another source of funding for the Organisation was Steve Jobs. The "Love Serve Remember Foundation," which was established in the late 2000s, has as its goal the preservation and propagation of Neem Karoli Baba's teachings.

Fig. 13.12 Kainchi Dham Neem Karoli Baba Ashram

In the 2021 documentary "Windfall of Grace", a compelling mix of narratives from unassuming, rural Indian devotees to well-known American devotees are presented. Through their utter devotion to Neem Karoli Baba, these expressions aim to highlight both the differences and similarities between the two contrasts. Their meetings with Baba led to significant changes in their spiritual practices, life goals, and paths.

A small temple complex known as Kainchi Dham is located on the banks of the Kosi River in the Kumaon region of Uttarakhand. On the recommendation of Steve Jobs, Zuckerberg, the founder of Facebook, visited Neem Karoli Baba's ashram in Kainchi. At that time, Facebook was going through a tough time. The place came to the limelight when Mark Zuckerberg told Prime Minister Narendra Modi during a town hall meeting. The Facebook founder had arrived here with just a book in his hand and he was supposed to stay here for one day but he spent two days.

Apple founder Steve Jobs, with his friend Dan Kottke, visited the Ashram to meet Neem Karoli Baba. By then, however, the Baba had died. Hollywood actress Julia Roberts is also said to have been influenced by Neem Karoli Baba and was drawn to Hinduism because of him.

Fig. 13.13 Neem Karoli Baba in Meditation

Ramana Maharshi (30/12/1879–14/4/1950)

He was a Hindu philosopher from India. His real name was Venkataraman Iyer and later he was known as Sri Ramana Maharshi. He was born in Tamil Nadu, India's town of Turuchuli. He came from a traditional Hindu Brahmin family and was the second of four children. His mother was Azhagammal, and his father was Sundaram Iyer. He could recall everything after hearing it just once, which he used to memorize Tamil poetry. He had an extremely good memory. He left his uncle's house in Madurai six weeks after his near-death experience and travelled to the sacred mountain

Arunachala in Tiruvannamalai. Though he was not formally initiated as a sannyasin, he assumed this position and resided there for the rest of his life.

He attracted followers who flocked to him for darshan and viewed him as an avatar of Shiva. Later, in his ashram, guests received upadesa (spiritual instruction). Ramana Maharshi advocated self-inquiry, devotion, and surrender to the self as the basic approach to removing ignorance and maintaining self-awareness.

Venkataraman, in November 1895, concluded that the holy mountain, Arunachala, was a genuine site for him. He has come to terms with himself and inquired, "What is it that dies?" and concluded that although the body perishes, this "current" or "force" lives on. He then realised that this "current" or "force" was his Self, which he later came to refer to as "the personal God, or Iswara". He stopped caring about his schoolwork, friends, and relationships. He shunned company, preferred to be by himself, and visited the Meenakshi Temple every day, crying out to God for mercy while asking for blessings for bhakti.

He spent days in deep samadhi at Tiruvannamalai, where he was oblivious to bug and rodent attacks. He was found in the underground vault by the local saint Seshadri Swamigal, who made an effort to safeguard him. He was removed and cleaned up on the Patala-lingam vault after approximately six weeks. He stayed in the Subramanya Shrine for the following two months, becoming so unaware of his surroundings and body that food had to be given to him to keep him from starving.

Six months after arriving in Tiruvannamalai, in February 1897, Ramana Maharshi relocated to Gurumurtam, a nearby shrine. A sadhu by the name of Palaniswami went to see him shortly after his arrival and was deeply moved. After experiencing calm and joy, he decided to become Ramana Maharshi's constant attendant. In addition to providing physical security, he would also beg for alms, make meals for both Ramana Maharshi and himself and provide any necessary care.

Ramana Maharshi had disregarded his physical needs. Even the persistent ants that bit him were ignored by him. Ramana Maharshi gradually drew the attention of visitors who appreciated his silence and austerities. He always wanted isolation. He was not so happy when devotees were bringing offerings and singing praises. A bamboo fence was eventually constructed to keep him safe. Ramana Maharshi relocated to the Shiva temple at Pavalakkunru in September 1898. Even though his mother pleaded with him to go back, he refused. He settled down at Virupaksha Cave for the following 17 years, with a brief stay at Satguru Cave and Guhu Namasivaya Cave.

A government representative by the name of Sivaprakasam Pillai paid a visit to the young Swami in 1902 to learn the answers to his inquiries regarding "How to know one's actual identity." Answers to the fourteen questions posed to the young Swami Ramana Maharshi made him famous. These were the first teachings on Self-enquiry advocated by him. These teachings were subsequently published as Nan Yar? or in English, Who am I?

He received a lot of visitors, some of whom turned into followers. In 1907, Sri Ganapati Sastri, a revered Vedic scholar of his time who was well-versed in the Srutis, Sastras, Tantras, and Yoga, travelled to Ramana Maharshi.

Following his receipt of Upadesa, he referred to him as Bhagavan Sri Ramana Maharshi. From that point forward, Ramana Maharshi was recognized by this name. The first

Westerner to learn about Ramana Maharshi was Frank Humphreys, a police officer stationed in India in 1911.

Fig. 13.14 Ashram of Saint Raman Maharshi

Humphreys penned articles about Ramana Maharshi, which were originally printed in The World Psychic Gazette in 1913. His mother's health began to decline in 1920, and she passed away on May 19, 1922, with Ramana Maharshi sitting next to her. Ramana Maharshi resided in Sri Ramanasramam, the ashram that sprang up around the grave of his mother, from 1922 until he died in 1950.

"*Self Realisation: The Life and Teachings of Ramana Maharshi*," a biography of the spiritual master written by B. V. Narasimha, was released in 1931. In his book A Quest in Hidden India, Paul Brunton recalls how the Paramacharya of Kanchi forced him to meet Ramana Maharshi. Brunton referred to him as "one of the last of India's spiritual supermen," and he expressed his admiration for him.

I like him greatly because "he is so simple and modest when an atmosphere of authentic greatness lies so palpably around him; because he makes no claims to occult powers and hierophantic knowledge to impress the mystery-loving nature of his countrymen; and because he is so totally without any traces of pretension that he strongly resists every effort to canonize him during his lifetime."

Ramana Maharshi was introduced to a larger audience in the West thanks to the book, which became a best-seller. A little malignant growth was discovered on Ramana Maharshi's arm in November 1948, and the ashram doctor excised it in February 1949. A renowned surgeon performed another procedure in March 1949 while using radium when another tumour quickly surfaced. Ramana Maharshi was advised by the doctor that he needed to have his arm completely amputated below the shoulder to survive, but he refused. In August and December 1949, the third and fourth operations were carried out, but they simply made him weaker. As other medical systems were tried, they all failed and were abandoned by the end of March when followers lost all faith. Ramana Maharshi is reputed to have asked in response to followers who implored him to heal himself for the benefit of his followers, "Why are you clinging to this body so tightly? Let it go; where can I go? I'm present." Ramana Maharshi was too feeble to enter the hall by April 1950, and there were few visitors allowed. To catch one last sight, visitors would stream through the modest room where he spent his dying days.

His passing on April 14, 1950, at 8:47 pm, coincided with the sighting of a shooting star, which some of his followers perceived as a sign of synchronicity.

Several people think highly of him as an excellent, enlightened incarnate. He was regarded as captivating and drew a large following of followers, some of whom viewed him as the physical manifestation of Shiva. For the darshan of this holy person or God incarnate, many devotees travelled to meet Ramana Maharshi to get beneficial blessings. He insisted on being accessible to everyone who came for his darshan, even during his terminal illness.

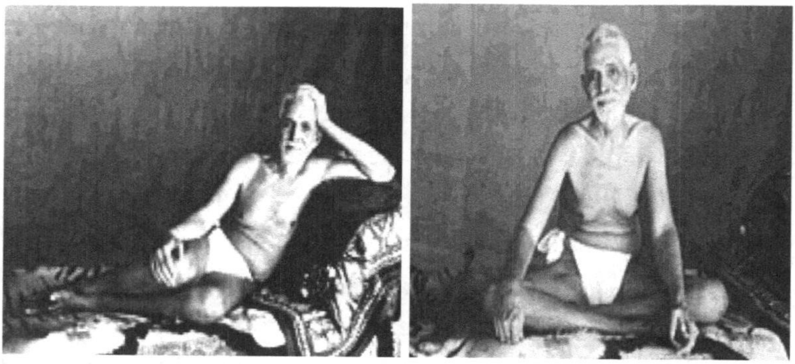

Fig. 11.15 Saint Raman Maharshi in Satsang

His followers placed a great value on anything he touched or used because "they regarded it to be prasad and that it passed on part of the power and goodness of the Guru to them." Others also attempted to touch his feet. The true feet of Bhagavan only exist in the heart of the devotee, Sri Ramana Maharshi said in response to a question about whether it would be possible to bow down before him and touch his feet. The only true bliss is to cling to these feet forever. Holding onto my physical feet will disappoint you because one day my physical body will vanish. Worshiping the feet of the Guru who is inside of oneself is the ultimate act of worship. His followers placed a great value on anything he touched or used because "they regarded it to be prasad and that it passed on part of the power and goodness of the Guru to them," according to a biography. Others also attempted to touch his feet; the true feet of Bhagavan only exist in the heart of the devotee, Sri

Ramana Maharshi said in response to a question about whether it would be possible to bow down before him and touch his feet. The only true bliss is to cling to these feet forever. Holding onto my physical feet will disappoint you because one day my physical body will vanish. Worshiping the feet of the Guru who is inside of oneself is the ultimate act of worship.

Later in life, Ramana Maharshi's everyday activities were constrained due to the sheer volume of his followers and their dedication. People should not touch him. Where precautions had to be taken. Ramana Maharshi made several attempts to leave the ashram and return to a life of seclusion. According to Vasudeva, Bhagavan declared while sitting on a rock that he would never return to the Ashram and instead would travel wherever he liked. He prefers to live in the forests so that he is not disturbed by the people. He tried to seclude himself from the people.

His devotees regarded him to be Dakshinamurthy, a divine form of Shiva. By giving darshan and sitting silently next to followers and guests, Ramana Maharshi provided "spiritual instruction," but he also addressed the inquiries and problems of people who sought him. Several of these question-and-answer sessions have been recorded, edited, and published by followers of Ramana Maharshi. A few works that Ramana Maharshi wrote himself or had been authored on his behalf and edited by him have been made public.

In his description of himself, Ramana Maharshi referred to it as a "force" or "Current" that descended in his death experience and continued for the rest of his life. A force, current, or energy centre acting on the body that persisted for the rest of his life, regardless of how stiff or active the body is, and remained connected to the body. This was the first time I became aware of the current, force, or centre that made up myself and kept me acting and moving. At the time, I was unaware of the identity of the current that belonged to the personal God or Iswara, as I used to refer to him. All I could sense was that the current was in control and not me. Ramana Maharshi used various terms to denote this Self. Sat-chit-ananda was the most frequently used by him which means "truth-consciousness-bliss". The individual ego, which Ramana Maharshi said to be fundamentally non-existent and was a creation of the mind, should not be mistaken with the real Self or real "I," as it conceals the authentic experience of the real self. Self-realization is another name for self-awareness.

The main approach of Ramana Maharshi's instruction to his followers was how to remove themselves from ignorance and abide by Self-awareness by sitting with them in silence and sparingly using words. Ramana Maharshi stated of this silence: "Silence is the true upadesa." This upadesa is wonderful. It is only appropriate for the most experienced seekers. The others are unable to fully utilise it for inspiration. As a result, they need words to communicate the truth. Truth, however, cannot be put into words and requires no justification. The only thing that can be done is to indicate it, but how?

Ramana Maharshi distinguished between samadhi and sahaja samadhi, according to Robert Forman. Samadhi is a momentary state of contemplation, whereas Sahaja Samadhi involves maintaining a "quiet state" while going about one's regular business. Ramana Maharshi consistently affirmed that samadhi merely suppresses the vasanas, or karmic imprints, rather than eradicating them. The vasanas, which give rise to a sense of a distinct self, can only be annihilated and sahaja samadhi can only be reached by being in Self-awareness.

His promoted self-inquiry was considered the quickest route to awakening. He also suggested the paths of bhakti and self-surrender to one's deity or guru which would finally converge with the paths of self-enquiry. Surrender is to be complete and desireless. It cannot be with hopes for relief or other benefits. It involves being prepared to accept whatever occurs. There is no individual self to yield; rather, there is a growing knowledge that there is no individual self to sacrifice. Practising is not meant to lead to realization but to rid oneself of ignorance.

Destroy the ego you possess. The alternative is to fully submit to the Lord and acknowledge one's helplessness. So long as the devotee desires something from the Lord, surrender cannot be considered complete. Love of God for the sake of love and nothing else, not even for the sake of salvation, is true surrender.

Ramana Maharshi placed a strong emphasis on one's self-realization journey. His authority was founded on his own life experiences, which were consistent with and typically related to Advaita Vedanta, the Upanishads, and Hinduism. Ramana Maharshi firmly advised followers against leading a life of renunciation and abandoning their obligations. Sri Ramana Maharshi responded to a devotee who thought he should leave his family, whom he referred to as "samsara" (an "illusion"), to sharpen his spiritual practice: What exactly is meant by samsara? Is it inside or outside the wife, kids, and other people? Does this sum up Samsara? Why did they do that? Please first determine what is truly meant by samsara. The decision to forsake them will then be discussed. Ramana Maharshi did not advertise himself as a guru. He also never claimed to have followers and never named any successors. Despite this fact, many people claim to have been impacted by him. Although some people who visited him claimed to have become enlightened through association, he never declared any living person to be liberated.

[*Some of the photos of the great masters and others given here are taken from the various internet sources, I record my sincere gratitude and thanks to them.*]

MY SEARCH FOR GOD

I believe that in the limitless sky, there is an unknown number of universes and in each universe, there are billions of Galaxies, and in each Galaxy, there are trillions of stars with millions of black holes within. There are millions of stars, where Earth-like exoplanets are in existence. Our earth is just one out of the millions of such living planets existing in the infinite universe. It is not at all possible to find out the total number of such living planets in the limitless boundary of space.

It is also not possible that such a beautiful and flawless universe is automatically created without a creator. Then who created the universe, and how is it maintained and governed? If one believes in God as the supreme creator, then he is not singularly overseeing and managing this vast creation. He has put a system in place. We have read in the book "Autobiography of a Yogi" where there is a discussion between Paramahansa Yukteswar who re-appeared in front of his loved disciple Paramahansa Yogananda in physical form after his death and informed him of his responsibility of being in charge of an exoplanet called "Hiranyaloka" which is another astral world. This indicates that the great enlightened persons (Rishis or Saints) become the demi-gods and are given the responsibility to look after the other exoplanets. They in turn report to their higher authorities which we may call the supreme God. In the Hindu system of belief, Lord Vishnu is the supreme God, who abodes in the highest Realm called Vaikuntha. This may be the reason that in our Hindu system, we have 330 million God and Goddess, who are constantly taking care of the Universe as well as all of us (This is just a personal opinion only).

Then who can become an enlightened person? Can any of us become a demi-God? The answer is Yes. A serious reading of this book with years of practice can certainly guide one towards His path to enlightenment. But the minimum requirement is that by then you must have completed the stock of Sanchita Karma. You must have come across great persons, who have infinite patience, are extremely cool, always positive in attitude, humble, absolutely have no ego, have no weakness for any materialistic things, polite, helpful, truthful, and fearless. When you meet such a great person, you can feel positive radiance emerging from their body. Meeting such people can be a lifetime opportunity. Such persons are not required to go to temples or churches, nor they are required to go to the Himalayas to become a Yogi. They are walking toward enlightenment by the practice of good karma. If one can develop these qualities, I am sure you are on the right track.

A simple test to know that you are stepping towards the right path of spirituality is to completely blank your mind. If you can totally blank it for a minute without any thought coming then you are much closer and if it can be for two minutes then you are an enlightened person.

GLOSSARY

AKASHIC WRITING: *The subconscious mind of a person born on earth writes his Karma (good or bad) under the name of the soul when he is in deep and dreamless sleep. These records are also known as hall journals. It is the record of all previous lives of a soul, whenever it has taken birth on earth.*

ASTRAL BEINGS: *It is the soul who has refused to become spirit beings as he does not care for the advice of the subconscious mind. His appearance is just like his physical body at the time of his death on earth. We call these lost spirits as Ghosts.*

AURA: *It is the field of energy surrendering a body of each and every individual with various colours and intensities reflecting the quality of a person. Some persons have the capacity to see the aura of others.*

AUTOMATED WRITING: *Some of the departed souls communicate with their known persons on earth through automated writing by moving a pen/pencil on the papers making it to be very good sentences. There are very limited such books available till date in the world.*

HALL OF LEARNING: *It is like a library for learning in the spirit world, where all information on the laws of GOD, the Universe and everything about Gods creation is documented. The soul can understand these higher things, depending on its quality.*

HALL OF REST: *A person meeting sudden death is usually in trauma state. In the hall of rest, they are given the healing rays to calm down and to be in peace.*

REALMS: *The persons on death are placed in various realms or the planes of living or existence for the spirits that are numbered from 1. Realm 1 is the darkest of all with very unhealthy living conditions and higher realms are brighter as the number increases. Higher numbered realms are charming places for stay.*

SILVER CORD: *It is a ray of light connecting the spirit with the earth body. If it is cut, the life of the physical body is gone.*

SOUL: *It is the spirit body controlled and guided by the subconscious mind which remains in the physical body of a person. The physical body is guided by the physical mind or the conscious mind. For good persons, the subconscious mind controls the conscious mind while for evil persons the subconscious mind becomes dormant.*

SPIRIT: *It is the soul with subconscious mind.*

SUBSONSCIOUS MIND: *It is the inner spiritual mid that guides the soul. It remembers* **all previous lives of a person.**

DISCLAIMER

The author does not claim any responsibility and/or any liability and gives no warranty or assurance on the occurrence or completeness or timelines of the messages and contents given in this book.

It is the sole responsibility of the reader for any acts he is taking or practising following the reading of this book. The writer of this book should not be responsible for any action taken by the reader.